Ethnic and Intercommunity Conflict Series

General Editors: **Seamus Dunn**, Professor of Conflict Studies and Director, Centre for the Study of Conflict, and **Valerie Morgan**, Professor of History and Research Associate, Centre for the Study of Conflict, University of Ulster, Northern Ireland.

With the end of the Cold War, the hitherto concealed existence of a great many other conflicts, relatively small in scale, long-lived, ethnic in character and intra- rather than inter-state has been revealed. The dramatic changes in the distribution of world power, along with the removal of some previously resolute forms of centralised restraint, have resulted in the re-emergence of older, historical ethnic quarrels, many of which either became violent and warlike or teetered, and continue to teeter, on the brink of violence. For these reasons, ethnic conflicts and consequent violence are likely to have the greatest impact on world affairs during the next period of history.

This new series examines a range of issues related to ethnic and inter-community conflict. Each book concentrates on a well-defined aspect of ethnic and inter-community conflict and approaches it from a comparative and international standpoint.

Rather than focus on the macrolevel, that is on the grand and substantive matters of states and empires, this series argues that the fundamental causes of ethnic conflict are often to be found in the hidden roots and tangled social infrastructures of the opposing separated groups. It is through the understanding of these foundations and the working out of their implications for policy and practical activity that may lead to ameliorative processes and the construction of transforming social mechanisms and programmes calculated to produce longterm peace.

Titles include:

Stacey Burlet
CHALLENGING ETHNIC CONFLICT

Ed Cairns
THE ROLE OF MEMORY IN ETHNIC CONFLICT

T. G. Fraser
THE IRISH PARADING TRADITION

Colin Knox and Padraic Quirk
PEACE BUILDING IN NORTHERN IRELAND, ISRAEL AND SOUTH AFRICA

Colin Knox and Rachel Monaghan
INFORMAL JUSTICE IN DIVIDED SOCIETIES
Northern Ireland and South Africa

Brendan Murtagh
THE POLITICS OF TERRITORY

Marc H. Ross
THEORY AND PRACTICE IN ETHNIC CONFLICT MANAGEMENT

Informal Justice in Divided Societies

Northern Ireland and South Africa

Colin Knox
Professor of Public Policy
University of Ulster

and

Rachel Monaghan
Lecturer in Human Geography
University of Ulster

First published 2002 by
PALGRAVE MACMILLAN
Houndmills, Basingstoke, Hampshire RG21 6XS and
175 Fifth Avenue, New York, N.Y. 10010
Companies and representatives throughout the world

PALGRAVE MACMILLAN is the global academic imprint of the Palgrave Macmillan division of St. Martin's Press, LLC and of Palgrave Macmillan Ltd. Macmillan® is a registered trademark in the United States, United Kingdom and other countries. Palgrave is a registered trademark in the European Union and other countries.

ISBN 0–333–97236–8

This book is printed on paper suitable for recycling and made from fully managed and sustained forest sources.

A catalogue record for this book is available from the British Library.

Library of Congress Cataloging-in-Publication Data

Knox, Colin, 1933–
    Informal justice in divided societies : Northern Ireland and
    South Africa / Colin Knox and Rachel Monaghan.
      p. cm. – (Ethnic and intercommunity conflict series)
    Includes bibliographical references and index.
    ISBN 0–333–97236–8 (cloth)
      1. Vigilance committees – Northern Ireland. 2. Vigilance committees –
    South Africa. 3. Death squads – Northern Ireland. 4. Death squads –
    South Africa. I. Monaghan, Rachel. II. Title. III. Ethnic and intercommunity
    conflict series (Palgrave (Firm))

    HV6322.N67 K56 2002
    364.1'34–dc21   2002073393

10   9   8   7   6   5   4   3   2   1
11   10   09   08   07   06   05   04   03   02

Printed and bound in Great Britain by
Antony Rowe Ltd, Chippenham and Eastbourne

To Veronica and Frédéric

Contents

List of Figures

Acknowledgements

The authors wish to acknowledge funding received under the ESRC Violence Research Project (Grant L133251003). We would also like to thank all of those who gave generously of their time for interviews both in Northern Ireland and South Africa. Dermot Feenan assisted with some early aspects of the fieldwork and we received helpful comments from Brice Dickson and Patricia Mallon. Pete Shirlow and Victor Mesev (University of Ulster) kindly compiled the GIS maps from data gathered in the project.

1
Informal Justice in Context

Introduction

Northern Ireland and South Africa may, at first sight, appear to have little to offer in terms of comparative analysis beyond the rather superficial observation that both are 'divided societies' as the title of this book suggests. One point of comparison, however, is that both might be styled 'post-conflict' societies and, as a consequence, merit academic enquiry to uncover common characteristics which could promote policy learning both within and between Northern Ireland and South Africa and, more generally, other countries emerging from conflict. Both countries have new political dispensations and seek to eschew the legacy of bitter and bloody violence. The collapse of apartheid in 1989, lifting the 30-year ban on the African National Congress (ANC) and the subsequent release of political prisoners including Nelson Mandela, created a climate for political negotiation and change in South Africa. In the face of international financial/trade sanctions and ongoing mass resistance, the then State President F.W. de Klerk, moved to create internal stability. To external observers and an increasing number of white South Africans 'apartheid stood exposed as morally bankrupt, indefensible and impervious to reforms'.[1] The restrictions of apartheid began to be removed and political rights extended to black South Africans. These reforms paved the way for an interim constitution and the first multiracial democratic elections in 1994 which led to a Government of National Unity.[2] Nelson Mandela was elected President in May 1994 and set out his vision for the attainment of a democratic, non-racial, non-sexist, peaceful and prosperous country in which he referred to four founding stones to build a new society. The first was national reconciliation and national unity, the need for blacks and whites to live together as equals, and as citizens bound together by a common destiny. Second, the establishment of a democratic system which ensured that all citizens have an equal right and an equal possibility to determine their future. This prohibited the option of tyranny and dictatorship, and guaranteed the fundamental rights of all. Third, to end the enormous race and gender disparities in wealth, income and opportunity inherited from the past which detracted from the achievement of the goals of national unity and reconciliation. Fourth, the rebuilding and modernising of the economy and setting it on a high and sustainable growth path to end poverty, unemployment and underdevelopment. Mandela argued 'we must refer to the mood of the masses of our people who correctly expect that freedom must be attended by a better life for all. But because they are poor, these millions understand the effort and time it will take to graduate from walking barefoot to the comforts of a truly decent existence' (Mandela, 1996: 22).

The ANC-led government therefore embarked on a twin-track approach of reconstruction and development of the country and the democratisation of its institutions. The Reconstruction and Development Programme (RDP) has five major policy programmes: meeting basic needs (through provision of housing, piped water, electricity, rural health care etc.), developing the country's human resources, building the economy, democratising the state and society, and implementing the RDP. The government also set up the Truth and Reconciliation Commission (Promotion of National Unity and Reconciliation Act, No. 34 of 1995) to investigate gross human rights violations during the apartheid era, identify victims and perpetrators, grant amnesty in the case of 'political acts' where there was full disclosure, and recommend measures to prevent such violations occurring in the future. The ANC's success in the country's second democratic elections (June 1999)[3] gave the party an overwhelming mandate to accelerate a programme of 'transformation' under President Thabo Mbeki (Mandela's successor), aimed at tackling the significant socio-economic problems facing South Africa: unemployment, AIDS, crime and education. In his inauguration speech he regretted that some South Africans were 'forced to beg, rob and murder to ensure that they and their own do not perish from hunger'. The legacy of political resistance, often violent, deployed to make the townships ungovernable during apartheid has created a culture tolerant of citizens taking the law into their own hands.

Northern Ireland's transition to 'peace' has been more recent and capricious. The signing of the Belfast Agreement in April 1998 and its subsequent endorsement in referenda by its electorate (71.2 per cent) and voters in the Irish Republic (94 per cent) heralded a political solution to the seemingly intractable problems which bedevilled the province for 30 years. Pivotal to the success of this transition to a power-sharing executive, with an inclusive system of decision making (parallel consent or a weighted majority), was the eschewal of violence by participating parties. Signatories to the Agreement had to affirm their commitment to six fundamental principles[4] of democracy and non-violence – to 'democratic and exclusively peaceful means of resolving political issues' (Belfast Agreement: section 4:1, 1998). The British and Irish governments formally resolved their historical differences through the general and mutual acceptance of the principle of consent – Northern Ireland is part of the United Kingdom, and will remain so, as long as a majority wishes. The Irish Constitution (articles 2 and 3) was amended to reflect this understanding and power was devolved (December 1999) to a locally elected Northern Ireland Assembly with a wide range of executive and legislative powers. The Agreement also contained measures designed to create a 'normal and peaceful society in Northern Ireland'. The most significant included the early release of political prisoners, parallel reviews of the policing and criminal justice systems, new independent Human Rights and Equality Commissions, and a commitment from participants to total disarmament of all para-military organisations by working with the independent International Body on Decommissioning. Failure to resolve the arms issue (prosaically described as 'no guns, no government') led to temporary suspensions of the Northern Ireland Assembly and Executive in February 2000, August and November 2001, a political impasse, and the re-imposition of Direct Rule from Westminster. The status of devolution remains tentative contingent on a resolution of the arms issue.

Comparing Northern Ireland and South Africa

While there have been several important comparisons made at the macro political level between Northern Ireland and South Africa, there is a paucity of public policy learning across the two countries. In terms of the former, McGarry (1998), for example, draws attention to work which compares the conflicts and argues that there are significant differences in considering the two cases (Adam and Moodley, 1993; Adam, 1995; Dickie-Clark, 1976; Giliomee and Gagiano, 1990; Guelke, 1994; Macdonald, 1986; and Taylor, 1994). The most important of these contextual differences is that while South Africa's conflict took place largely within a single state, Northern Ireland's occurs within a wider

British–Irish space. Other differences include the fact that the South African conflict, unlike Northern Ireland, is not about the legitimacy of the state, hence the objectives of political violence differ in both countries. Moreover, the degree of disparity between the majority–minority communities isn't at all comparable and the scale of the problem is quantitatively different.

South Africa has 43.7 m people, 77 per cent of which are African, 11 per cent white, 9 per cent coloured, and 3 per cent Indian/Asian. Figures from the 2000/2001 South African Survey published by the South African Institute of Race Relations highlight the fact that 57 per cent of the population lived in poverty in 1996. Officially, South Africa had an unemployment rate of over 23.3 per cent in 1999, although if people not actively seeking work were included, this would rise to some 36 per cent, and a gross domestic product of $4290 per capita. By international standards, in particular the African continent, South Africa is not poor, it is a middle income country. These figures however disguise major disparities. More than 3 m households (out of 10.7 m) still have no electricity, and 8 m people still have no access to clean water. As one observer suggested 'South Africa is really both a first-world country and a third-world country, the rich part mostly white, the poor part mostly black' (Grimond, 2001: 3). Northern Ireland, by contrast, is a small region of the United Kingdom with a population of 1.7 m people, of which 38.5 per cent are Catholics,[5] average gross earnings were £360 per week in 2000, its gross domestic product for 1999 was £17 000 m or £10 050 per capita,[6] and its unemployment rate at Spring 2001 was 6.2 per cent of the Northern Ireland workforce (Northern Ireland Annual Abstract of Statistics, 2001). Comparing the two countries: the Human Development Index for the United Kingdom (including Northern Ireland) is 0.931 and for South Africa 0.716.[7]

The theoretical basis for comparison, however, according to Connor (1990) is that both countries exhibit fundamental differences over national identity or 'ethno-national' dimensions. An ethnic group has been defined by Cashmore (1995: 102) as 'a group possessing some degree of coherence and solidarity composed of people who are, at least latently, aware of having common origins and interests'. Once the consciousness of being part of an ethnic group is created then distinct languages, religious beliefs and political institutions become part of that ethnicity. The fundamental conflict in Northern Ireland and South Africa is, according to Connor, between ethnic groups over national identity. McGarry and O'Leary (1995: 354) concur on Northern Ireland – 'explosive national conflicts arise between politically mobilised ethnic communities. Territory, sovereignty and national esteem are their media. Land, power and recognition are their bloody issues. Northern Ireland has been the site of such ethno-conflict'.

Donald Woods (1995), immortalised in the film *Cry Freedom*, argued that there are several further points of comparison. Both countries have had crises of legitimacy in terms of government, have gone through civil turmoil and have been held up as examples of outdated and malign approaches to sharing political power. South Africa, and latterly Northern Ireland, have changed to democratic consensual government through an inclusive political process. Central to this was the Constitution of the Republic of South Africa, 1996, drawn up by the Constitutional Assembly which reaffirmed South Africa as a constitutional and republican state. The Belfast Agreement in April 1998 acknowledged the substantial differences between the political parties but accepted their respective legitimate aspirations (to remain part of the United Kingdom or to become a United Ireland). They agreed to 'strive in every practical way towards reconciliation and rapprochement within the framework of democratic and agreed arrangements' (Belfast Agreement, 1998: 1). Converting the democratic ideals enshrined in the Constitution/Agreement respectively into practice provides further points of comparison.

In South Africa this has involved a radical overhaul of the machinery of government at every level, a major programme of reconstruction and development, and moves towards openness and a culture of human rights. In chapter two of the Constitution,[8] human rights bind all legislative and executive bodies of the state at all levels of government. They apply to all laws, administrative decisions taken and acts performed during the period in which the Constitution is in force. Similar provisions have been made in Northern Ireland through the independent Human Rights Commission established as a result of the Belfast Agreement to promote and protect the human rights of everyone. This involves the preparation of advice for the British government on what rights could be added to the European Convention on Human Rights to form a Bill of Rights for Northern Ireland. The main purpose of the Bill of Rights is to establish and guarantee the relationship between the state and its citizens. One section of the Belfast Agreement considers 'rights, safeguards and equality of opportunity', within which it highlights reconciliation and victims of violence as a key focus. South Africa addressed this issue through the Truth and Reconciliation Commission which attempted to uncover the cause, nature and extent of gross violations of human rights under apartheid based on 'a need for understanding but not vengeance, a need for reparation but not retaliation' (Promotion of National Unity and Reconciliation Act, 1995). Northern Ireland did not opt for a Truth and Reconciliation Commission but instead established two units within government[9] to 'promote models of community healing and to enable growth in confidence and empowerment for individual victims and survivors' (Northern Ireland Executive Programme for Government, 2001: 2.2.2).

Similar comparisons also exist in the area of urban renewal. The President of South Africa has pledged resources to job creation, crime and violence, health and 'generally improving the quality of life of millions of our people who lead desperate lives' (Mbeki, 2001: 8). Integrated development programmes have been targeted in the poorest areas to deliver housing, roads, water, sanitation, schools, clinics, magistrate offices and police stations.[10] Although the needs are of an entirely different order in Northern Ireland, the devolved government is, through a policy of 'targeting social need', attempting to tackle the problem of social exclusion. This policy has three complementary elements: a focus on the problems of unemployment and increasing employability; tackling inequalities in health, housing and education, and the problems of disadvantaged areas; promoting social inclusion by government departments working together and with partners outside government (Office of the First Minister and Deputy First Minister, 2001). In short, both countries offer opportunities for comparative analysis on policies dealing with the legacy of societies riven with violence, inequality, treatment of majority–minority communities and building inclusive democratic institutions.

Violence: comparative learning

For the purposes of this book, however, the focus of our attention is on comparative policy learning in the area of tackling violent crime, in particular paramilitary and vigilante violence, with which both countries have become synonymous. In South Africa official statistics are difficult to validate. The then Minister for Safety and Security (Steve Tshwete) placed a moratorium on the release of crime statistics in July 2000 for one year, ostensibly because of problems with their reliability, but according to critics, such as the Democratic Alliance, to hide the worsening state of crime in the country. The number of crimes, especially rape, carjacking, serious assault, housebreaking and common robbery has been increasing since 1996, and the trend has been sharply upwards since 1998. Though the murder rate has been falling, the rates for other kinds of violent crime have all been rising. In 1999, about a third of all reported crimes were violent, and the number had increased by over 9 per cent in 1998. The 2000/2001 South Africa Survey shows that while recorded crime increased by 24 per cent between 1994 and 2000, the number of prosecutions dropped by 23 per cent and the number of convictions went down by 19 per cent. Of the 2.58 million cases which were reported to, or recorded by, the police in 2000, only 8.2 per cent ended in conviction of the perpetrators. Convictions for serious crime were even worse: 2 per cent for carjacking, 3 per cent for aggravated robbery, and 8 per cent for rape. While levels of recorded crime have increased, the criminal justice system has been less effective. In short, violent crime is growing faster than any other and the majority of criminals never get caught. The South Africa Survey further records gang-related crime. Police statistics show that there were 316 gang-related shootings in 1999. This might not, however, reveal the extent of such crime since there is significant non-reporting. Some 70 per cent of crime in the Western Cape is believed to be gang-related. Vigilantes killed 137 people between January 1999 and March 2000. There was evidence of support for vigilantism. *Mapogo-a-Mathamaga*, the country's largest vigilante group had an estimated 50 000 members in January 2000. According to Terence Corrigan one of the writers of the 2000/01 South Africa Survey:

> Persistent crime resulted in many people turning to vigilantism. South Africa is no longer threatened by violent instability, but insecurity arises from other types of violence: gang activity, urban terrorism, vigilantism, and feuding in the taxi industry. Such violence may not have political objectives (although this is often suspected), but it shares some characteristics of political violence. It suggests a level of organisation, is perceived to target certain people or groups systematically (unlike 'random' crime) and can become a 'way of life' for both victims and perpetrators. (Corrigan, 2001: 2)

All of this has led to calls for extreme measures to tackle extreme circumstances. Two MPs (Stanley Mogoba and Michael Muendane) from the Pan Africanist Congress (PAC) have called for cutting off the offending limbs of criminals. Both claim to respect the legal process and suggest that limbs should be cut off after people were tried in court. The inability of the police to deal with crime is a major concern. Thompson has argued that the Mandela government inherited a 'white-and-black police force trained to maintain white supremacy, one that frequently tortured or even murdered its victims' (Thompson, 1999: 87). Many of its officers were deeply corrupt and lacked basic skills to undertake conventional police work. He claims that nearly one-quarter of the total police force is functionally illiterate and little progress has been made in terms of improving their ability to do the job.

In an attempt to explain the high crime rates in South Africa, one view is that crime is a legacy of apartheid and therefore a development challenge that can be countered by alleviating poverty and disadvantage. Steinberg (2001) goes further by arguing that the crime wave, while originating in the violence of apartheid, is primarily due to the failure of South Africa's democratic state to impose moral and institutional authority. In other words, the politics of exclusion and estrangement that characterised apartheid continue today. Simpson (2001), from the Centre for the Study of Violence and Reconciliation, contends that because there is a gangster culture, it is 'premature to talk of South Africa as a post-conflict society'. He notes the 'snail's pace nature of transformation' and the fine and often blurred line between the 'socially functional' violence of resistance and the 'anti-social' violence of criminality. He argues that the growth in youth-based criminal activity and organisation, not re-emerging political resistance, represents 'the gravest threat to an embryonic human rights dispensation' (both authors cited in Pelser, 2001: 80–2 reviewing Steinberg (2001)). This resonates hugely with increasing levels of anti-social behaviour and criminal activity in Northern Ireland.

While of a different scale, the latest crime figures in Northern Ireland show a similar deterioration. The number of shootings increased in 2000/2001 to 331 compared to 131 during the previous 12 months. Bombings also increased from 66 in 1999/2000 to 177 in 2000/2001. This is the highest level of shootings and bombings since the 1994 Provisional IRA and loyalist cease-fires. Eighteen people were killed in the conflict compared to seven in 1999/2000, all of whom were civilians (as opposed to police or army personnel). The number of people injured as a result of the security situation rose by more than 25 per cent, from 878 in 1999/2000 to 1101 in 2000/2001. Violent crime, defined in the statistics as offences against the person, sexual offences and robbery, increased by 160 over the same period. Of particular concern, however, is the number of paramilitary-style attacks (so-called 'punishment' beatings and shootings) now standing at an all time high of 332 in 2001 (this figure is provisional and may be subject to minor change). All of this in an era of cease-fires, peace and political agreement.

While not oblivious to the ongoing and increasing violence, the British government rationalises this as 'an imperfect peace', or what former Secretary of State Mo Mowlam described as 'an acceptable level of violence'. Quite how 'acceptable' is defined is unclear, but the notion that a society riven with violent conflict can be more tolerant of murder, shootings and bombings is the implication of this description which can become self-fulfilling and encourage acquiescence in the *status quo*. Instead, the government argues that its role is to create the political context in which violence becomes a thing of the past and the aims of paramilitary groups have been superseded by political progress. The British government has attempted to do this in several ways. First, by securing the political institutions which are the democratic core of the Belfast Agreement – devolved government through the Northern Ireland Assembly and the Executive. Second, the implementation of the Patten Report on police reforms including the introduction of legislation to amend the Police (Northern Ireland) Act 2000 and reflect more fully Patten's recommendations. Third, the implementation of the Criminal Justice Review so that the criminal justice system has the confidence of all parts of the community and delivers justice efficiently and effectively through a fair and impartial system which encourages community involvement, where appropriate. Fourth, a progressive rolling programme reducing levels of troops and military installations, as the security situation improves. And finally, further progress in implementing the Agreement's provisions on human rights and equality.

In practice, the British government's ability to deliver democratic stability has made faltering progress. The on–off nature of devolution (through suspensions of the institutions) demonstrates the fragility of the peace process and how contingent it is on the resolution of issues such as policing, decommissioning and demilitarisation. Some Unionists, for example, are challenging historic moves by the IRA in putting a quantity of weaponry verifiable beyond use, as insufficient. The establishment of a new Police Service of Northern Ireland (replacing the RUC from November 2001) accountable to a Policing Board, has not secured the agreement of Sinn Féin. Stable governance is far from secure. Dr John Reid (Northern Ireland Secretary of State) declared:

> We are on a journey from violence to democracy. For those who are making that change from violence to politics, including Republicans, we have shown patience. We don't underestimate how far they have come. We understand the historical and ideological enormity of that challenge. But ultimately we all face a stark choice. The ballot box,

or bomb and the bullet. There is no mix 'n' match in a democracy. (Secretary of State's Speech to Labour Party Conference: 3 October 2001)

The research for this book would contend, however, that there *is* in fact a 'mix 'n' match' in the democracy that is Northern Ireland but the government simply chooses to ignore it in the interests of what they perceive as the broader collective good of securing a long-term political settlement.

This brief overview of the two countries suggests several things. First, communities, which have been brutalised during conflicts over a long period, become desensitised to violent crime. Second, within conflict settings, crime can be differentiated into 'political' and 'normal' crime. The former could include informing and collaborating with the 'enemy' even though such activities would not necessarily be deemed as criminal by the state. In contrast, 'normal' crime would include break-ins, muggings, rape, car theft, drug-dealing etc., criminal offences necessitating action by the formal justice system. When the legitimacy of the state and effectiveness and impartiality of its organs (the security forces and legal system) are integral to the nature of the conflict, however, this fore-closes recourse to the usual channels by which communities seek to tackle 'normal' crime. Third, and as a direct consequence, communities develop their own responses to crime, informal justice mechanisms, which will be heavily influenced by the violent environment within which they live. In Northern Ireland these are located within working-class communities while in South Africa they are confined to the black townships. These mechanisms can be divided into two types, punitive sanctions meted out by agents of informal justice, paramilitaries in the case of Northern Ireland and vigilantes in the South African context, and secondly, non-violent restorative justice schemes. In Northern Ireland, restorative justice is a relatively recent approach taken by working-class communities whereas in South Africa's townships it has a long history.

This book will therefore consider in detail key aspects of the so-called informal justice system in two divided societies. It will begin by conceptualising informal justice and locating it within the wider literature on political violence (remainder of this chapter). We will examine, both historically and contemporarily, how the informal justice system operates through paramilitaries and vigilantes (Chapter 2), experiences of the victims of summary justice (Chapter 3), and the response of communities to this type of violence within their midst (Chapter 4). We consider how public bodies and non-governmental agencies react to the existence of informal justice (Chapter 5) and alternative ways of tackling the causes of communal violence (Chapter 6). The emerging debate is then located more broadly in a discussion on how informal justice aligns with international human rights standards and violations thereof (Chapter 7) before drawing some conclusions and policy implications from the research undertaken for this book (Chapter 8).

In general terms, therefore, we attempt to:

- Document the nature of the informal justice systems in Northern Ireland and South Africa.
- Identify reasons for the prevalence of this activity.
- Record and understand the perception of communities to this type of violence.
- Evaluate the response of voluntary/NGO and statutory agencies.
- Assess possible strategies for the prevention or reduction of summary justice within the wider context of human rights abuses.
- Draw some tentative policy implications based on the two case study countries – Northern Ireland and South Africa.

We now consider the concept of informal justice within the context of the literature on political violence in both countries and elsewhere (North and South America).

Conceptualising informal justice

Informal justice refers to those acts committed outside the boundaries of the formal criminal justice system. Such acts usually involve collective violence and are often described as vigilantism. Vigilantism is a problematic concept in that there has been little serious attempt to conceptualise it. As Johnston (1996) notes, 'the problem is that everyone has an opinion on what vigilantism is, but no one has taken the trouble to define it' (Johnston, 1996: 220).

For some scholars such as Black (1984) and De la Roche (1996) vigilantism is merely a synonym of social control. According to Black, some activities, which are regarded as criminal by the state, are often modes of conflict management involving the pursuit of justice and may entail punishment, even capital punishment. Thus vigilantism can be viewed as both social control and self-help. For Black, social control refers to any process by which individuals or groups define or respond to the deviant behaviour of others. It can involve a variety of phenomenon ranging from a frown or scowl to a verbal reprimand, to physical expulsion from a group, to violence. Self-help is defined as the handling of a grievance or dispute by unilateral aggression. In many tribal and traditional societies it is the primary mode of social control and would include assassination, feuding, fighting, maiming and beating. When similar actions are taken in modern societies they are labelled as crime but can still be understood nevertheless as social control and self-help.

De la Roche (1996) argues that collective violence, when unilateral and non-governmental, occurs in four main forms: lynching, rioting, vigilantism and terrorism. Each form can be distinguished from the others in terms of liability (individual versus collective) and degree of organisation (low versus high). In cases of lynching and vigilantism, only the person responsible for the grievance is held accountable or liable. In contrast, in instances of rioting and terrorism, a group or members of a group or other social category such as a religion or political party, are collectively held liable for the conduct of an individual or group. Furthermore the level of organisation involved can differentiate the various forms of collective violence. Lynching and rioting have a relatively low level of organisation while vigilantism and terrorism involve a high level of organisation. This can be seen in Figure 1.1.

For others, vigilantism represents a sub-category of political violence. Rosenbaum and Sederberg (1976) attempt to explain vigilantism as violence designed to maintain the established socio-political order and subsequently label it as establishment violence. They argue that 'vigilantism is simply establishment violence. It consists of acts or threats of coercion in violation of the formal boundaries of an established socio-political order which, however, are intended by the violators to defend that order from some form of subversion' (Rosenbaum and Sederberg,

LIABILITY

		Individual	Collective
ORGANISATION	Low	lynching	rioting
	High	vigilantism	terrorism

Figure 1.1   Four Forms of Collective Violence
Source: De la Roche, 1996: 10.

1976: 4). Using this wide-ranging and over-inclusive definition they construct a typology of ideal types of vigilantism based upon the intended goal of the action: crime-control, social-group-control, and regime-control. Crime-control vigilantism is directed against those individuals who are suspected of committing acts that would be punishable by the formal system but who are not punished because of inefficiencies, corruption or leniency within the formal criminal justice system. Examples of this type of vigilantism would include the elimination of suspected petty thieves or drug dealers by groups of private citizens. Social-group-control vigilantism is undertaken by a communal group who feel threatened by another group advocating or seeking a redistribution of resources or values. The catalyst for such vigilantism 'is usually the attempt of a low-ranked group to rise above its socially prescribed position' (Rosenbaum and Sederberg, 1976: 13). The early activities of the Ku Klux Klan can be seen as social-group-control vigilantism. The final ideal type is that of regime-control vigilantism. Unlike the previous two types of establishment violence, which involve the use of violence to preserve the *status quo* and are aimed outward at threatening elements within society, regime-control vigilantism is concerned with altering the regime for the better, for example *coups d'état*. Thus vigilantism is seen as a conservative phenomenon undertaken by groups and is basically negative given that its essential aim is to suppress, or in some cases to eliminate, any threats to the *status quo*.

Brown (1975) and Abrahams (1998) also consider vigilantism to be a conservative and group phenomenon. Brown defines vigilantism as referring to 'organised, extralegal movements, the members of which take the law into their own hands' (Brown, 1975: 95–6). Abrahams, while conceding that vigilantism is not an easy concept to define, constructs an 'ideal type' thereby identifying general characteristics of the phenomenon. He suggests that vigilantism,

> typically emerges in 'frontier' zones where the state is viewed as ineffective or corrupt, and it often constitutes a criticism of the failure of state machinery to meet the felt needs of those who resort to it. It is a form of self-help, with varying degrees of violence, which is activated instead of such machinery, against criminals and others whom the actors perceive as undesirables, deviants and 'public enemies'. (Abrahams, 1998: 9)

Although acknowledging that vigilantism is a form of self-help, Abrahams contends that it is conceptually quite different from self-help of the 'simple oppositional kind' such as feud, revenge or vendetta, in that these occur between structurally equal individuals or groups.

A key criminological contribution to this debate is made by Johnston (1996) who provides a definition of vigilantism as,

> a social movement giving rise to premeditated acts of force, or threatened force, by autonomous citizens ... Such acts are focused upon crime control and/or social control and aim to offer assurances (or guarantees) of security both to participants and to other members of a given established order. (Johnston, 1996: 232)

Johnston argues that it is possible to draw a distinction between two modes of vigilantism: one having a focus on 'crime control', the other being concerned with 'social control' or the maintenance of communal, ethnic or sectarian order and values. Paramilitary groups in Northern Ireland, he suggests, may undertake dual forms of vigilante engagement – 'punishment' attacks against those accused of criminal deviance (for example, joyriding and burglary) and those accused of communal deviance (for example, breaching paramilitary organisation rules). Importantly, Johnston (1996: 229) notes that vigilantism is a reaction to real or perceived deviance, distinguishing it from mere 'establishment violence'. Hence he represents the actions of paramilitaries involved in 'punishment' squads in Northern Ireland as vigilantism, whereas the actions of the same groups involved in shooting Catholics/Protestants, soldiers, police and bombing buildings is described as acts of political (establishment) violence, which 'have no direct function in the internal regulation of social deviance'. Johnston concludes that vigilantism is a subject awaiting criminological analysis and draws attention, *inter alia*, to the need for research on the relationship of vigilantism to other forms of policing. The suggestion from scholars thus far that vigilantism is *either* a sub-category of political violence *or* must be differentiated completely from violence which is politically motivated, merits a review of the wider literature on the relationship both in Northern Ireland and South Africa.

Political violence and informal justice

Both Northern Ireland and South Africa are replete with literature on political violence which concentrates on two broad areas – firstly, trying to establish the facts or data about the levels, distribution and sources of violence (Murray, 1982; Poole, 1993; Sutton, 1994; Jeffrey, 1997; Bornman, van Eeden and Wentzel, 1998; South African Institute of Race Relations, 1998; Truth and Reconciliation Commission, 1998; Fay, Morrissey and Smyth, 1999) and secondly, examining the causes of, or motivation for, violence (Haysom, 1990; White, 1993; O'Duffy, 1995; Patel, 1997; Bornmann, 1998; Sullivan, 1998). What is largely absent, however, in terms of Northern Ireland is research on the nature of the relationship between paramilitary groups and the communities over which they exert social control. There are, however, notable exceptions including the work of Burton (1978), Hillyard (1985), Cavanaugh (1997) and Silke (1998). In terms of South Africa, an emerging literature exists on informal justice including Hund and Kotu-Rammopo (1983), Seekings (1989), Burman and Schärf (1990) and Crais (1998). However, most of this research deals with the apartheid era and not with the 'new' South Africa.

Northern Ireland

Northern Ireland, for obvious reasons, has been the subject of several studies on political violence. In general the literature concentrates on the two broad areas mentioned above. In the first category, Poole (1993) and Murray's (1982) spatial analysis of violence, Sutton's index of deaths (1994) and Fay, Morrissey and Smyth's (1999) database of location and organisations primarily responsible, are typical examples. The value of this work has clearly been in trying to establish a reliable and comprehensive database with disaggregated statistics which allow depth analysis of trends.

In the second category, studies have examined the motivation for political violence as a way of informing the political debate and proffering advice to the British government. O'Duffy (1995), for example, looked at the variation in targeting and intensity of paramilitary violence in Northern Ireland and explained it as ethno-national rather than 'sectarian' or 'communal'. In an empirical study, Sullivan (1998) considered the changing dynamics of violence (measured by killings) during two phases (1969–80 and 1981–94) in Northern Ireland. His work updated a study undertaken by White (1993) who researched the causes of political violence in the first phase of this period.

In an ethnographic study undertaken in loyalist and republican communities in Belfast, Cavanaugh (1997) argued that the main cause of political violence was not materialism (socio-economic inequalities), culture or religion but the absence of national state legitimacy. She claimed that 'the levels of republican violence are most affected by organized and unorganized state repression, while loyalist violence is most affected by republican violence and activated when loyalists feel threatened' (Cavanaugh, 1997: 45). She contended that the absence of state legitimacy has fostered support for, and tolerance of, paramilitary groups within communities.

What is significant about Cavanaugh's work is that she posited the community, not as a passive entity, but integral to the analysis of political violence in Northern Ireland. As part of that analysis she suggested civil society in Northern Ireland was characterised by a strong sense of community, ethnic separatism, and a tradition of loyalism and republicanism in both its cultural and political forms. 'With basic security needs left unfulfilled and fear of identity loss prevalent in both republican and loyalist communities, strong intra-communal infrastructures have evolved which protect and promote community cohesion' (Cavanaugh, 1997: 46). This strong communal cohesion, she argued, demands social order and control constructed through 'alternative legalities to that of the state'. She concluded:

> Paramilitary involvement in social control is tolerated, even demanded, but communal support is conditional... For both loyalist and republican paramilitaries to maintain credibility they must meet communal demands to control hooding, drugs and petty crime. Administering 'rough justice' however, risks alienating or reducing the paramilitant's support base... These findings illustrate the complexity of the relationship between paramilitant and community. (Cavanaugh, 1997: 49)

Cavanaugh concurred with research undertaken by Burton (1978), which suggested that paramilitaries and their communities had a 'see-saw' relationship, and to describe it as one forged through 'naked force' was too simplistic. Silke's work (1998) is more detailed both on the range of methods used by paramilitary vigilantes and their motives. He argued that their activities revolved 'around a practical need to control criminal behaviour as perceived by the community, and to control behaviour within that community which may threaten the authority of the paramilitaries' (Silke, 1998: 151). Drawing on previous work by Hillyard (1985) and Sluka (1989), he distinguished between these two categories as 'punishable' offences – community or civil crime (theft, drug-dealing, joy-riding, vandalism, muggings and so on), and political crime (public criticism of the paramilitaries, collaboration with the security forces and so on). He added that maintaining alienation between the community and security forces was also an important function of vigilante activity. Silke (1999a) further explored the problems which vigilantism raised for Sinn Féin as a political party and argued that 'if they step away from "community policing" they risk losing much of the political support they currently enjoy'. If, however, they do not step away from it he suggested 'they stifle the possibility of genuine growth' (Silke, 1999a: 89). This is a bold assertion implying that Sinn Féin's political support is predicated on a single issue – their propensity to address communal violence.

The complexities of the community–paramilitary relationship are also obvious from a study by Brewer *et al.* (1998), which looked at the role played by local communities in civil unrest and crime management. The researchers challenged some preconceptions about informal policing by paramilitaries as a means of social control in a study of two areas in Belfast. Therein, they found localised evidence of the extended family network, a sense of neighbourliness and community identity 'which extends beyond the policing role of the paramilitary organisations'. In fact, they argued the role which paramilitaries play in local crime management 'is heavily conditional upon the survival of community structures' (Brewer *et al.*, 1998: 576 and 581).

South Africa

Similarly South Africa has also generated a number of studies on political violence. The South African Institute for Race Relations (SAIRR) provides facts and figures for a range of issues including violence and crime as part of its annual survey of South Africa. Although there are statistics for fatalities of political violence, no figures are available for crimes arising from informal justice as the South African Police Service does not maintain separate records on different methods of murder. The work of Jeffrey (1997) looking specifically at KwaZulu-Natal, the Truth and Reconciliation Commission (1998) and Bornman *et al.* (1998) try to establish the facts or data about the levels, distribution and sources of violence.

The other area of research has been concerned with the motivation for the political violence. Haysom (1990), for example, examined the use of violent, organised and conservative vigilante groups by the police in the townships during the apartheid years. Haysom argued that the 'operation of vigilante groups in South Africa's black areas since 1985 is an expression of the militarisation of South Africa' and that 'it is a low intensity civil war which appears to be conducted at arm's length from an aggressive state' (Haysom, 1990: 64). Such groups were used by the apartheid state to neutralise anti-apartheid resistance in the townships. In contrast, the work of both Bornmann (1998) and Patel (1997) deal with the political violence of the post-apartheid South Africa. Bornmann addresses the issue of group membership as a possible decisive factor of violence and conflict, while Patel looks at the causes of conflict in the taxi industry.

In terms of the literature on informal justice, Hund and Kotu-Rammopo (1983) in their exploratory study of Mamelodi (a township outside Pretoria), found a number of different and competing dispute-settlement and peace-keeping mechanisms in existence. They contend that,

> The township was composed of different sets of social relations, each of which forms a distinct sub-system with its own perceptions of justice and its own methods for securing it. What this means is that 'justice' in the township operates within a developing system that is marked by the continuing conflict of different values and loyalties. (Hund and Kotu-Rammopo, 1983: 179)

This idea of a number of competing structures operating at any one time was also found by Burman and Schärf (1990) in their study of townships in Cape Town. They suggest that at no time since the establishment of the colonial state has there been a universally accepted adjudicative and enforcement mechanism that has accommodated the needs of the indigenous population. Subsequently this has led to a plurality of structures and practices. In selecting a forum for settling disputes 'people will try to avoid discredited or impotent courts' and 'a court must offer acceptable remedies and be able to enforce its judgements if it is to keep its credibility as a possible forum' (Burman and Schärf, 1990: 735).

The changing nature of informal justice mechanisms in South Africa is also obvious from the work of Seekings (1989) and Crais (1998) who attempt to explain the emergence and proliferation of 'people's courts' in 1985–86 in light of historical antecedents. 'People's courts' arose at a time of intense political conflict and struggle and were aligned to anti-apartheid elements within the townships. They addressed both 'civil' (for example, theft, rape and gangsterism) and 'political' (for example, collaborating, ignoring a consumer boycott or a stay-away) crimes. As Crais notes 'the literature has tended to see people's courts as recent, urban phenomenon that emerged *de novo* in the context of political struggle. In doing so the literature has stressed function over process, structure over history, snapshots of brief moments over sustained analysis over time' (Crais, 1998: 49). Other countries also provide insights into the operation of informal justice.

The Americas

There is a body of literature examining informal justice elsewhere in the world, in particular North and South America. Brown's (1975) work examines the history of violence and vigilantism in the United States of America (USA). For Brown, the key to understanding why Americans have resorted so frequently to violence as a means of resolving conflict lies in the country's past: 'Our history has produced and reinforced a strain of violence, which has strongly tinctured our national experience' (Brown, 1975: vii). Patterns of violence (for example the American Revolution and the Civil War) have accompanied every stage and aspect of the country's national existence. Much of this violence has been socially conservative and designed to preserve the *status quo*. Thus violence 'has been the instrument not merely of the criminal and disorderly but of the most upright and honorable' (Brown, 1975: 4). Lynch mobs, vigilante movements and other related extralegal bodies arose in response to the absence of effective law and order in the frontier region (1767–1850). In frontier areas vigilantism filled a void. According to Brown, vigilantism or neo-vigilantism also existed in areas where the formal system of law and order was functioning satisfactorily. Neo-vigilantism (post-1850) was a response to 'the growing pains of post-Civil War industrial and urban America' (Brown, 1975: 24). It was aimed at reducing the cost of local government in the area of law and order and targeting those problems that were being dealt with too slowly, or not at all, by the formal system. Subsequently vigilante action acted as a process of community reconstruction through the recreation of social structure and values. For example, a vigilante hanging served as a graphic warning to all potentially disruptive elements that community values and structure were to be upheld. Much of the vigilantism experienced in the USA was of an organised nature and the group or movement usually disbanded once the problem of disorder had been dealt with. In some cases, such as the Bald Knobbers of the Missouri Ozarks (1885–86), intervention by outside authorities was required to put an end to the vigilante actions.

In contrast vigilantism in South America has been of a more varied nature. Both Martins (1991) and Benevides and Fischer Ferreira (1991) examine the phenomenon of lynchings (defined as citizens' action against another citizen suspected of having committed a crime or violated some social norm) in Brazil. According to Martins, it is possible to differentiate between those lynchings that occur in the state capital cities and their environs, and those that occur in the smaller towns of the interior. In the former, lynchings are carried out mainly by the poor and working-class while in the latter, lynchings and attempted lynchings are undertaken by the middle-class who are critical of the formal criminal justice system (police and the courts). This criticism of the formal criminal justice system has also manifested itself in lynch mob attacks on police stations and courthouses. Lynchings in the capital cities are a response to the crimes to which the poor and working-class are subjected to and a demonstration of their desire for justice. Lynchers 'do not want to continue to be the helpless victims of robbery, rape and murder' (Martins, 1991: 25) and one lynching is likely to lead to another. The lynchings of the interior towns, on the other hand, are the preserve of the middle-class and are undertaken to maintain their position and protect their society from outsiders. Despite these differences, similarities between the two types of lynching exist, namely:

> In both types of lynching there is a conservative or reactionary motivation; both types deny self-defense to the victim; both eliminate trial by an impartial judge and the right of appeal. For a victim of lynching, the verdict is final ... Lynching represents a punitive act that denies its victim the right to a judgment about the relative severity of an alleged crime. It also denies the lynch victim an opportunity to pay a penalty short of death. All alleged infractions become equal – whether petty larceny or murder. (Martins, 1991: 24–5)

Benevides and Fischer Ferreira (1991) also distinguish between 'anonymous lynch action' and 'communal lynchings'. Anonymous lynch actions occur in large Brazilian cities and those involved are strangers who act individually and not as a community in the lynch action. The origins of such actions are unknown and are usually initiated by shouts of 'stop thief'. In contrast, communal lynchings occur in the smaller towns or cities and involve broad popular mobilisation within a particular community or locale. Communal lynchings involve a degree of co-ordination, planning and leadership. Both types of lynchings 'represent moments in which citizens' feelings of impotence and rage [against the formal institutions of society] reach a peak' (Benevides and Fischer Ferreira, 1991: 43).

The work of Gitlitz and Rojas (1983) and Palomino (1996) examines the *rondas campesinas*, peasant vigilante committees found in the mountains of northern Peru. Gitlitz and Rojas address the reasons behind the appearance of the *rondas* and their exact nature. In brief, the *rondas* are vigilante committees that emerged in the mid-1970s in response to the increasing criminal activity of professional cattle rustlers together with the theft of community goods such as educational equipment. By 1983 there were some four hundred groups patrolling the roads, trails, pastures and fields in northern Peru. Gitlitz and Rojas argue that the '*rondas* are essentially the spontaneous creation of small peasant farmers, who have organised on their own, largely without help from outside, in response to a concrete, specific, shared and vital economic problem' (Gitlitz and Rojas, 1983: 165). This 'vital economic problem' was cattle rustling. The police, it is argued, have not been able to deal effectively with this problem because of a number of factors, including the geographical location of cattle farming and the distances involved, plus suspicions of widespread corruption amongst government officials who are believed to be collaborating with the rustlers. Palomino's work updates our knowledge of the *rondas*. He distinguishes between two types of organisation in the *rondas campesinas*; firstly the organic self-generated vigilante committees described by Gitlitz and Rojas, and secondly, the Self-Defence Committees or anti-subversion armed *rondas campesinas* created by the government of President Fujimori in the early 1990s.

These two types of organisation differ in terms of the way in which they are established and the functions they perform. The popularly generated or organic *rondas* are formed after agreement amongst the residents of a particular village or town and deal with a range of problems including cattle rustling, petty theft, family and land disputes, and even crimes like rape. They attempt to resolve conflicts and sanction the wrongdoer either by repossessing the stolen goods or cattle or resorting to physical punishments such as whippings or cold night-time baths. As Palomino notes, 'the objective is not only to punish the individual physically or economically but also morally. To do this, the castigated are usually forced to walk naked through town with signs hanging from their necks stating the acts they have committed' (Palomino, 1996: 116) – there are resonances with Northern Ireland. In contrast the Self-Defence Committees are organised by the army and provided with military training and uniforms. They are then assigned to patrol a determined area, for a set period of time, usually not more than 15 days, that has been recently visited by subversives. The Brazilian State's policies towards the *rondas* has shifted over time. Initially the government opposed their activities but since the mid-1980s they have been recognised as autonomous organisations and provided with weapons although they are ultimately under the administration of the state structure and subject to political authority.

Notwithstanding this wider literature on informal justice and, in conflict settings, its relationship with political violence, there is a dearth of material on the role that communities play in our understanding of informal justice in Northern Ireland and South Africa and a lack of knowledge about the dynamic between them and the paramilitaries and vigilantes. Kennedy (1995), for example, points out that although the 'brute facts of communal violence are well known … what is less well known is the degree of "internal" paramilitary repression (in the form of beatings, shootings and mutilations) which developed in the shadows of the larger conflict' (Kennedy, 1995: 67). Similarly, Hund and Kotu-Rammopo note 'despite the need for it, there has been remarkably little research on problems of justice in African urban areas' (Hund and Kotu-Rammopo, 1983: 179). As the political landscape changes to a post-conflict era, a number of questions arise from the existing work of researchers. How realistic is the distinction made between civil and political crimes perpetrated by paramilitaries or vigilantes on communities? In Northern Ireland is the bulk of paramilitary vigilantism directed at the former, as Silke claims? Jennings, for example, suggests that paramilitaries are economically motivated and that they will 'devote more time to gangster activity, to recoup their losses from terminating political violence' (Jennings, 1998: 307). Have the paramilitaries and vigilantes alienated their communities by administering 'rough justice', as referred to by Cavanaugh (1997) and Burman and Schärf (1990)? Understanding the relationship between paramilitary and vigilante groups and communities has become even more important as the scale and ferocity of internal repression increases and, in the case of Northern Ireland, has become inextricably linked to political developments. In short, in a new post-conflict environment what is the ongoing *raison d'être* for vigilante and paramilitary groups administering informal justice in South Africa and Northern Ireland respectively? These are the questions we seek to address in subsequent chapters. Before looking at substantive issues, however, we trace the historic roots of informal justice.

2
Agents of Informal Justice

Informal justice in Ireland: a historical overview

Prior to colonisation by the English in the sixteenth century,[11] the indigenous Irish population had developed their own set of customary laws, customs and institutions embodied in the Brehon Laws. As Davitt explains:

> 'Brehon' in Irish means judge, and an Irishman would speak of the 'Brehon' law just as you would say the national law or the law of the land; now, however, we speak of the Brehon law in the same way as we speak of the Draconian code, and to signify the old law of Ireland, before the days of conquest began. The Brehons were the judges, next in importance to the chiefs, and their persons were sacred. (Quoted in Cashman, c. 1885: 194)

This system acted as both a legal and a social code ensuring the smooth running of the rural hierarchical communities found in Ireland at this time. Accordingly, the legitimacy and authority of the system was dependent on the cohesiveness of the community. The hierarchical nature of the community resulted in the status of the victim and offender being taken into account when sentences were passed. Other factors considered included the extent of the damage and any accompanying circumstances such as provocation. Sentences aimed to restore harmony and to re-integrate the offender into the community. Subsequently, the Brehon courts did not rely on physical punishment, and fines were given for most offences including murder. Expulsion from the community was reserved for habitual criminals and perpetrators of 'vile' crimes (see Ginnell, 1894). As to what constitutes a 'vile' crime remains unclear as Ginnell fails to offer a definition: 'In the case of certain peculiarly vile crimes, which need not be further specified here' (Ginnell, 1894: 191). Thus the Brehon system can be seen to have espoused a restorative approach to justice as opposed to merely exacting retribution on behalf of the victim and larger community. With colonisation the system was suppressed and eventually died out around the beginning of the seventeenth century following the extension of English law to Ireland.

Informal justice systems were also developed by secret organisations in the eighteenth and nineteenth centuries. Organisations such as the Whiteboys, the Rightboys and the Ribbonmen were exclusively agrarian in origin and enjoyed the support of the rural population. Subsequently they were primarily concerned with protecting those who worked on the land, namely tenants, labourers and small holders from arbitrary acts by landholders. In addition, they opposed the payment of dues they felt were 'illegal', for example taxes or tithes levied for the establishment of the Protestant Church (see Donnelly, 1978; Alter, 1982; Bell, 1996). In terms of their activism, they pulled down fences, filled in ditches, killed cattle, burned houses, physically assaulted landowners and their agents and took action against 'collaborators' or informers. For example, individuals suspected of informing had part of their lips and tongues cut off. In some cases, sinister public warnings were given. Donnelly (1978) notes the Whiteboys 'erected gallows, made coffins, and dug graves in the public roads, all obviously intended as portents of the fate awaiting those who refused to obey their mandates' (Donnelly, 1978: 29). These agrarian secret organisations emerged particularly in times of economic depression or hardship and tended to disappear once conditions improved.

The nineteenth century saw the emergence of revolutionary agrarian societies associated with the Irish national movement. These societies were concerned with securing fundamental changes in Irish agrarian conditions. To this end they worked closely with tenant farmers and refused to recognise the legitimacy of the British system of justice. For example, the Irish National Land League organised resistance to bailiffs and established alternative arbitration courts known as Land League courts. These courts sought to impose a 'moral law', which entailed rents being withheld, evicted farms being kept empty, unilateral fixing of new rents, and the ostracism or community boycott of landlords. Transgressors of this 'moral law' were subject to a range of 'punishments' including the firing of warning shots into people's houses, the infliction of injuries to the person, for instance ear-clipping or gun-shot

wounds to the legs, and in some cases death (Forester, 1988). The government eventually imposed martial law and outlawed the Land League
in 1881. However, violent agrarian agitation continued through the
1880s until it dwindled away (Alter, 1982).

In parallel to the development of revolutionary agrarian societies, the
Irish Republican Brotherhood (IRB) was formally constituted in 1858.
The IRB was a secret political society solely focused on the national
question, the removal of British rule and the establishment of an Irish
Republic. Following an unsuccessful rebellion in 1867, they established
a Supreme Council, which claimed political authority in Ireland. In subsequent years the IRB formed provisional governments, adopted consti-
tutions and decreed their enactments as the laws of the Irish Republic.
Like the Irish Land League, the IRB refused to recognise the legitimacy
of the British system of justice and dealt with local disputes. Laws of
membership and secrecy governed individuals within the organisation.
Violations of these codes were met with violence, for example those
suspected of being 'traitors' were executed (Ó Broin, 1976).

Increased agitation by Irish nationalists continued throughout the
nineteenth and early twentieth century. In the 1918 General Election,
Sinn Féin won 78 out of the 100 Irish seats and subsequently declared
itself the provisional government of Ireland, Dáil Éireann. In August
1919, Sinn Féin established a scheme of national arbitration courts
to deal with land disputes. These courts required the consent of both
parties in order for them to work. Although intended as a national
measure, the scheme was only fully operationalised in West Clare and
relied upon Sinn Féin personnel with moral authority in the local area
(see Macardle, 1965). These courts were replaced by Dáil Courts, which
operated simultaneously with the 'official' courts between 1920 and
1922. The Dáil Courts dealt with a spectrum of offences ranging from
rowdyism, theft, property damage, licensing laws, bank and post office
robberies. Judges were able to order the return of stolen property, the
payment of restitution or fines, beatings, banishment from the area
and, given the non-existence of Dáil Éireann gaols, the removal of a
guilty party to an island for the duration of their sentence (Kotsonouris,
1994; Connolly, 1997). The organisation of the Dáil Courts was hierarchical and they operated at the Parish, District and Supreme Court level.
The Parish Courts dealt with claims of less than £10, petty crime and
eviction from low rent accommodation. Evidence was gathered and presented to three judges elected from the local community. As representatives of the local people, judges took their duties very seriously as
it was considered a great honour to be elected. As Kotsonouris (1994)

notes, the Parish Courts were central to the acceptability of the system and were very much 'consumer-driven' as they provided a cheap and immediate access to justice. Furthermore, they tended to operate on the basis of conciliation; this is in part reflected in the range of 'punishments' open to them and a local need for solidarity and affability. Accordingly, they received public support and had little difficulty enforcing their decrees and, where required, Irish Republican Army (IRA) Volunteers imposed the sentences of the court. In 1922 the Free State government was established and the British court system in Ireland passed to the Saorsta Éireann. Subsequently, the Dáil Courts were suppressed. With the passing of the Dáil Éireann Courts (Winding-up) Act 1923, the Dáil courts were declared illegal and their decrees rendered unenforceable.

Informal justice in South Africa: a historical overview

Prior to colonial conquest and expansion in the mid-nineteenth century,[12] the indigenous African population had developed their own set of laws, customs and institutions. These processes sought reconciliation of disputing parties and the restoration of harmony within the community. If an offending party was found guilty, they were shamed and then re-integrated into the community. Colonial conquest and subsequent rule did not however result in the elimination of such structures. Within the rural areas, a dual system of state (formal and colonial) and non-state (informal and indigenous) courts operated. This was due in part to the early isolation of magistrates and the small number of police in service. In areas where local chiefs were in opposition to the new 'alien laws', they were largely unenforceable. In addition, there was reluctance from locals to use the new courts and many continued to take their disputes to their chief. A number of reasons have been suggested for this including a dislike and fear of the colonial power, a preference for familiar institutions, loyalty to community leaders and a fear of a community backlash (Burman and Schärf, 1990). These alternative courts were proving difficult to displace and their continued existence posed an ongoing challenge to the state.

The state's response was to co-opt the chiefs under their control and amend their functions so that they became an integral part of the administration system of colonial rule.[13] Rural chiefs were given jurisdiction over matters of 'black law and custom', while magistrates' courts implemented Roman-Dutch law. With the start of urbanisation in the mid-1920s, the government established Commissioners' Courts in the townships.[14] It was hoped that these courts would provide a simple and inexpensive apparatus for settling disputes between blacks and that those involved would have their cases tried by experts in indigenous law and custom. However, this was not the case and 'fundamentally, the Commissioners' Courts created 'poor law for poor people' (Brogden and Shearing, 1993: 138). The accused were assumed to be guilty and usually plea bargains were forced upon them. A government enquiry also found evidence of bribery and irregularities in the taking of guilty pleas.[15]

From 1948 onwards the police and judicial institutions enforced the state's (National Party's government) policy of racial discrimination. Subsequently the police were primarily concerned with enforcing liquor and pass laws, and suppressing dissident political activity rather than fighting 'normal' crime and settling disputes. The courts were responsible for upholding apartheid legislation, thus they were seen as a tool of the apartheid state and township residents did not use them voluntarily. Furthermore, they were generally expensive and inaccessible to the black population and imposed upon them an alien moral code. Indeed some practices classified by the formal system as crime, for instance the illicit brewing and sale of beer, were not viewed as crime by blacks. Furthermore, other activities such as the provision of information to the state (informing) or going against the *makgotla* (community courts) broke local moral codes that required community sanction in the townships but did not transgress the laws of the state (Hund, 1988).

Within the townships there was little state control and the absence of a police presence together with rising violent crime and theft meant that a dispute settlement and policing vacuum was created. This vacuum was left to the communities themselves to fill. Hence in many townships especially in the Transvaal and the Orange Free State areas, community-based courts or *makgotla* emerged to fill this vacuum. The *makgotla* represented an attempt to revive traditional rural courts within a township setting. Their social base comprised immigrants from the rural areas and working-class adults. They advocated a morally conservative code emphasising respect for elders and the importance of kin. Like the rural courts they modelled themselves upon, they were concerned with the restoration of harmony and the re-integration of offenders into the community.

Crime in the townships was seen as the result of disrespectful and undisciplined children and there was a reliance on corporal punishment to remedy this. One such example is Soweto's *makgotla*, which developed in the Meadowlands area between 1969 and 1974, in response to a number of break-ins, rapes and assaults. It combined vigilante patrols with regular courts, and was primarily concerned with juvenile delinquency and family disputes. Its leader, Sinah 'Madipere' Makume stated:

> I believe naughty children should be sjambokked. So if children under 18 are brought to us for disciplining, we sit as a *lekgotla* [singular of *makgotla*] and thrash out the problem, giving the child (a chance) to defend himself. If the kid is found guilty, we let the parents lash him in front of us so the child cannot fight back. (Quoted in Seekings, 1989: 121)

The *makgotla* received much support from the township residents, but over time some, including the one in Soweto, lost their community support base because of their increasing arbitrariness and brutal practices. Their policing became more violent and their sentencing increasingly severe. For instance, in Soweto, a 19-year-old youth was sentenced to 100 lashes with a sjambok and later died from his injuries (Seekings, 1989). The activities of the *makgotla* to an extent minimised the workload of the police in the townships and relieved the state courts of some township cases. The state tolerated the *makgotla* so long as they did not pose a threat to apartheid and even encouraged its members to join the police as reservists.

In other townships, especially in the Western Cape, street committees developed. These usually comprised respected male residents who were directly elected by street residents. Street committees settled domestic disputes and served as spokespersons to the local Administration Boards (responsible for the day-to-day running of areas where black Africans lived) on issues such as housing, roads and lighting. Township residents also came together to form patrols, for example, in Guguletu, a township near Cape Town, a group known as the *Amasolomzi* was established to patrol the area at night. Its members were usually middle-aged heads of households. On apprehending troublemakers they were encouraged to hand them over to the police for prosecution or to the street committees if they could deal with the matter (for more details see Burman, 1989).

In 1976 the state decided that half the curriculum in African schools was to be taught in Afrikaans. In Soweto 15 000 pupils joined in a march against this decision and a number of pupils lost their lives after being confronted by the police. School boycotts spread countrywide with the youth assuming a prominent position in the struggle against apartheid. Subsequently much of the informal justice exercised in the townships became political in nature. The politicised youth or 'comrades' increasingly saw the *makgotla* and the street committees found in the Western Cape, as instruments of the apartheid state. In response, the 'comrades' developed new models of informal justice centred around people's courts. Such courts were clearly linked to the political struggle against apartheid and were viewed as alternatives to its structures. This new political morality advocated discipline, organisational accountability, recognition of the true enemy (the state and its surrogates), and an understanding of the damage that crimes against the oppressed caused, namely that they were diversive and counter-productive to the struggle. Those found guilty were given punishments of a community service nature; sometimes this also involved a measure of reparation, while more serious cases received limited physical punishment, such as 30 lashes. Thus as Schärf and Ngcokoto (1990: 350) observe, 'the main aim of such exercises in "people's justice" was to show the wrongdoers that they had not been abandoned by their community'.

Although many of the practices of the people's courts, for instance the re-integration of the offender and the restoration of community harmony, have their roots in traditional African concepts, those within the new courts placed their emphasis on a 'popular' mandate as opposed to a traditional one. Indeed, their practices also challenged a number of traditional concepts such as notions of authority and patriarchy. Subsequently people's courts took action against elders, and against men on behalf of women. By 1987, there were some 400 people's courts in operation in South Africa (Brogden and Shearing, 1993).

Over time these courts gained a reputation for predetermined guilt of the accused, instant redress, engaged in wide-scale human rights abuses and were often referred to as 'kangaroo courts'. They administered beatings and whippings with a sjambok, with sentences up to 300 lashes and in some cases even death. In the mid-1980s, the 'necklace' method of dealing with those people identified as 'sell-outs', 'collaborators' or 'informers' was introduced. This involves the placing of a petrol-filled tyre around the victim's neck, which is then set alight. It is estimated that some 350 to 400 people were killed by this method of execution between 1985 and 1990. A further 500 were necklaced between 1990 and 1994 (Minnaar, 1995). Individuals involved in the practice highlight the summary nature of the activity: 'we did not even care to interrogate ... If it is said you are an informer, that was it. We did not want to interrogate and find a person innocent' (Cikicane, a necklacer from a Port Elizabeth township quoted in Nomoyi and Schurink, 1998: 158). The 'comrades' also policed the stayaways in addition to the consumer and rent boycotts, taking action against individuals who dared to break them. For example, when a stayaway was called township residents were not allowed to leave the township in order to go to their place of work (hence the name stayaway), individuals found in violation of this call often had their houses burnt down.

The mid-1980s also saw the emergence of conservative and pro-*status quo* vigilante groups, known as *mabangalala* (for a detailed account of their development see Haysom, 1986). These groups were violent, organised and received varying degrees of police support. They were politically directed in the sense that they sought to neutralise individuals and groups which opposed the apartheid state and its institutions, for instance civic associations, youth groups, trade unions and women's groups. Members of the *mabangalala* included local elites such as businessmen and elders plus their supporters, urban gangsters and policemen who had seen colleagues attacked or killed. Many of those involved had a vested interest in retaining the *status quo* as their power and influence rested on their ability to reward supporters either through clientelism or gangsterism. The number of such groups mushroomed during 1985 in both urban and rural settings. Within the townships these included the *witdoeke* (Crossroads, Cape Town), the *Amabutho* (Umlazi, Natal), the *Phakatis* (Thabong, Orange Free State) and the *Ama-Afrika* (Kwanobuhle, Eastern Cape), while in the rural areas these included *Inkatha* (KwaZulu) and the *Mbokodo* (Kwandebele). These groups provided violent opposition to those who opposed the homeland regimes and suppressed the development of organised resistance.

The *mabangalala* claimed the lives of hundreds of people, left thousands homeless and in some areas created an acute refugee problem. By 1988, more than 90 per cent of unrest related deaths were caused by vigilante violence and by 1992, some 6–7000 people had died as a result of such attacks (Murray, 1994). This violence tended to be portrayed by the government and media alike as 'black-on-black violence'. As Haysom (1990: 63) notes, 'in 1988 more than twice as many persons died as a result of vigilante and counter-vigilante violence in the Greater Pietermaritzburg area than died in Beirut during the same period, that is, 682 compared with 312'. The attacks by the *witdoeke* in May 1986, resulted in 58 deaths, the destruction of 7000 homes and created 70 000 refugees in the informal settlements of Nyanga, Nyanga Bush and Portland Cement, areas in which there was support for the ANC (Haysom, 1989). Eyewitnesses reported police acquiescence of the destruction. They were seen escorting the *witdoeke* and firing tear-gas and shotguns at residents who attempted to resist the attackers or tried to save their possessions (see Cawthra, 1993). The police in this case actively supported the *witdoeke* in their attack on anti-apartheid supporters while also failing to offer protection to those targeted.

In other cases the police directly sponsored and established groups to work on their behalf, were active members of such groups and regularly failed to investigate their criminal activities. In addition to aiding *mabangalala*, the police also stood accused of using criminals and gangs to control townships or to create within them a situation of lawlessness either through direct support or inaction against their activities (Schärf, 1990). In the Port Elizabeth township of Missionvale, the police were utilising criminals as 'Peacemakers' to control the area who then engaged in a campaign of robbery, rape and theft (Missionvale Action Committee, 1991).

Self-Defence Units (SDUs) were established in many townships from 1983 onwards as a response to co-ordinate the actions of the 'comrades', provide protection from the security forces and to counter attacks by the *mabangalala*. These units were supported by the ANC and were often directed by members of its armed wing, *umkhonto we Sizwe*. Initially they were to hand offenders over to the people's courts for punishment but often exacted summary justice.

We now examine the agents of informal justice and explore the changing nature of such 'justice' throughout the period of 'the Troubles' and in post-apartheid South Africa.

Contemporary informal justice in republican areas

Since the beginning of 'the Troubles' alternative or informal justice and policing mechanisms have developed in Catholic working-class communities. Citizen Defence Committees (CDCs) were established in most areas and provide the earliest example of organised activities. Their primary aim was to protect Catholic enclaves from loyalist attacks. To this end they erected and supervised barricades and mounted foot and car patrols. As Connolly (1997) notes,

> modern self-policing was a spontaneous community self-defence response, not something initiated or controlled by a revolutionary organization. Probably the earliest example of self-policing was that in and around the barricades in 1968 at a time when the IRA was a moribund organization. (Connolly, 1997: 21)

With the introduction of internment without trial, the Catholic Ex-Servicemen's Association[16] supplemented the activities of the CDCs in Belfast and supervised the barricades in places such as Ballymurphy (*The Tatler*, 1972).

In the nationalist areas of the Bogside, Brandywell and Creggan in Derry the local defence association set up a 'police force' to deal with petty crime. 'Punishment' usually took the form of a stern lecture regarding the need for solidarity in the area. In the early 1970s for a brief period, the Free Derry Police operated independently of republican paramilitaries, with its chief being a former international footballer who had given up his career to undertake the position (McCann, 1993). In contrast, in the 'no-go' areas of nationalist Belfast the republican para-militaries assumed an early policing and justice role (Munck, 1984; Silke, 1999a). The Provisional IRA, formed as a result of a split in the republican movement in December 1969, is the most active of the republican paramilitaries in the area of informal justice. In the late autumn of 1970, the IRA launched a purge of 'anti-social' elements in the Ballymurphy area. Those targeted included alleged local criminals, minor drug abusers, teenage girls suspected of fraternising with British soldiers and anyone believed to be connected to, or having sympathy with, the state. Many were forced to leave the area, others were sub-jected to a variety of 'punishments'. For example, a local woman was tarred and feathered and left tied to a lamppost while two local 'gang-sters' Arthur McKenna and Alexander McVicar were shot dead (Cusack and McDonald, 1997). The IRA's decision to assume a policing role is based, in part, upon a need to ensure the organisation's own security and survival particularly from informers. As Burton (1978) notes,

> informing is particularly threatening. It attacks the fabric of the com-munity in its capitalization on what cannot be controlled, the public nature of knowledge...Systematic informing would rip the district apart and smash its tentative organizations, laying it open for a Protestant or British Army takeover. (Burton, 1978: 35)

Furthermore, 'people's courts' also operated in 'no-go' areas. These courts consisted of committees of locally elected people who would come together to deal with neighbourhood disputes and minor criminal offences. The concept of community courts was debated openly at the time (early 1970s) in the local republican press and stressed a restorative justice approach (*Andersonstown News*, 1973b, 1973c). Sentences handed down by the 'people's courts' were of a community service nature. However, these courts were relatively short lived owing to a number of factors including harassment of committee members by security forces, insufficient resources, the partiality of neighbours, and sanctions imposed by neighbours, did not carry the same legitimacy and weight as those imposed by the IRA.

A special IRA unit established to deal with crime, and the republican youth movement, Na Fianna Éireann, undertook early policing activities (Hillyard, 1985; Munck, 1988). Incidents were investigated and those found guilty were subject to a variety of 'punishments'. Individuals deemed responsible for house and shop break-ins were compelled to re-imburse their victims and return stolen goods. In cases involving children, the IRA approached the parents and requested greater parental control (*An Phoblacht*, 1971). In situations where an alleged offender refused to co-operate or had ignored previous warnings, then they were liable for 'suitable punishment'. The most usual type of 'punishment' meted out by the IRA at this time was a 'kneecapping', the shooting of an individual anywhere in the leg. As Munck (1988: 44) notes, 'the "hard core" criminal is pursued relentlessly, the ordinary hood is to be reformed'. Individuals suspected of informing were dealt with most severely and their 'punishment' depended on the type of information passed on to the security forces, in some cases they were 'kneecapped' but usually they were shot dead. Reports in both the *Andersonstown News* (1973a: 2) and *An Phoblacht* (1974b: 3) carry details of such shootings:

> with three men from the area being shot in the leg in the past two week period, it seems evident that the provisional Irish Republican Army have now begun the new 'get tough' tactics which have been expected for some time.

> The Provisionals claimed responsibility for shooting a man in the knee in Derry's Creggan Estate for alleged 'touting'.

In February 1975, the IRA declared a cease-fire that was to last into the following year. With the ending of this cease-fire, the 'incident centres' established by Sinn Féin to monitor breaches of the truce, evolved into 'advice centres'. These centres were labelled locally as 'Provo Police Stations' as they were easily accessible to the local community, and people took their complaints to them. This development marked a shift in the administration of informal justice in republican working-class areas. Informal justice was taken out of the hands of the IRA field commanders and moved to the control of the emerging Sinn Féin. According to Joe Austin, a Sinn Féin councillor for north Belfast, once a crime or incident of 'anti-social behaviour' has been reported to Sinn Féin and the details recorded, an investigation was launched by the Civil Administration Officers (CAOs) assigned to deal with the case. After all the details were collected and information gathered from local people verified, a decision would be made regarding the next step. If an offender had been identified, they would be brought before the CAOs and allowed to defend themselves, although in practice this did not always happen owing to limited resources and demands upon the system. A further decision would then be taken as to whether a warning should be issued or if the case should be passed to the IRA for them to carry out a 'punishment' (Human Rights Watch/Helsinki, 1992).[17] If the offenders were not known, then a warning would often be placed in local newsletters, the republican press and sometimes via a leaflet drop in the area. The IRA has, over the years, developed a graduated scale or tariff system consistent with the seriousness of the offence under consideration. This tariff ranges from warnings, threats, curfew, fines or restitution, placarding, tarring and feathering, beatings, shootings, exiling and ultimately death (Silke, 1998). The 'punishment' ordered, in theory, is influenced by mitigating factors such as age, gender, past criminal record and family background, particularly those from a strong republican tradition. In some cases those accused are told to turn up at a certain time and place in order to receive their 'punishment' – 'punishment' beating/shooting by appointment. Failure to do so often results in a harsher 'punishment'. In practice, however, the level of 'punishment' can be arbitrarily brutal or lenient, depending upon whether the offender was 'connected' in some way to known paramilitaries or influential members of the republican movement. Furthermore, some individuals have been punished as a result of mistaken identity.[18] For example, John Brown a 79-year-old senior citizen was mistakenly identified as a paedophile and shot in both knees and ankles. In a small number of cases the IRA has publicly apologised to the person concerned or placed an apology in the local republican press.

The IRA appears to have been reluctant to shoot women and those found 'touting' or informing and/or fraternising with the 'enemy' were often tarred and feathered or had their heads shaved (*An Phoblacht*, 1974a; Morrissey and Pease, 1982). It has been suggested that within the republican community there existed a reluctance 'to accept wounding as a legitimate form of punishment for female offenders' (Morrissey and Pease, 1982: 164). The 'disappearance' of Jean McConville by the IRA in December 1972 from her home in Belfast's Divis flats is contrary to this and may explain why her body has never been recovered. The IRA contends that Mrs McConville admitted to being an Army informer

(*An Phoblacht*, 1999), a claim strongly contested by relatives. Her body has never been found despite recent digs for the 'disappeared'.[19] Burton (1978) suggests that tarring and feathering represents an expulsion ritual in that the punished individual knows that they are to leave the area. A further reluctance to shoot those aged 16 or under can also be detected, as an anonymous youth worker explains,

> the rule is that the Provos don't 'punish' – that is, don't shoot or severely beat – kids under sixteen. Some of our younger kids have been 'branded' – that is, made to stand against a lamppost, or outside church on a Sunday, with a placard around their necks saying, 'I am a hood', or 'I am a joyrider'. It's the softest option the Provos can take – public shaming. (Quoted in Human Rights Watch/Helsinki, 1992: 47)

Other 'punishments' used against those 'too young to be kneecapped' include curfewing, tar and feathering, being tied up and publicly painted and the punishing of parents. For instance, a 39-year-old father was shot after 'repeatedly ignoring IRA warnings to discipline two of his sons who had been involved in persistent acts of anti-social behaviour' (*An Phoblacht/Republican News*, 1982a: 3). Republicans' use of shootings as a 'punishment' peaked in 1975 with 139 being recorded by the Royal Ulster Constabulary (RUC). Silke (1999a) suggests the peak can be attributed to the cease-fire of 1975 in that Sinn Féin was attempting to establish itself as a political power in nationalist areas and that there were more IRA Volunteers available to mete out 'punishments'.

With the adoption by the IRA of a cellular structure, an IRA Auxiliary Unit made up of former prisoners, low-calibre members and new recruits took over responsibility for 'punishments'. Other IRA members regard them with distaste: 'They're … the dregs of the organization, people who aren't any good at anything else but beating people up' (quoted in Silke, 1998: 62). In addition to physical 'punishments', the IRA can order people out of a local area, city, Northern Ireland or Ireland. The exiling or expulsion of alleged criminals can vary in time from six months to a year and so on. In some cases, people are ordered out indefinitely. Both a leeway period of between 24 and 48 hours and an 'or else' threat usually accompany expulsion orders. These orders are attractive to paramilitaries as they remove undesirable elements from the community and are less brutal than other forms of 'punishments'. Males, females, youngsters under 16 and, in some instances, whole families have been exiled.

Not only does the IRA take action against alleged criminals but it also punishes its own members for disobeying orders or breaching internal codes. 'Punishments' range from a beating for leaving a gun out of an armoury to being shot for 'bringing the movement into disgrace', this would include self-gain robberies or misusing the organisation's name. To this end, an internal police force known as the 'Nutting Squad' was established which deals with matters concerning IRA Volunteers. According to a former-IRA member, they 'are the ones who put a hood over the heads of informers before 'nutting' them with a shot in the head and leaving their bodies at border crossings' (Collins, 1998: 142). In addition, the IRA has also targeted other republican paramilitary groups. In the 1970s, the IRA launched purges against the Official IRA[20] in some parts of Belfast and in October 1992 took action against the Irish People's Liberation Organisation (IPLO).[21] The IPLO had a history of criminal activities including a gang rape of a woman in the Divis flats complex and involvement in the growing drug trade. The IRA's action resulted in the execution of one IPLO member and the shooting of a further 20 members with assault rifles in Belfast (*An Phoblacht*, 1992). The IPLO disbanded shortly after this.

Throughout the period of 'the Troubles' the IRA has sought alternatives to physical 'punishments'. This can be seen in Figure 2.1 in terms of fluctuations of the number of individuals punished. In 1982 the IRA embarked upon a reconsideration of its policy of 'punishment' after acknowledging that shootings do not solve the problem of rising crime (*An Phoblacht/Republican News*, 1982b). A wide-ranging debate occurred within republican circles, and in nationalist areas generally, as to how to combat crime. Physical action was still taken but against mainly persistent criminals, an identifiable hard-core element. In contrast, the young 'hood' was to be involved in a process of dialogue with the republican movement as to the consequences of their behaviour for their victims and larger community. They were spared 'punishment' if they made a public commitment to desist from their previous activities and gave a written undertaking to the IRA. If this undertaking was broken then they could expect to be dealt with more severely. By 1984 the crime problem in nationalist areas had increased and letters began appearing in the republican press calling for the IRA to reconsider its policy on hoods, which it responded to. More recently the IRA and Sinn Féin have thrown their support behind Community Restorative Justice projects, which are being established in republican areas and are detailed in Chapter 6.

The use of 'punishment' beatings has escalated since the early 1980s and in 1996 172 were recorded by the RUC. This sharp increase

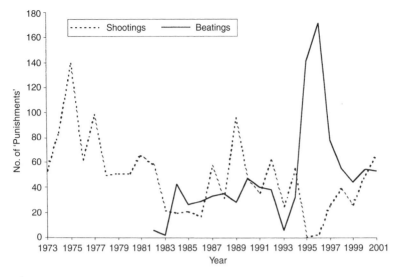

Figure 2.1 'Punishment' by Republicans
Source: RUC/PSNI Statistics.

coincided with the IRA ending its cease-fire with the Canary Wharf
bombing on the 9 February 1996 (the cease-fire was restored on the 19
July 1997). Overall, the general increase in the number of beatings and
corresponding decrease in the number of shootings is linked to the IRA's
maintenance of its cease-fires since 1994. This change reflects moves by
the organisation not to implicate its political representatives in charges
that the cease-fires have been broken, leading to their exclusion from
the peace process and subsequent participation in the power-sharing
devolved Executive. Indeed, in 1994 the year in which the cease-fires
were declared, there were no reported 'punishment' shootings by republicans although beatings increased by over 400 per cent. Since 1996 the
trend has reversed with an increasing number of republican shootings.
The IRA have also been linked to the execution of at least 11 drug dealers since 1994, which have been claimed by a group calling itself Direct
Action Against Drugs. Furthermore, in August 1999, they were directly
implicated in the murder of Charles Bennett, a suspected informer. The
then Northern Ireland Secretary of State, Mo Mowlam, ruled that while
the IRA had breached its cease-fire, the cessation as a whole had not
broken down and no sanctions were taken against Sinn Féin.

A shift in policy towards punishing women and young people under the age of 16 can also be observed. The IRA has taken to physically punishing women. In 1985, they executed alleged informer, Catherine Mahon; her body was found with that of her husband's in an entry in the Turf Lodge area of Belfast. According to RUC/PSNI statistics no females were shot in the period between 1990 and 2001, although this is contrary to the IRA's claim of executing Caroline Moreland in July 1994 for informing (*An Phoblacht/Republican News*, 1994). For the period between 1989 and 2001, 23 females received 'punishment' beatings. The RUC/PSNI is unable to provide a gender breakdown of victims prior to 1989. Young persons under the age of 16 are also liable for more physical 'punishments'. For example, a 16-year-old boy was beaten with hurley sticks and iron bars by at least seven masked men in Newry, while a 15-year-old was beaten with hammers and baseball bats in a nationalist area of Derry (*News Letter*, 1999; Rodgers, 1999).

It should be noted that the IRA is not the only republican paramilitary group to mete out 'punishments'. The Official IRA also 'kneecapped' alleged criminals in the early 1970s, indeed a number of individuals received 'kneecappings' from both the Officials and the Provisionals. The Irish National Liberation Army (INLA),[22] although publicly distancing itself from a law and order role, has shot a number of alleged criminals and informers dead. For instance, in April 1984 John George, an alleged criminal, was found shot dead at his home in Twinbrook. The INLA has also taken action against its own members suspected of informing. In June 1991, it executed INLA member Gerard Burns; his body was found at the back of a house in Ballymurphy. The now defunct IPLO also undertook similar 'punishment' actions. More recently, the Continuity IRA[23] has moved into the administration of informal justice and claimed responsibility for a 'punishment' beating and the exiling of a drug dealer.

Contemporary informal justice in loyalist areas

Since the early 1970s loyalist paramilitaries have assumed a policing role in the communities in which they operate. The largest loyalist paramilitary group, the Ulster Defence Association (UDA), was in fact established in 1971 as a result of the amalgamation of Protestant vigilante groups/defence associations in Belfast. The UDA adopted as its motto *Codenta Arma Togae*, meaning 'law before violence' and sought 'to see law restored everywhere, including the "no-go areas" of nationalist Belfast' (Boulton, 1973: 145). The UDA assumed the role of area defenders against attacks from Catholics and the IRA, mounted roadblocks, patrolled the streets and gathered evidence against petty criminals. The Ulster Volunteer Force (UVF)[24] also adopted a policing role. For example, it established a special patrol group in the Shankill area of Belfast. If an individual was caught by the patrol then they were either warned to stay out of trouble or handed over to the police. Patrols by paramilitaries were not designed to usurp the RUC/PSNI but to assist them. Paramilitaries reserved the right to mete out their own form of justice if the police and courts did not adequately deal with offenders.

Like their republican counterparts, loyalist paramilitaries take action against those involved in 'political' and 'normal' crime. Incidents can be brought directly to the paramilitary group or they become aware of an incident themselves. Most groups claim to carry out an investigation before deciding upon whether or not an individual will be punished. Unlike the IRA, who have different units assigned to deal with 'internal' and 'external' discipline, loyalist paramilitaries employ the same personnel, usually Active Service Units (Bell, 1996). The accused have little chance to defend themselves. Loyalists also punish individuals who are perceived to have offended their members in some way – behaviour that causes offence can range from stealing a member's wallet to sleeping with his wife/partner. Loyalist paramilitaries have used many of the same methods of 'punishment' as republicans, including warnings, placarding, tar and feathering, beatings, shootings, exiling and execution. However, the use of warnings by loyalist groups is not widespread. As one interviewee explains,

> two car loads came and got me and took me away and they stabbed me, left me with thirty-six stitches in the stomach, and told me to come back at seven o'clock [for a beating] ... In fact, when they took me away I thought I was just going away to be questioned because I hadn't done anything. (Interview with a 'punishment' beating victim, September 1999)

Offences of a sexual nature attract harsh 'punishments' and those punished are usually shot or badly beaten. In one case, an ex-Presbyterian minister given a warning by the police for possession of an illegal homosexual pornographic video, died as a result of injuries sustained from a UVF 'punishment' beating. For many loyalist groups, drug dealing is seen as an acceptable way to raise funds, although the leaders of the main loyalist paramilitaries publicly deny this. Silke (1999b) suggests that the vast majority of internal 'punishments' by loyalist paramilitaries involves money, such as swindling, skimming funds from the group, payment of misappropriate 'cuts' or self-gain robberies. Members suspected of informing are usually executed. For example, in November 1981 the Ulster Freedom Fighters (UFF), a cover name used by the UDA, shot dead Arthur Bettice, a UDA member, at his home in the Shankill. Some paramilitary members join the organisation to avoid being 'punished' either by the group they joined or by a rival grouping. An interviewee subjected to a 'punishment' attack by one loyalist paramilitary group joined another group as it 'sort of offered me protection from these other guys' (interview with a 'punishment' beating victim, September 1999). Once a member, it is very difficult to leave a paramilitary group given the illegal nature of their activities.

Actions are also taken against rival groups – in recent times these tend to be centred on feuds involving drugs. Feuds between the rival loyalist paramilitary groups are nothing new as Bruce (1992: 124) notes, 'like any two competing organisations, the UDA and UVF have rarely been on good terms for long'. In the early 1970s disagreements were limited to fist fights but in March 1975 this escalated into a more violent feud in Belfast involving shootings and bombings (for a discussion of the reasons for the feud see Cusack and McDonald, 1997). Following UVF bomb attacks on the homes of a number of UDA men, the east Belfast UDA issued a press statement condemning the use of bombs against them:

> we ask the loyalist community to try and imagine the depraved mind of the UVF 'loyalist', planning and assembling a bomb to plant in a Protestant home ... While we reserve the right to, and indeed will, take retaliatory action against the UVF or any splinter group connected with them, we will not, repeat not, be drawn to the depths of depravity by bombing loyalist homes and endangering of innocent women and children. (Cited in Bruce, 1992: 126)

More recently, a feud linked to a drugs and turf war developed between the UDA/UFF and the UVF on the Shankill and spread to other areas of Northern Ireland including Ballymena, Carrickfergus and Coleraine (see O'Neill, 2000 for details of the background to the feud). Seven men lost their lives in the feud that lasted from July until December 2000 and unlike the 1975 feud, 'innocent women and children' were endangered. An 11-year-old girl was shot in the back in Coleraine and more than 281 households in the Shankill area approached the Housing Executive[25] for assistance after being forcibly evicted from their homes or decided to leave, in fear of intimidation

(Kelly, 2000; Thornton, 2000; Murray, 2000). British soldiers were re-deployed in the areas affected by the feud.

In the period between 1973 and 1985 RUC statistics show that loyalist paramilitaries carried out 317 'punishment' shootings and beatings. Between 1986 and 2001 this figure had increased to 1710 (see Figure 2.2). It should also be noted that RUC/PSNI statistics only record cases reported to them, an under-estimate of the problem – this is also true of republican 'punishments'. The use of 'punishment' beatings over 'shootings' has been visible since the cease-fires of 1994 by the major loyalist paramilitaries. As Winston (1997: 123) notes this 'change came about as a result of the cease-fire emphasis on removing the gun from the political picture'. Like their republican counterparts, loyalist paramilitaries have tried to deflect criticism from their political representatives regarding the maintenance of their cease-fires and have increasingly resorted to 'punishment' beatings as opposed to shootings. However, recently an increase in shootings can be observed. In the year 2001, recorded numbers of 'punishment' shootings (121) exceeded the number of beatings (91). This increase can, in part, be explained by the failure of Northern Ireland Secretaries of State to rule that 'punishment'

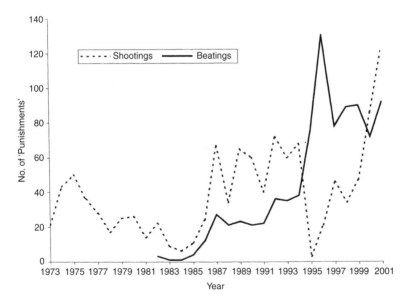

Figure 2.2 'Punishment' by Loyalists
Source: RUC/PSNI Statistics.

shootings and beatings constitute a breach of the cease-fires. Further-more, there are a number of loyalist paramilitary groups that are not on cease-fire, for example, the Orange Volunteers who may be engaged in 'punishment' attacks.

Owing to a relative lack of detailed information about specific loyalist informal justice mechanisms, it is unclear whether groups like the UVF or UDA have ever developed specific policies towards punishing females and young people under the age of 16. Only two women have received a 'punishment' shooting between 1990 and 2001 according to the RUC/PSNI. A further 30 are recorded as having been beaten by loyalist paramilitaries in the same time period. A victim of a 'punishment' beating explained that on his housing estate the UDA as a rule do not physically punish females: 'They don't beat girls ... If you're a girl you're all right' (interview with a 'punishment' beating victim, January 2000).

In recent years loyalists have punished young people under the age of 16. In March 1999 a 13-year-old was beaten with baseball bats by a gang of masked men and told to leave Northern Ireland. In August of the same year, six men armed with hammers beat a 15-year-old. In some instances, those 'punished' receive more than one beating through the course of their teenage years. Like their republican counterparts, senior paramilitary figures are not exactly enthusiastic about meting out 'punishments' and cite pressure from the communities that support them to assume a policing role. The role played by communities is considered in greater detail in Chapter 4.

In summary, therefore, considering the informal justice systems operating in both communities, police statistics show that between 1973 and the end of December 2001 there have been 2564 paramilitary 'punishment' shootings (an average of 91 per year) of which 45 per cent have been perpetrated by loyalists and 55 per cent by republicans. From 1982 to the end of December 2001 there have been 1833 beatings (an average of 96 per year), 47 per cent of which have been carried out by loyalists and 53 per cent by republicans. Statistics on paramilitary-style attacks were not collated before 1973 in the case of shootings and 1982 for beatings, and police admit that official figures are thought to under-estimate the true extent of the problem by as much as 30–50 per cent because victims are reluctant to report incidents for fear of paramilitary reprisal.

Overall, the figures show there was a significant increase in beatings and concomitant decrease in shootings following the cease-fires of August and October 1994. This reflected moves by paramilitaries not to implicate their political representatives in claims that their cease-fires had broken down, particularly on the republican side with their public avowals of non-violent alternatives. Since 1996 beatings have decreased but still remain higher than pre-cease-fire levels, and shootings are escalating year-on-year. In short, the situation is getting worse. There is no information available of charges brought against perpetrators. Offenders are charged with crimes such as common assault, grievous bodily harm and actual bodily harm, hence it is impossible to ascertain successful police prosecutions. The Chief Constable of the Police Service of Northern Ireland has confirmed that the Provisional Irish Republican Army (IRA), Ulster Defence Association (UDA) and Ulster Volunteer Force (UVF), all of which have declared cease-fires, are behind many of these attacks. He highlighted the distinction that they make between 'a cessation of military operations and some distorted view that this sort of barbarity doesn't come within these terms' (MacKay citing Chief Constable, 1999: 351). In October 2001 the government concluded, in the wake of violence in the North Belfast area that the UDA, Ulster Freedom Fighters (UFF) and LVF were no longer maintaining their cease-fires and specified these organisations.[26] The central role played by para-militaries in these attacks is cynically demonstrated by their complete cessation (on the republican side) during the Clinton (former USA President) visits to Northern Ireland in 1994 and 1998 and the Mitchell (USA Senator) review on the implementation of the Belfast Agreement in November 1999.

Transition and post-apartheid South Africa

The period covering the negotiation of a political settlement to the holding of the country's first democratic elections witnessed an increase in overt political violence within South Africa. Statistics reveal that 16 022 people lost their lives as a result of political violence between 1990 and 1994 (SAIRR, 1998: 51). The same period also saw a dramatic rise in crime in general. According to published figures by the Institute for Security Studies, the transition years of 1990 to 1994 showed a 7 per cent decrease in the murder rate but increases in rape (42 per cent), robbery (40 per cent), vehicle theft (34 per cent) and burglary (20 per cent) (Shaw, 1996: 159).

In the same period, people's courts continued to operate and employed varying degrees of punishment. In the township of Alexandra, a woman accused of assault was fined R200 and received a further sentence of a hundred lashes when she could not pay the original fine (Maluleke, 1990). A further example is the sjambokking of a man for speaking on behalf of a defendant at the people's court (Moses, 1990). Others were given death sentences or died as a result of their injuries (Rider, 1992). In Guguletu, a man was beaten to death after being accused of stealing clothes while in another incident an alleged taxi thief was stoned and set alight. Although alive when the police intervened, the gathered crowd refused initially to allow the man to be taken to hospital and he later died of his injuries (*Citizen* Reporter, 1992). Given the reputation of people's courts for brutality and summary justice, anti-crime committees were established within the townships. These committees were primarily concerned with reducing crime but without the excesses of the 'comrades'. In some areas training programmes were established and guidelines issued, and they operated with varying degrees of success (see Minnaar, 1995 for examples).

The election of a democratically elected government in 1994 has not resulted in the eradication of vigilantism. The post-apartheid period has witnessed the open emergence of vigilante organisations such as PAGAD and *Mapogo-a-Mathamaga*. These groups are made more interesting by the fact that they are not confined to the black townships. It has been suggested that PAGAD is the first organised manifestation of vigilantism in the new democratic dispensation (Nina, 1996). PAGAD emerged towards the end of 1995, after a series of meetings between like-minded individuals from within the coloured and predominantly Muslim community living in the Western Cape. This community lives mainly in the townships of the Cape Flats, which are characterised by the existence of gangs, some of which have long histories. It is estimated that there are up to 80 000 active gang members in the Cape belonging to some 137 gangs (figures quoted by Superintendent Al Heylinger, Commander of the Police Gang Investigation Unit, cited in White Haefele, 1998). Crime including murder, rape and drug abuse are daily experiences for the people living and working in these townships. Residents talk of 'the community being on hold', dictated to by the gangs, and how it is 'the innocent who are behind bars' held to ransom by vigilantes (group interview, Manenberg, November 1999).

The organisation's acronym evolved after a meeting at which one participant declared: 'We are ordinary people and we are against gangsterism and drugs. So why not call ourselves People Against Gangsterism and Drugs?' (cited on PAGAD's website, http://www.pagad.co.za/what.htm). Subsequently, PAGAD articulated a number of stated aims and objectives:

- To propagate the eradication of drugs and gangsterism from society.
- To co-operate with, and to co-ordinate the activities of similar minded people and groups.

- To encourage the incorporation of these people and other groups into PAGAD's campaign.
- To generate funds to realise their stated aims.

Initially PAGAD embarked upon an intensive awareness campaign, lobbying local churches, mosques, civic groups, youth clubs and community radio stations for support. They held candlelight vigils, distributed pamphlets and went door-to-door with their message. As their support grew, house meetings gave way to large-scale public meetings and protests. In addition to educating the community, PAGAD entered into consultation with the government and its various departments. In May 1996, 3000 PAGAD supporters marched to Parliament and delivered an ultimatum to the Minister of Justice, Dullah Omar. They demanded the government take action against the drug lords and gangs within the following 60 days. This action was to include the reintroduction of the death penalty for drug dealers, the confiscation of their assets, bail to be set at R10 000 for drug users and denied to drug dealers, first time offenders should be dealt with more severely and that greater control measures be introduced at harbours and airports. If, however, no such action was taken, then PAGAD would be forced to take the law into their hands (for more details see White Haefele, 1998). Following this action, 'ultimatum marches' were conducted to the homes of alleged drug dealers and gangsters. These marches culminated with a 24-hour warning or ultimatum to the individuals concerned to stop dealing in drugs and/or to desist from gang-related crime or 'face the mandate of the people'. According to police figures, PAGAD organised 54 'ultimatum marches' between the start of August and the end of December 1996 (figures cited in Le Roux, 1997).

PAGAD acknowledges that it holds large-scale public meetings and protests, stages marches to the homes of alleged drug dealers and gangsters, and issues warnings and ultimatums to individuals involved in drugs and gang-related crime. However, the organisation denies that it is involved in drive-by shootings, petrol and pipe-bombings and other shootings, although its members were captured on film shooting and then setting alight Rashaad Staggie, a leader of the 'Hard Livings' gang in August 1996. A leaked military intelligence report suggests that between March and July 1998 PAGAD targeted 86 alleged drug dealers and succeeded in killing 24 (South African Press Association-AFP, 1999). Furthermore, police attribute 188 out of the 667 violent attacks recorded in Cape Town in 1998 to PAGAD, and arrested 28 suspects with links to the organisation (Hartley, Jordan and Heard, 1999).

Its members have been charged with a range of offences including sedition, murder, attempted murder, possession of illegal firearms, malicious damage to property and public violence. In December 1999, Dawood Osman became the first member of the group to be convicted and sentenced for murder. He was found guilty on four counts of murder and two of attempted murder following a shooting incident at the Waterfront involving members of the Junior Mafia gang.

Attacks have not been confined to drug dealers and gang members. Individuals who have dared to criticise PAGAD's methods have also been targeted. For example, Dr Ebrahim Moosa, an academic at the University of Cape Town, had his home bombed after criticising on the Muslim radio station Radio 786 their vigilante tactics. He has since left South Africa and is on extended sabbatical in the USA. The media have also been targeted as a result of their reporting of PAGAD activities. In November 1996, both the *Cape Times* and *Cape Argus* were threatened with a boycott while the news agency *Reuters* suspended its Cape Town operations in October 1999 after staff received death threats. The police and the courts have also been subject to PAGAD's attentions. PAGAD allege police collusion with drug dealers and gangs, and complain that the courts release them on easy bail terms. The relationship between PAGAD and the police has further deteriorated following a police clamp down on their activities. For example, in December 1996, the police tried to stop a protest march at Cape Town's international airport; violence ensued and gunfire was exchanged between protesters and the police. Furthermore, five policemen were shot and wounded by PAGAD supporters at Bellville Magistrates' Court during a bail hearing for protesters arrested at the airport (for more details see Le Roux, 1997). In January 2000, a pipe bomb exploded at Wynberg Magistrate's Court where two PAGAD members were due to appear at a bail hearing. Pieter Theron, a magistrate who had heard cases involving PAGAD was assassinated at his home and witnesses due to give evidence against PAGAD members have been killed (MacGregor, 2000; Lovell, 2000).

PAGAD continues to operate a dual strategy of non-violent protest and violent activities. Despite the deaths of a number of their supporters as a result of gang reprisals and police actions, PAGAD still continues to hold public meetings and undertake often-violent actions against drug dealers and gangsters. A recent report by Dixon and Johns (2000: 21) found that,

> PAGAD's less committed supporters have gradually melted away. For them the 'fad' of fighting gangsterism and drugs has passed. PAGAD

has emerged from these experiences a smaller, leaner organisation, but also a stronger one with a more active, more purposeful, membership.

In addition to PAGAD, another organised vigilante group, *Mapogo-a-Mathamaga* (hereafter referred to as *Mapogo*) has also emerged. The group was established in August 1996 in the Northern Province by a group of business people in response to increasing levels of crime and the murder of eight businessmen. Its support base has grown substantially from 100 members initially to a figure of around 50000 with some 90 branches operating not only in the Northern Province but also in Guateng, Mpumalanga, the North-West, in the Free State and in the Northern Cape. This support base is multi-racial, with 10000 white members. Many of these are farmers who tend to live on isolated homesteads. In the past farmers have been targeted by criminals in often extremely brutal attacks (Lubisis, 1999). Monthly subscription rates vary from R50 for pensioners, R500 for businesses and schools, R1200 for shops to R10000 for off-licences.

Early activities of *Mapogo* included apprehending alleged suspects who would then be handed over to the police. After the release of a number of these suspects, the group has resorted to more punitive sanctions against criminal behaviour. If a paid up member of *Mapogo* becomes a victim of crime, they will contact the group, recount the incident and name suspects. Suspects are then are picked up by the group and subjected to an interrogation usually involving violence. John Magolego, the group's leader, publicly advocates corporal punishment as a means of combating crime and views the penal system as an easy option for those found guilty by the formal courts: 'The medicine is the only thing that works. Criminals like going to jail. They get three meals a day. If they go to jail then at least they must sit on very sore buttocks' (quoted in Duval Smith, 1999: 5). This 'medicine' usually involves the sjambokking of an alleged criminal until they confess. In some instances, suspects have died as a result of the beating they sustained and there have been allegations that suspects have been dragged behind vehicles or thrown into crocodile-infested rivers in order to obtain confessions. Given the multi-racial nature of the group, white suspects have also received *Mapogo* 'medicine'. One such case involved the five-hour ordeal of a Grobersdal shopkeeper who was sjambokked after being accused of handling stolen goods (Duval Smith, 1999). Suspects are denied due process, presumed guilty and not given an opportunity to defend themselves or refute the allegations made against them. Members of the group have been accused of murder, attempted murder, kidnapping, common assault and assault with intent to cause grievous bodily harm but, to date, few members (approximately 14) have been convicted. Further to its crime-solving activities, the group has moved into the area of crime prevention by offering services, usually provided by private security firms, such as the protection of property and patrolling. Takers have included schools and churches.

In Khayelitsha, a township on the outskirts of Cape Town, ex-combatants of the liberation struggle have come together with ordinary citizens and taxi drivers to fight crime. In October 1998 they formed the Peninsula Anti-Crime Agency (PEACA) and set up offices in a disused shipping container in the Site C area of the township. There are no joining fees or subscription charges and its membership is estimated at around 1500. The organisation claims it limits its crime-fighting functions to handing over suspects to the police and ensuring damages or reparations are paid to victims of crime (interview with Chair of PEACA, November 1999). For example, in July 1999, its members 'arrested' three men in connection with the murder of a shopkeeper and handed them over to the police. Local residents queue up outside the container to register their complaints and/or to report a crime. The group can receive up to a hundred complaints a day. In order for a case to be taken by PEACA a fee has to be paid. The fee charged will depend upon either the location of the crime scene or the whereabouts of suspects. Moneys paid cover the hire of local taxis as members do not have access to other forms of transport (e.g. their own cars or group-owned vehicle). This fee can range from R50 for a crime/complaint in Khayelitsha to R340 for a journey to Hermanus, a town some distance away. Once a case is opened, PEACA launches an investigation. This involves visiting crime scenes and speaking to witnesses and suspects. Cases are heard at PEACA's offices and decisions are taken by five 'judges'. These 'judges' preside over all matters and are predominantly unemployed members of the community with no formal legal training. The local community police forum and SAPS personnel view the groups as a vigilante organisation. PEACA contend that allegations of criminal activity by its members are part of 'a smear campaign' against them and claim that they have 'been shunned by some members of civil society who stigmatised [them] as a get together of common criminals because of its refusal to toe a particular political line' (PEACA, 1998). According to its own Code of Conduct, PEACA members 'shall be expected to respect the Constitution of the country and all the government laws' (PEACA, 1998). However, PEACA has been accused of taking the law into its own hands and beating suspects. Eight members of the group have been arrested with four senior officials detained in custody on charges of assault and abduction (Gophe, 1999). The group has approached a number of non-governmental organisations (NGOS) in the Cape Town area for training but NGOs have been wary of getting involved with the group, given its vigilante activities.

In addition to the organised manifestations of vigilantism such as PAGAD, *Mapogo* and PEACA, in some townships taxi associations have assumed an anti-crime role at the behest of the community. This was the case in Guguletu (in June 1998) following the deterioration of the community–police relations in the area as a result of a *Cape Times* journalist losing an eye after a police beating. The community, outraged by this incident, together with a growing feeling that the police were not taking their complaints seriously, turned for justice to the Cape Amalgamated Taxi Association (CATA), which operated in the township. On taking a complaint, the taxi-drivers would arrest the suspect/s in the case, convene a kangaroo court, usually physically assault the accused during questioning in order to obtain a confession and/or information regarding the location of stolen goods and then mete out punishment upon pronunciation of guilt. Punishments included sjambokking, parading the suspected criminals naked through the township or dragging them behind vehicles. Many suspects have been severely injured and required hospital treatment. In one instance the taxi-drivers allowed a film crew from the South African Broadcasting Authority to film their handling of a rape case. Television viewers witnessed the alleged suspects being stripped and severely beaten and sjambokked by not only the taxi-drivers but also the girl that was raped. Community tension and frustration with the police have decreased somewhat. Certain personnel have been removed from the police station and a delicate relationship has been established between the community and the police through the auspices of the local Community Police Forum (interviews with Danile Landingwe, Guguletu Community Policing Forum, November 1999, and Superintendent Johann Conradie, Head of Crime Prevention, Guguletu Police Station, November 1999).

In contrast, mob justice, spontaneous in nature, has occurred in both the township and city centre settings. Such occurrences are rapid responses to crime and may involve local neighbours and residents in the townships and/or passers-by who just happen to witness a crime. In some instances, those present convene kangaroo courts but this is not always the case. The justice meted out is often of an extremely brutal nature and deaths are common. Examples in the townships include the stoning to death of a motorist after he had run over and killed a two-year-old child in Carletonville; the severe beating of an alleged rapist by women in Chatsworth (Durban) and the necklacing of four immigrants accused of gangsterism in Ivory Park (Midrand) (South African Press Association, 1999; Williams, 1999; Reuters, 1999). In the Berea area of Johannesburg, a suspected mobile phone thief was beaten unconscious by 'a mob of furious women' after he was caught by two passers-by. In a similar incident in nearby Hillbrow, again involving the theft of a mobile phone, the suspect was beaten and stripped naked before being rescued by the police. One of those involved in the beating said: 'Next time we will make sure a snatcher is dead before the cops arrive. They're the ones preventing us from killing thieves' (quoted in Nxumalo and Valentine, 1999: 3). In some cases members of a suspected criminal's family or the family home are targeted. Their houses are either destroyed or burnt and often the families subsequently leave the area as a result of intimidation (interview with the mother of an alleged rapist and murderer, November 1999). In February 1997, the mother of an alleged criminal was stoned to death for the deeds of her son by a crowd of 4000 in the township of Mamelodi, near Pretoria (Amupadhi, 1997).

Informal justice in both Northern Ireland and South Africa has, therefore, historic antecedents based on a self-help culture in the face of an oppressive state and ineffective formal criminal justice system. This history of self-reliance, immediacy of response and punitive retribution in both countries has considerably influenced the contemporary response to communal violence. There are significant differences in the way in which informal justice operates in republican and loyalist communities in Northern Ireland. In part this has to do with the fractured nature of loyalism and increasing propensity for paramilitary feuding between groups. In South Africa, the emergence and growth of vigilante groups in response to increasing crime is recognition that the formal policing and criminal justice systems are perceived as failing. The legacy of political violence in both countries has influenced the ways in which 'normal' crime is dealt with and cultivated a tolerance accepting of increasingly brutal treatment of alleged offenders. Despite political advances at the macro level, the reality is that either little has changed in terms of criminal activity at the grassroots or things have become significantly worse. Set alongside this is a distrust or lack of faith in the state's ability or unwillingness to tackle paramilitaries/vigilantes, and conditions are ripe for reliance on community 'protectors'. We examine in greater detail reasons why communities support informal justice in Chapter 4, but before that we consider the victims of informal justice.

3
The Victims of Informal Justice

Victims of political violence

The plight of the victims of political violence in Northern Ireland and South Africa and the enduring suffering of their families has assumed much greater public prominence. Some see this new-found concern by governments for victims in both countries as no more than a necessary part of the political and public relations exercise undertaken in light of unpopular policies (with victims) linked to the wider unstoppable agenda for a peace deal in Northern Ireland and political stability in South Africa. Such policies include the political prisoners' early release programme in Northern Ireland and the granting of amnesty to individuals disclosing full details of their gross violations of human rights under the apartheid regime in South Africa. Preconceived notions of perpetrators and victims have been politically contested in ways which suggest there are those who are 'deserving' or 'undeserving' of victimhood status. This chapter will consider one category of victim, those subject to informal justice. These victims have become expendable and legitimate targets for violence in both Northern Ireland and South Africa. They are expendable in the sense that any attempt to deal with the problem in a serious way would have widespread political ramifications for parties currently in government. They are legitimate in that victims' culpability derives from the communities within which they live and their 'punishment' is meted out by agents (i.e. paramilitaries and vigilantes) acting on the communities' behalf.

Who are the victims?

Definitions of violence according to Richardson and May (1999) revolve around culpability, victimisation and what is deemed socially appropriate behaviour in particular contexts. Accordingly, the notion of deserved-ness or the idea that 'to a greater of lesser extent a person 'deserves' the violence they experience, is not only related to understandings of the social contexts in which violence is thought likely to occur, but is also mediated through the social characteristics of the victim' (Richardson and May, 1999: 309). They exemplify this by considering violence against lesbians and gay men, who because of their marginalised and stigmatised status are likely to be perceived as a potential threat, for example through the spread of AIDS. Because their culpability is in doubt, they are unlikely to be seen as innocent victims of violence. Conversely, Christie (1986: 18) describes the 'ideal victim as a person or category of individuals who, when hit by crime, most readily are given the complete and legitimate status of being a victim'. Elderly victims of robberies, burglaries and assaults, children who are sexually abused, victims of medical negligence, come close to the 'ideal victim'. Similarly Edgar and O'Donnell's research on assaults in prisons highlights the fact the 'the victim's attributes, attitudes or behaviour significantly increases the likelihood of assault' (Edgar and O'Donnell, 1998: 636). Miers' (2000) research draws attention to victims' self empowerment in the face of their frustration with the criminal justice system, reinforced in the United Kingdom by the Conservative government's 1980s market ideology of 'do-it-yourself' justice or private responsibility for crime pre-vention. The excessive or misplaced exercise of direct justice, he argues, 'threatens rather than supports, the claimed values implicit in the crim-inal justice system, as well as the values implicit in claiming the status of, or being labelled, a victim' (Miers, 2000: 83). Similarly, South Africa has witnessed both the birth of a burgeoning private security industry providing safety and security for a price and the continuance and devel-opment of township alternatives including resident patrols, vigilante actions and the formation of organised vigilante groups. We now consider victims of political violence in both countries.

Northern Ireland

The concern for victims of 'the Troubles' and their families has recently received a greater amount of public attention and subsequently become a policy issue of some importance for the British government and local political parties alike. The clearest evidence of this was the appointment of a Victims' Commissioner in November 1997 by the then Secretary of State, Mo Mowlam, to 'look at ways to recognise the pain and suffering felt by victims of violence arising from the troubles, including those who have died or been injured in the service of the community'

(Bloomfield, 1998: 8). Similarly, politicians signing up to the Belfast Agreement believed it was 'essential to acknowledge and address the suffering of the victims of violence as a necessary element of reconciliation' (Belfast Agreement, 1998: 18). The Victims' Commissioner reported in April 1998 (Bloomfield, 1998) with a series of economic, welfare, counselling and support measures aimed at those with injuries or relatives of the dead. These included the appointment of a Minister for Victims (Adam Ingram) to be the 'listening ear' for victims of the troubles; establishment of a new trauma unit; a victims' liaison unit to drive the process forward; grants to community and voluntary sector to implement the report's proposals; an educational bursary scheme to provide assistance to children and young adults who lost a parent or had become a victim of the troubles in some other way; and a memorial fund for victims who suffer financial hardship. The Prime Minister pledged £5 m as a down-payment to support the recommendations flowing from the Victims' Commissioner's report.

Victims and their families were somewhat cynical of the government's new-found concern, describing it as 'too little, too late'. Some viewed such moves as no more than a necessary part of the political and public relations management of the political prisoners' early-release programme[27] within which victims were mere pawns in the wider agenda for a peace deal. Typical of this view is Robert Sergeant whose father was killed in the Mount Inn Bar in North Belfast. He had to seek psychiatric help to deal with the trauma of having to identify his father's face which was still bloody from the head and neck wounds inflicted by the gunman. He did not qualify under the victim support scheme and commented: 'I am literally struggling week-to-week while prisoners are getting assistance and being released. I have suffered mentally; support for victims of trauma has come many years too late' (Purdy, 1998: 4). Despite palliative comments from the Minister for Victims that 'the release of prisoners is bound to bring home the grief, reopen the suffering and all my concern is focused on the human feelings of victims directly affected', this was seen by some as a deft political gesture in anticipation of the outcry over prisoner releases (Ingram, 1998). Providing economic assistance to victims also acted as a counterbalance to the well-organised and funded ex-prisoners' welfare and training programmes, many of which had benefited from public funds. Given the importance ascribed to victims in the unfolding political agenda, the IRA also felt compelled to provide information to families on burial places of 'the disappeared'; those murdered and secretly buried during 'the Troubles'. Although offered as a gesture of good faith on the part of republicans, it subsequently proved counterproductive under the full glare of negative publicity surrounding unsuccessful digs carried out mainly by the Garda Siochána (Republic of Ireland police force). Three bodies were uncovered but the absence of precise informa-tion on the whereabouts of other secret graves led to efforts being abandoned, much to the distress of the victims' families.

South Africa

Likewise in South Africa, the process of a negotiated peace attempted to address the plight of victims of political violence. Moreover, it involved the acknowledged need to deal with past human rights violations. The African National Congress (ANC) began calling for a truth commission prior to the first democratic elections in 1994. This followed three inter-nal commissions (the Stuart, Skweyiya and Motsuenyane) into alleged human rights violations by the ANC-in-exile, which found that gross human rights violations had taken place in some of the ANC camps in Tanzania and other parts of Southern Africa. The National Executive Committee (NEC) of the ANC, while accepting these findings, expressed the view that these violations should be seen within the context of human rights violations committed in South Africa over a consider-able period of time. The NEC, in its response to the Motsuenyane Commission's report in 1993, called upon the government 'to agree, following discussions with the ANC and other political and non-governmental organisations, to set up, without delay, a Commission of Inquiry or Truth Commission into all violations of human rights since 1948' (quoted in Boraine, 2000: 12). It was generally believed that national unity and reconciliation could only be achieved if the truth about past violations was publicly known (Truth and Reconciliation Commission of South Africa, 1998; Boraine, 2000). Following lengthy discussions and deliberations, the new democratic government of South Africa introduced the Promotion of National Unity and Reconciliation Act, which established the Truth and Reconciliation Commission (TRC) in 1995. The Act emphasised a 'victim-centred approach' stressing the importance of victims to the proposed process and their right to tell their stories of suffering and struggle. The TRC sought to promote national unity and reconciliation by:

- compiling as complete a picture, as possible, of the causes, nature and extent of the gross violations of human rights committed in the period between 1 March 1960 and 10 May 1994;
- granting amnesty to perpetrators of such violations in exchange for full disclosure of all relevant facts relating to acts with a political objective;

- establishing and making known the fate or whereabouts of victims, by providing them with the space to recount their victimisation;
- recommending reparation measures in respect of victims; and
- suggesting mechanisms to prevent future violations of human rights.

During the lifetime of the TRC more than 21 000 statements were taken from people who believed that they had suffered gross violations of human rights and some 7000 perpetrators applied for amnesty. At the time of publication of the TRC's Report in 1998, amnesty had only been granted to 150 applicants with a further 2000 cases outstanding.

The issue of amnesty has caused much controversy and resentment. Mary Burton, a member of the TRC, suggests that 'considerable anger is directed by victims and survivors towards the concept of amnesty. Such people have a profound sense of being deprived of their rights, the right to justice and the right to bring civil claims' (Burton, 1998: 21). Individuals granted amnesty cannot be prosecuted for their actions, nor can victims or their families sue them for damages. Furthermore, individuals already convicted and imprisoned could be set free. For example, three members of a six-person Azanian People's Liberation Army (APLA)[28] team who attacked the Heidelberg Tavern (Cape Town) in December 1993, killing four people and injuring another five, applied for amnesty. One of the applicants was serving a 27-year sentence for the attack. The three successfully argued that the tavern was targeted because it was frequented by members of the security forces and received amnesty in July 1998. Amnesty was viewed as the price to be paid for peace:

> The provision of amnesty, however unfair it seems to some victims was the product of a political deal. Had a vengeful victor overthrown apartheid, the perpetrators indeed might have been tried and punished. But as Mr Omar [Justice Minister] points out, the country's interim constitution, which guarantees amnesty for political acts, was really a peace treaty. Amnesty was the price of securing peace and cooperation in the negotiated collapse of white rule. As it is, the guilty will have to pay something; the humiliation of a public confession. (*The Economist*, 1996: 59)

The TRC's final report notes that much of the public outcry over certain amnesty decisions occurred in cases where the victim was white and the perpetrator was black, for example the murder of Amy Biehl.[29]

The TRC was also tasked with providing measures aimed at granting reparations to victims, facilitating their rehabilitation and restoring their human and civil dignity. Reparation was seen as an essential counterbalance to amnesty and included financial (e.g. interim and individual grants), symbolic (e.g. a national day of remembrance and reconciliation) and institutional reparations (e.g. medical and educational support). Paul Setsetse, a representative from the Ministry of Justice has publicly acknowledged that final reparations are not imminent and that 'the government is looking at the situation in a broader context: how best can it restore the dignity of victims of violations of human rights. It's not about money. It's about restoring the dignity of victims and there are many ways to do it' (quoted in Merten, 2001). Interim reparations of between R2000 and R6000 (£200 and £600 respectively) have been paid to victims who are in urgent need from the President's Fund (established to administer financial reparations). According to government figures, R42 million has already been paid to 13 504 victims (Merten, 2001). The TRC recommended that victims or their relatives receive a yearly payment of between R17 000 (£1700) and R23 000 (£2300) for six years, the estimated cost of this is R3 billion. This is in addition to symbolic and institutional reparation measures. The Fund stands at R824 million following a government commitment of a further R500 million in the 2000/2001 budget. Victims' groups are becoming increasingly frustrated over the government's apparent lack of action. Speculation is mounting that victims will receive a single payment of R45 000, based on dividing the Fund between the numbers of victims. Ntombi Mosikare, the deputy manager of Khulumai, a survivor support group, responded to this by saying: 'If this is really the final reparation, we are not happy with it. It's not even half of what the TRC recommended' (Merten, 2001).

This new emphasis on those who have suffered has generated a fundamental debate about who precisely are the victims of political violence in Northern Ireland and South Africa. This debate includes informal justice mechanisms by working-class communities in Northern Ireland and township residents in South Africa.

Victims and perpetrators – ambiguity and contestation

Northern Ireland

The victim/perpetrator dichotomy is fraught with problems when considering political violence in Northern Ireland. Definitions of 'victims' abound. The Victims' Commissioner defined them in two ways – those who have died as a consequence of conflict; and the surviving injured and those who care for them, together with those relatives who mourn the dead (Bloomfield, 1998: 2.2 and 2.13). In a parallel commission established in the Republic of Ireland to review whether the services within its jurisdiction met the needs of those who had suffered from the conflict in Northern Ireland, a narrower interpretation was adopted. Victims were defined as 'those directly affected by acts of violence, rather than indirectly affected by the troubles in general' (Wilson, 1999: 5). The more legally based UN definition of a victim[30] is 'anyone who has suffered harm as a result of violation of criminal laws, regardless of whether a perpetrator has been identified or is being dealt with by the criminal justice system'. A victim may include, where appropriate, the immediate family or dependants of the direct victim and others who have suffered harm in intervening to help victims or prevent victimisation (Criminal Justice Review Group, 2000a: 322).

While these definitions may appear theoretically plausible, in practice however the term 'victim' has become contested and politicised, resulting in an ambiguous distinction between victim and perpetrator. Smyth, for example, poses the question whether 'we are all victims' by drawing on the Victims' Commission Report which states 'no-one living in Northern Ireland will have escaped some degree of damage' (Bloomfield cited by Smyth, 1998: 34). Smyth dismisses this 'as neither a viable or advisable way to approach the past' but goes on to argue:

> Many of us have given support to acts of violence by our covert support or at least for not vocalising opposition … The direct use of violence may have been the role of relatively few in the society, but the few cannot carry out their acts of violence without the support of the many. Therefore there is merit in the idea that we are all perpetrators to some extent. (Smyth, 1998: 41)

The ambiguity around victimhood status is compounded in Northern Ireland because one of the protagonists to the conflict is the British government. Hence when the state is either directly or indirectly involved in violence, the status of the victims is often contested. Ní Aoláin's (2000) research into 350 deaths caused by agents of the state between 1969 and 1994 illustrates this and several examples serve to highlight the point. The events of Bloody Sunday (Derry/Londonderry, January 1972), in which 13 men were shot dead and a further 13 injured from gunshots by the soldiers of the Parachute Regiment, have been defended as a legitimate response to a sustained gun and bomb attack on the

British Army by the IRA. The Coroner (Major Hubert O'Neill), on the other hand, stated 'the Army ran amok that day without thinking what they were doing. They were shooting innocent people'. Whether the state was perpetrator or victim of violence is the subject of an ongoing enquiry into the affair launched by Tony Blair in January 1998.

Rolston's (2000) research presents not only a comprehensive account of examples of 'innocent' victims such as the case of Robert Hamill, beaten to death by a loyalist mob in Portadown town centre in April 1997, but also summarises incidents including Mairéad Farrell preparing for a bombing mission in Gibraltar and Patrick Kelly's attack on an RUC barracks. He argued that it would be too easy to focus on the 'innocent' victims of violence and leave out the latter 'as somehow fouling the humanitarian pitch' (Rolston, 2000: x). Rolston goes on to describe the differential treatment of victims as 'deserving' and 'undeserving'. The latter he argues 'are presumed to be less than innocent, or worse, downright culpable, implicated in their own suffering' (Rolston, 2000: xi). Hence a hierarchy of victims exists, top of which are the 'innocent' – usually women and children killed by paramilitary violence, to the bottom which are members of paramilitary groups killed by state force. This hierarchy is legitimised through media reports describing innocent victims has having 'no interest in politics' or just 'going about their daily work'. Rolston suggests this leads to the social construction of the 'ideal victim', central to which are two key elements – 'innocence' and 'passivity'.

The legitimacy of victim status has therefore been challenged. When Victims' Minister Adam Ingram met with families of the IRA members shot dead while on 'active service' in 1987 by the SAS at Loughgall ('undeserving victims' according to Rolston's hierarchy), a major row erupted. The victims' pressure group FAIR (Families Acting for Innocent Relatives) claimed that 'these people were not victims – they caused the troubles'. Sinn Féin rebutted that no section of the population had a monopoly on suffering and the grief of all relatives (paramilitaries or their victims) was indistinguishable. The incident exemplifies the contested notion of what the Ulster Unionist Party described as 'genuine victims of terrorism'. By contrast Le Vine has argued 'that 'victims' are not necessary to definitions of terrorism, but more important, where 'victims' are involved, their 'innocence' (or 'guilt') may be largely irrelevant to the fact that they became 'victims' in the first place' (Le Vine, 1997: 55).

South Africa

In contrast to the broad definitions of victims that exist in Northern Ireland, the TRC's mandate limited its focus to those victims of gross human rights violations defined as 'the killing, abduction, torture or severe ill treatment of any person' perpetrated by 'any person acting with a political motive'. In its final report, the TRC notes that,

> This definition is a reminder that the responsibility for building the bridge between a dehumanising past and a just and democratic future does not belong to the Commission alone. Furthermore, in making its own limited contribution, the Commission had to walk a tightrope between too wide and too narrow an interpretation of gross violations of human rights. The Commission would have neither the lifespan nor the resources to implement a broadly constituted interpretation. Too narrow an interpretation, on the other hand, might have added insult to the injuries and injustices experienced by the many victims who would have been excluded. (Volume 1, Chapter 4: 60)

Furthermore all victims regardless of the status of the perpetrator were to be treated by the TRC even-handedly. For example, people made to eat inedible goods such as detergent, raw food and cooking oil by the comrades for defying a consumer boycott were to receive the same consideration as individuals abused by the security forces. Not that perpetrators are necessarily 'wrongdoers'. It appears there are certain circumstances when perpetrating violence can be seen as 'acceptable'. Although the ANC were accused and found guilty of gross human rights violations, the TRC made it clear that its struggle against apartheid was justified, including the use of armed force. There could be no equivalence, it argued, between evils of the apartheid system and the abuses, however serious and including murder, which the ANC members committed. The state as a perpetrator of violence is not uncommon and its role may not always be overt. The role of anti-apartheid vigilantes or *mabangalala* such as the *witdoeke* discussed in Chapter 2 was politically directed and became a mode of repression adopted by the governing regime.

It is generally acknowledged in post-apartheid South Africa by government and scholars alike that victims of both political and criminal violence have the potential to become perpetrators (Department of Safety and Security, 1996; Hamber, 1998b). The government's National Crime Prevention Strategy (NCPS) states that 'victimisation itself lies at the heart of much retributive crime ... Victims of past or current criminal activity if untreated, frequently become perpetrators of either retributive violence or of violence displaced within the social or domestic arena' (Department of Safety and Security, 1996: 4.10.1). This position is further compounded by the perceived marginalisation of victims of crime and an emphasis on offenders and their rights within the criminal justice process. Such perceptions, when coupled with historically-rooted problems of popular credibility and legitimacy of the criminal justice agencies (e.g. the police and the courts), have contributed to the continuance of informal justice mechanisms in the townships and formation of vigilante groups such as PEACA and *Mapogo-a-Mathamaga*.

The distinction between victim and perpetrator has therefore become blurred. Victims of crime and/or concerned township residents have taken the law into their hands and in doing so have become perpetrators. Those targeted for such actions, allegedly suspected of being criminals, have in turn become victims themselves. The following case is illustrative of this. In February 2001, local residents in the Pimville area of Soweto (a township in Johannesburg) on apprehending a criminal gang stealing chairs from a church attacked them with bricks and stones leaving three members of the gang dead and another severely injured. The residents argued that they were the victims, as the gang had been terrorising the neighbourhood and had committed a series of rapes, car hijackings, house break-ins and thefts. According to the law, the residents were the criminals and the police duly arrested and charged twelve of them in connection with the killings. They have since appeared before a local magistrate's court and been released on bail while the case is pending.

Thus the status of victims of violence in Northern Ireland and South Africa has become differentiated with examples of complete role reversal. The terms 'victim' and 'perpetrator' have therefore taken on new meanings. Their gradation is a direct result of living in a conflict ridden society in which the role of violence and tolerance in its usage have been redefined.

'Deserving' victims of paramilitary and vigilante violence

Northern Ireland

Nowhere is this ambiguity between victim and perpetrator more clearly illustrated than in the case of so called 'punishment' attacks carried out by paramilitaries on those engaging in 'anti-social behaviour'. As discussed in Chapter 2, paramilitaries claim they take action against petty criminals involved in burglary, car thief, joy riding and target more serious criminals such as alleged drug dealers and paedophiles. They administer 'justice' through a tariff system of warnings, threats, curfew, beatings, shootings, exiling and ultimately execution (Silke, 1998). Those subjected to beatings and shootings are fearful of involving the security forces in case of paramilitary reprisal and hence there is large scale under reporting. In addition to physical 'punishments', paramilitaries also exile individuals by forcing them to relocate (usually in England/Scotland) under threat of serious injury or death. Paramilitary groups, particularly republicans, rationalise their activities as policing their own communities in the absence of a 'legitimate police force'. Communities are discouraged from going to the police as the experience is that charges will be dropped against the perpetrators in return for low-level intelligence information useful to the RUC/PSNI. Loyalist paramilitaries, on the other hand, tend to engage in 'punishment' attacks as much to maintain discipline amongst their own members as to 'police' their areas (Silke, 1999b). A typical view of how communities react to the perpetrators of crime in their areas and the role played by paramilitaries is as follows:

> The informal justice system as it operates here and now isn't an arbitrary one. People aren't shot, for example, just for stealing a car. You're talking about maybe someone with a history of crime stretching two or three years and it's a last resort. The community puts pressure on the paramilitaries to go and deal with these people. They go through the whole process of curfews, warnings, and then at the end of it, it's expulsion or punishment. The paramilitaries have no prisons to lock them up in but they're given chances time and time again. There is a certain element that no matter what you do, they're going to go in that direction, and once they're excluded from this community they come back hell bent on revenge. They systematically wreck it by burning cars in the middle of the road, attacking people's houses seeking revenge. It becomes a war basically between the community and these individuals. So the paramilitaries are usually forced into a decision where they have to take punitive action against them. (Focus group interview, Twinbrook/Poleglass (Belfast), September 1999)

This sense of victimisation, particularly in the Greater Belfast area where many 'punishment' attacks occur, is indeed a 'rational' response when viewed in the context of crime statistics. The Police Authority for Northern Ireland which monitored the performance of the RUC during 1998/99 found 'that many categories of crime are on the increase while police performance in tackling this has not always been as effective as anticipated' (Police Authority for Northern Ireland, 1999: 9). The report noted that the number of violent crimes[31] rose by 21.2 per cent, recorded crimes increased by 27.9 per cent and crimes against the person went up by 33.2 per cent. The Northern Ireland Crime Survey (1998), which reported fears of crime and perceptions of the likelihood of becoming a victim, recorded higher victimisation rates (26 per cent) in Belfast than other parts of Northern Ireland (West Northern Ireland had the lowest rates at 19 per cent). Catholic respondents (24 per cent) had higher victimisation rates than Protestants (20 per cent) (Northern Ireland Office, 1999b).

This suggests communities are being victimised by those seen as anti-social elements and are vulnerable because of the failing in the formal policing system. Fear of crime is not therefore 'irrational', and because 'justice' is administered through third party paramilitaries, people appear to be more punitive towards lawbreakers. This is somewhat at odds with victims' attitudes towards treatment of offenders highlighted in early British Crime Surveys (Hough, 1986; Walklate, 1989). In the prevailing circumstances of Northern Ireland the distinction between victim and perpetrator is ambiguous at best. The victim is redefined as the perpetrator of some previous crime(s) against the community and the 'punishment' depicted as the means of attaining 'fair' retribution. The labelling of the 'victim' as 'perpetrator' may be compounded by their subsequent treatment under the law.[32] The Secretary of State is empowered to refuse or reduce compensation if the victim was in any way responsible through provocative or negligent behaviour for the incident in which he/she was injured. The Victims' Commissioner described this provision in law as 'lending weight to a pernicious conclusion that it was really his/her own fault' (Bloomfield, 1998: 27).

The majority of victims of paramilitary violence are men under 30 (30 per cent are under 20 years of age and 53 per cent between 20–29) who are beaten or shot in urban paramilitary heartlands, the areas in which they live (Kennedy, 2001: 100). These individuals are identified as the 'type of person' who is likely to be involved in 'hooding' (anti-social behaviour) and therefore a 'deserving' victim of paramilitary violence. The result is that the culpability of the paramilitaries as perpetrators of violence is significantly reduced through their role as community protectors. Moreover, both the organs of the state and the media can reinforce the status of victims as 'deserving' of violence. In the case of the former, one official from the Northern Ireland Compensation Agency explaining how they processed claims for injuries sustained by a paramilitary attack, said: 'we don't assume with every other applicant that they're going to have a lengthy criminal record but with a "punishment" attack I think we maybe do have a predisposition to think "there will be a criminal record here" ' (interview with Compensation Agency official, December 1998). In the latter *The Mail on Sunday* ran an article claiming young men were voluntarily undergoing 'kneecapping' by punishment squads to earn compensation which would fund holidays and settle debts (Foggo, 2000). Despite the absence of evidence to support this assertion, the paper went beyond characterising these young men as 'deserving' victims by portraying their injuries as self-inflicted.

The 'deserving' status of victims is further reinforced by pragmatic shorthand in the use of the terms 'perpetrators' and 'victims'. Put simply, paramilitaries carry out 'punishment' beatings and those at the receiving end are victims. Therein lies a number of problems. The use of the term 'punishment', as Kennedy (1995) suggests, is value-laden in that it carries a presumption that the victim somehow deserves what is meted out by the paramilitaries. Moreover, it can conjure up an image of chastisement, threatening behaviour and minor physical violence. This point is taken up in a parliamentary debate on the issue:

> The term 'punishment beating' sounds like a modest extension of neighbourhood watch – at the very worst some vigilante group modestly beating up drug dealers or vandals. Let us make it absolutely clear what is going on in Northern Ireland. We are talking of mutilation, and of beatings in which every bone in the victim's body is deliberately broken. It is intimidation of the very worst sort, and often leads to exile. (MacKay, 1999)

Such emotive language must however be set in the context of the collapse in the bipartisan political approach to Northern Ireland affairs in Westminster. A parliamentary debate on 'punishment' attacks formed the basis of a motion in the Commons to halt the early release of paramilitary prisoners and afforded anti-Agreement Unionists and Conservatives a platform to embarrass the government. This represents the politicisation of the kind of differentiated victim status described previously by Rolston (2000). Conservative Party support for victims of paramilitary violence (the 'ideal victim') must be set alongside their ambivalence in endorsing the Labour government's inquiry into the events of Bloody Sunday.[33]

The term 'victim' can disempower those who have been the subject of such attacks and beatings. There is what Beattie and Doherty (1995) describe in their accounts of paramilitary-related violence, as the 'subtle negotiation of blame' away from the perpetrator to the victim. In a television interview by the hospital bedside of a 13-year-old boy beaten by the paramilitaries, for example, his mother stated while he might be 'bad' like any other local young person, 'other kids do it and they don't get batons taken to them'. The onus is shifted to the victim to defend the reasons why they might have been attacked, an *a priori* assumption of guilt popularly expressed as 'he/she didn't get it for nothing'.

South Africa

Likewise in South Africa, the ambiguity between victim and perpetrator is often evident in cases of vigilantism undertaken by victims of crime, townships residents or organised groups tasked with crime control. Such agents of informal justice impose a variety of usually punitive sanctions against people suspected of involvement in crime (e.g. stoning, sjambokking, beating, destruction of house/shack). Communities are reluctant to report crimes to the police given the perceived ineffectiveness of the criminal justice system and through fear of being targeted by criminals. The following case is illustrative of this point. Oyama Rwaxa, a resident of Pimville apprehended two members of a criminal gang breaking into a neighbour's house and handed them over to the police. Two weeks after the incident Rwaxa was abducted by nine armed men (members of the criminal gang) and assaulted (for more details see Skosana, 1999). Individuals on the receiving end of vigilante attacks are also reluctant to report the matter to the police fearing re-victimisation by the community should they further incur its wrath. The recourse to vigilante action by community members is viewed by many as the only effective course of action open to them (this will be explored in greater detail in Chapter 4). For example, residents in the Winnie Mandela squatter camp in Tembisa (East Rand) pooled their financial resources to raise bail for Johannes Manamela who was on remand accused of murder. Manamela assumed that his relatives had paid his R4000 bail. On his release from prison he was abducted and tried before a people's court, which sentenced him to die. Some of the individuals who had made contributions had themselves been recent victims of crime. As Johannes Motaung explains, 'I donated R22 when I heard what was going to happen to him. The idea of paying bail for criminals and then killing them is liked by everyone. We want them to know that we will get them in the end. We are always told that there is a shortage of police. We will protect ourselves' (quoted in Khupiso and Hennop, 1999). This is not an isolated incident and residents in other areas affected by crime have raised the bail of alleged criminals or have waited for them to secure their own release before taking action against them.

According to a recent analysis of crime statistics by the Institute for Security Studies (ISS) in the post-apartheid period (1994 through to 1999) the overall number of recorded crime has increased and violent crime has increased consistently since 1994 (Schönteich and Louw, 2001). Victimisation studies such as the National Victims of Crime Survey and ISS's own victim surveys have shown that crime 'does not affect all citizens uniformly – race, class and gender are significant determinants of the nature of victimisation in South Africa' (Louw and Shaw, 1997: 12). Louw and Shaw contend that the wealthy (whites) are more likely to be victims of property crime, while the poor (blacks) tend to be the victims of violent crime and to a lesser extent are victims of property crime. This also reflects the findings of the Human Sciences Research Council's national survey, which concluded that a much higher proportion of those found in the lowest income quartile reported being victims of violent crimes than those in the higher income brackets (Human Sciences Research Council, 1995). In the specific case of rape, victims according to South African Police Service (SAPS) estimates are concentrated among the poor and 95 per cent of rapes were reported by African women in 1995 (Cited in Louw and Shaw, 1997).

Areas inhabited by the poor are also less likely to possess the types of infrastructural development such as street lighting, public telephones and urban planning that can reduce the incidence of crime. Given their financial circumstances, the poor are less able to install security measures (e.g. lockable doors, window grills, electronic alarms and high fences). Furthermore, police resources have historically been located in white areas. Taken together, these factors contribute to the disadvantage experienced by the poor in relation to policing and crime control. For the residents of townships, fear of crime and victimisation is a daily reality and many see the victims of vigilante attacks as 'deserving' of the treatment they receive. A number of studies have found, not only support for vigilante actions but also for more draconian measures to be adopted by the state. Schurink (1998) found in her study of four Greater Midrand communities that overall the necklacing of an alleged criminal by a group of people was considered the least serious of crimes relating to murder or attempted murder. In the poorest community, that of Ivory Park (an informal settlement/squatter camp), necklacing received the lowest ranking. Schönteich's survey of public attitudes to punishment in the Eastern Cape has led him to argue that,

the potential for members of the public to engage in vigilante activity is considerable. While few respondents admitted to participation in vigilante activities, many indicated their willingness to do so under certain conditions. Respondents also took a draconian approach towards the punishment of criminals, with a majority favouring a reintroduction of the death penalty, corporal punishment for juveniles, and forced manual labour for prisoners. (Schönteich, 2000)

This description of paramilitary violence in Northern Ireland and vigilantism in South Africa serves to reinforce some of the key explanatory factors for victimisation outlined by Sparks (1982). He argued that if the victim facilitated crime by placing himself/herself at special risk, initiated the events which led to being assaulted, and was vulnerable due to illegal activity, this provided assailants with a degree of impunity and increased the likelihood of victimisation. This would typically apply to joyriding, a euphemistic term for stealing cars and driving them recklessly at high speed often to attract the attention of the paramilitaries or police – an ongoing problem in urban areas of Belfast. Those who engage in violent crimes and vandalism are at a greater risk of being victims (Wittebrood and Nieuwbeerta, 1999). Victimisation, in turn, increases the probability of violent offending (Baron and Hartnagel, 1998). In short, victims become perpetrators of violence, either directly or vicariously.

In summary, victims of political crime in both Northern Ireland and South Africa have become integral to their political 'solutions'. The many victims of violence have been acknowledged, albeit belatedly, as worthy of at least equal status to other protagonists in the conflicts. The early release of political prisoners in the case of Northern Ireland and the Truth and Reconciliation Commission in South Africa were key elements in securing and copper-fastening 'peace' agreements (Belfast Agreement and the Interim Constitution respectively). In both countries, victims of political violence have viewed measures to secure their support for the constitutional agenda as inadequate and tantamount to a political sop. This wider debate about victimhood has prompted differentiation between those considered to be 'deserving' and 'undeserving' victims of political violence. Labelling a victim of political violence as 'deserving' depended on one's support for, or standpoint on, the 'war against the British' or 'anti-apartheid struggle'. The political controversy over degrees of victimhood will continue to reflect the wider debate about the acceptability of the cause which rendered them victims. It is unlikely, for example, that RUC personnel who lost their lives in-service will ever be seen as victims from a republican perspective. Rather, dead IRA volunteers are characterised as victims of British occupation. A shared view of victimhood therefore becomes difficult to reach because the status of victims is differentiated according to a scale which reflects their political ascription in the conflicts in Northern Ireland and South Africa.

It is within this context that our discussions of the role of victims and offenders in the informal justice system become similarly ambiguous. Communities, in the absence of what they perceive as protection from the police and enforcement of the law through the judicial system, must protect themselves against crime. They therefore define themselves as victims of crime. In taking the law into their own hands, however, they become perpetrators. Because they do so in the interests of the common good of their community's safety, there is a subtle shift of blame away from their involvement in, or association with, violent acts towards those accused of committing crime. Labelling the perpetrators as 'deserving' reinforces this. As Richardson and May (1999) have argued in a different context, the evaluation of victim status can significantly influence assessment of the degree of culpability attributed to perpetrators. Because communities identify the victim as 'deserving', then the culpability of the perpetrator (in this case paramilitaries or vigilantes) is abated. The question 'who is the victim?' in these circumstances is apposite. Communities who see themselves as victims of crime can justify the use of violent retribution. If that retribution can be vested in 'third parties' – paramilitaries or vigilantes, this offers an arm's-length solution in which direct association with their violent methods is not required. Broad community support for the process of informal justice is all that is needed. Perpetrators become community protectors operating with a populist mandate to uphold the law outside the parameters of the formal justice system, providing no safeguards for the rights of victims. In these 'abnormal' circumstances, communities can assume the moral high ground and detach themselves from the punitive actions of paramilitaries and vigilantes yet, at the same time, demand harsher sentences for offenders. Paramilitaries and vigilantes can be seen to be protecting their communities yet simultaneously using the informal justice system to exert violent control and further their own self-interests. The dynamics of the relationship between protectors and the communities they purport to protect forms the substance of the next chapter.

4
The Community Response

Crime in Northern Ireland and South Africa

Informal criminal justice mechanisms have evolved to counter crime and 'anti-social behaviour' in the working-class areas of Northern Ireland and in the townships of South Africa. In Northern Ireland, paramilitaries exercise social control and 'police' their own people, taking action against individuals involved in crime and 'anti-social behaviour'. In South Africa, a number of mechanisms have emerged over the years including the *makgotla* based on traditional rural courts, the people's courts of the 'comrades', street committees, spontaneous mob justice and, more recently, the activities of groups like PEACA and *Mapogo-a-Mathamaga*. These mechanisms have emerged in Northern Ireland and South Africa to fill the policing vacuum created by the political conflict. Furthermore, both countries are marred by a 'culture of violence', a legacy of the political conflict they have experienced. Political oppression and repression by the State and its surrogates, together with the often violent social control exercised by the paramilitaries in Northern Ireland and the 'comrades' in South Africa, have further desensitised the communities to violence. This chapter will examine community condonation of informal justice and offer explanations as to why communities continue to support such mechanisms.

The Northern Ireland security forces have prided themselves on having a lower rate of 'ordinary' crime than other parts of the United Kingdom, even allowing for evidence of under-reporting particularly amongst republicans. In 1994, for example, Northern Ireland had a lower crime rate than in any of the 43 police forces in England and Wales. This, however, disguises a high level of violent crime, referred to in Chapter 1 and confirmed by a Home Office report on international crime statistics, which showed that Northern Ireland's percentage increase (28 per cent) in recorded crime was second only to South Africa where it rose by 37 per cent in 1998. Northern Ireland also experienced the largest rise of the 29 countries examined in the report in the area of recorded violent crime, with an increase of 21 per cent, while England and Wales, and Ireland recorded decreases of 6 per cent and 17 per cent respectively (Barclay and Tavares, 2000). One explanation suggested by the Northern Ireland Police Authority was that reduced levels of security force activity provide greater opportunity for criminals. The Chief Constable of the RUC/PSNI in his 2000/2001 report noted: 'levels of crime, in particular violent crime, remain a concern. Figures for the year under review show a total of 119 112 offences recorded by the police'. At the same time, the overall clearance rate fell from 30.2 per cent to 27.1 per cent. The Chief Constable drew attention to paramilitary violence:

> Paramilitary activity persists, even by mainstream terrorist organisations. These organisations although they continue to adhere to their definition of a cessation of military operations, have continued to engage in a whole range of criminality. (Chief Constable RUC/PSNI 2000/2001 Annual Report: 18)

He exhorted 'people of influence' – elected representatives and community leaders, to bring their influence to bear so that the 'control of paramilitaries is weakened and the misery which they inflict on ordinary decent people, is brought to an end'.

The parallels with South Africa are outlined by one observer:

> Northern Ireland could be risking a surge in non-political organised crime, as members on both sides of the sectarian divide exploit the weaknesses of peacetime policing. Urban guerrilla movements such as the African National Congress's *Umkontho we Sizwe*, the Ulster Volunteer Force and the IRA have routinely resorted to bank robbery, protection rackets, and smuggling to fund their military campaigns against the ruling power. When, as was the case in South Africa, the movement becomes the dominant political force, many of its former operatives find themselves unable to adjust to life on the side of the law. Instead, they stay in the shadows, and sometimes join forces in lawlessness with the very men who, when they served apartheid's police structures, were given the task of fighting them. (Kiley, 1999: 17)

South Africa has been described as a 'crimo-generic society', the origins of which can be traced to its apartheid past (Shaw, 1996). Transgressions of pass laws were classified as crime and those involved in the liberation struggle justified the use of violence as a legitimate means to an end. Subsequently, politics and crime have been closely interlinked. Police figures show that crime had actually begun to increase in the decade prior to the ending of apartheid (1980–90), for example, murders increased by 32 per cent, rape by 24 per cent, and burglary by 31 per cent (Shaw, 1996: 159). In the post-apartheid era, crime has continued to rise – as detailed in Chapter 1. In the period between 1990 and 2000, police data for the number of recorded crimes to the person showed a dramatic increase. For example, assaults rose by 121 per cent, rapes by 160 per cent, and robbery by 223 per cent. For the same period, the number of recorded crimes to property also increased, housebreakings were up 75 per cent and theft of motor vehicles by 47 per cent (South African Police Service, 2001). The only crime to have experienced a decrease is that of murder; this is due to declining levels of political violence. As Shaw notes,

> Increases in crime from 1990 are consistent with the experiences of other countries undergoing transition to democracy: as change proceeds, society and its instruments of social control – formal and informal – are reshaped. The result is that new areas for the development of crime, which are bolstered by the legacies of the past, open up. (Shaw, 1996: 156)

What appears to have happened in Northern Ireland as the conflict developed is that the boundaries between so-called 'normal' and 'political' crime have become blurred, leading to community frustration with the formal system of criminal justice yet, at the same time, fear of the influence exerted by paramilitaries. Questions are now being asked as to whether these erstwhile community protectors have become oppressors and what, if any, is their ongoing role in an era of 'peace'. We now examine in some detail the response of communities to crime both pre- and post-conflict.

Community response to crime in Northern Ireland

Paramilitaries in republican areas of Northern Ireland have assumed the role of community 'police' from the very beginning of 'the Troubles', in what they describe as the absence of a legitimate police service (Munck,

1988; Kennedy, 1995; Monaghan, 2002). Not only do republican communities see the RUC/PSNI as an instrument of the British state which they do not recognise in Northern Ireland, but point to its religious composition (8 per cent Catholic from just under 40 per cent of the overall population) and treatment of the minority community (Hamilton and Moore, 1995; O'Rawe and Moore, 1997). They cite cases such as Robert Hamill, beaten to death by a loyalist mob and witnessed by police who allegedly failed to intervene. They claim RUC/PSNI collusion with loyalist paramilitaries, most notably in killings of high profile nationalist/republican figures such as human rights lawyer Rosemary Nelson and solicitor Pat Finucane, and accuse the police of exploiting young petty offenders in return for intelligence information gathering. In contrast, within the loyalist communities, the RUC/PSNI are seen as legitimate but ineffectual, part of a system of criminal justice which cannot react quickly enough and exact retribution deemed appropriate by victims of crime. Conway (1997) points to significant differences in loyalist and republican paramilitary policing. In the former he suggests they are more involved in policing their own organisations for reasons such as internal disputes and informing. Young people involved in anti-social crime, rather than being marginalised, are often persuaded to either 'join-up' or, at the very least, contribute part of the proceeds of their criminal activity to the paramilitaries.

Communities have turned to paramilitaries for protection against crimes committed in the areas they control. Officially when community members complain an investigation is carried out and, if substantiated, followed up by a 'punishment' graduated on a scale or a tariff system. The reality is that blame and guilt may be established through little more than hearsay and the level of 'punishment' can be arbitrary – mitigating factors include whether the accused 'is connected' (related or linked in some way) to known paramilitaries referred to in Chapter 2.

Community endorsement and support for the system is outlined by two interviewees:

> The RUC don't come into our areas so we have to look to the republican movement for policing. Because we don't have cells to lock offenders up, the system evolved from there. In the '70s they dropped breezeblocks on them and nobody complained. As a matter of fact, I don't think they are doing enough to them now.

> No person will go to the RUC. They will either go to representatives of Sinn Féin, community representatives or members of the IRA to actually get it dealt with. If somebody's caught joyriding in the area,

they're going to face the courts, probably get out on bail, more likely get a suspended sentence, and they're free to go out again, start joyriding, terrorising the community again. If they go through the informal system, action will be taken immediately, whether it's exiling, their legs broke[n] or kneecapped. That's tackling the problem, getting to its core. (Focus Group interviews, Belfast, September 1999)

All of this ignores available evidence that a number of people have been mistakenly identified by 'punishment' gangs who perpetrate these criminal acts. Boys as young as 13-years-old have been hospitalised through paramilitary beatings, and the process is also used to settle grudges or internal feuds, euphemistically described as 'housekeeping' issues. The police tacitly acquiesce in a system which they know to exist and can exploit for intelligence gathering ('informing' from another perspective), particularly given the vulnerabilities of many of the young people targeted by paramilitaries. Hence communities are caught in a trap. Even though the Northern Ireland conflict reached a political and constitutional resolution through the Belfast Agreement, the associated reforms of the police and criminal justice systems have not (at the time of writing) been fully implemented or secured overall political support (particularly from Sinn Féin). A hiatus therefore exists. In republican areas the RUC/PSNI are anathema and communities still look to paramilitaries for community 'protection', yet their political leadership gave a commitment to the Mitchell principles of democracy and non-violence underlying the Belfast Agreement. In loyalist areas, which are factional in their paramilitary make-up and therefore less ideologically homogeneous, there is a more irregular approach to community 'justice'. This is best illustrated by a comment from one interviewee in a loyalist area:

Quite frankly, I don't want the paramilitaries to deal with anything. I want the police to have power to look after the community. As far as I'm concerned the paramilitaries have no place in Northern Ireland. I mean they were set up to protect one side and fight the other side. Well that's done. We've got peace now. They're big business. They're hiding behind this paramilitary protection and all this, but really they are extortionists into fraud and drugs. There's no place for them. They're kneecapping a young lad for housebreaking yet they are holding up post offices and banks. (Focus Group interview, Belfast, November 1999)

This remark traces the shift in community feelings from a stage when paramilitaries were seen to have a legitimate role to play in a conflict scenario. During this period communities were prepared to overlook racketeering, choosing to believe that this was necessary to fund the ongoing 'struggle'. As 'peace' developed they have become more intolerant, yet no less fearful, of the role played by paramilitaries. The line between 'ordinary' crime and 'political' crime is therefore indistinct and a frustration is palpable in that the formal system of criminal justice has been unable to keep pace with this shift in the attitudes of communities. An international report on armed groups argued that 'the distinction between politically motivated action and organised crime is fading away. All too often, the political objectives are unclear, if not subsidiary to the crimes perpetrated while allegedly waging one's struggle' (International Council on Human Rights, 1999: 6). This is particularly apposite in the case of loyalist paramilitaries whose political objectives might broadly be described as defenders of the Union with Great Britain but, in practice, they have been the countervailing forces to IRA violence. With the Union secured and the IRA maintaining a cease-fire, their current role is being questioned by those they claim to protect. What is the nature of the relationship between paramilitaries and these communities?

Paramilitaries and the communities

Understanding the nature of the relationship between paramilitaries and communities requires an appreciation of the circumstances within which these 'punishment' attacks take place. The current policing and criminal justice systems lack credibility in many of the working-class areas of Northern Ireland. People within these communities have become alienated from the state through their dealings with the RUC/PSNI and the formal system of criminal justice. On the republican side this alienation is, in part, ideologically driven through their lack of acceptance of a (mainly Protestant) British police force.

As one interviewee explained:

> The RUC first of all don't have my respect and don't have the respect of the vast majority of people in this area. My first memory was of British soldiers and peelers coming into the house trailing my sister out of bed, calling her a Fenian whore. I didn't know what a whore meant, didn't even know what a Fenian meant. I was only four years of age and through the culture and traditions that we've

been brought up with, it's not the thing to go and phone up the RUC and say 'I need help'. When you've seen the RUC coming into your houses week after week, coming into your community, abusing it, destroying it. They are not the guardians of the law, they have become the abusers. There's no way round it. You can't bring them to court. You try to and the charges are thrown out, you're told you're telling lies. There is no respect for the RUC. (Interview with 'punishment' victim, December 1999)

On the loyalist side it has more to do with what they perceive as the inefficacy of the existing system – perpetrators are dealt with too leniently or the process takes too long. This policing and justice vacuum has resulted in communities turning to paramilitaries as the alternative means of tackling criminal activity in their areas. This is described by a focus group participant in a loyalist community as follows:

Whilst I do not agree personally with physically hurting someone, at times it has proved purposeful in controlling things that went on within our community, simply because taking them to court doesn't work...I know young lads who were put on probation for stealing cars. The first week they went to the Probation Board they talked about the consequences of their actions for victims. The next week they were taken go-karting, then deep-sea fishing. The average mother cannot afford to send her kids to these activities. I then heard one young fella who hadn't been involved in crime ask 'how do you join the probation club for week-ends away?' People see these young lads who have committed quite serious crime being taken by the hand without punishment for their actions against the community. (Focus Group interview, Shankill (Belfast), November 1999)

Paramilitaries therefore claim to be responding to popular pressure and in turn engage in swift and often brutal 'punishments' carried out without regard for the human rights of the victim or due legal process. The system becomes self-perpetuating and reinforcing. It satisfies the response of communities for 'justice' and reinforces the dominant role of paramilitaries who wish to exert social control in their areas. This 'culture of violence' also means that communities are afraid to speak out against such activities. When young people in these areas become involved in criminal behaviour they are more likely to encounter paramilitaries than the police. Some see this as a challenge and part of a sub-culture of bravado amongst their peer group. Rarely however can they match the weaponry or force of organised paramilitary 'punishment' gangs who administer the informal criminal justice system under the guise of community 'police'.

What is difficult to understand however is the acceptance by some of the victims of their 'deserving' fate at the hands of paramilitaries, indeed even their compliance with the informal system. This has led, for example, to 'punishment' attacks and shooting being carried out by mutual arrangement between paramilitaries and victims, or 'punishment' by appointment, as referred to in Chapter 2. In one case the police chased two men involved in a robbery into a republican area. The paramilitaries, who had no knowledge of the robbery and were receiving none of the proceeds, accused the perpetrators of drawing the police into the area. One of those 'accused' takes up the story:

> I was put under house arrest by the paramilitaries and interrogated. They came in and put a statement of guilt in front of me. I said 'no, I'm not admitting my part in it, I didn't do it' and they said, 'you're being stupid here, you'll only end up getting shot'. From that moment I felt nothing but anger. There was a guy actually walked us round the entry (alley-way) and I said to him 'look, we're not going anywhere, we're going to take what we have to take and that's it'. We were actually waiting for the gunman to come round and shoot us. We decided at the end of the day it was a couple of bullets in the legs and at least after that there would be no comeback. A guy came ten minutes later with a gun. The first thing he said was 'lads, I'm sorry, I'm only doing what I'm told' and I said 'no problem' but at the same time was still very angry. He shot me in the back of the leg, it was just a thud, but the next shot flipped my whole body over. The sensation I always remember is how warm your own blood is. So he moved across and shot the other guy in the legs. He passed out. (Interview with 'punishment' victim, November 1999)

Such attacks do not recognise due process and summary justice carried out in this way, based upon accusation and hearsay, has led to notable 'mistakes'. In Strabane a masked squad of paramilitaries burst into a man's house and beat him with baseball bats and an iron bar before realising their intended target lived next door. They regrouped and inflicted multiple injuries on his neighbour. As one interviewee remarked:

> Obviously a lot of people were 'done' wrongly because people were prepared to stand up and give false evidence and there are also cases

of mistaken identity. I know a man who lives on this street. He was one of nine people who were kneecapped in this area in one night because they robbed a post office and they closed the post office down. It meant that all the locals had to go to the city centre to cash pensions, dole (social assistance payments) and family allowance. They went round and shot the nine of them on the basis of information from one person who had been involved in it. He named the other eight and one of the people he named was just a guy he didn't like! They didn't wait to question them, they just shot the other eight. (Interview with 'punishment' victim, December 1999)

One young man accused of assaulting and robbing a local insurance agent who collected money door-to-door describes the interrogation process by the paramilitaries and lack of due process.

They put it to me that I had robbed this person. They said 'look, you admit to us and we'll shoot you once, but see if you don't admit to it, I don't give a fuck because we have the proof and we have evidence here, and if we have to get people and bring them in, we're going to shoot you three or four times'. These guys say to you 'look, we're going to shoot you once', but when you lie face-down waiting for it, you still think they're going to shoot you in the fucking head or they're going to shoot you four times or whatever. (Interview with 'punishment' victim, December 1999)

All of this illustrates not only the graphic detail of 'punishment' incidents, but also the complex dynamic relationship which exists between communities and paramilitary organisations. As recorded crime continues to rise in Northern Ireland, communities have little option but to rely on paramilitaries for 'protection'. There is little confidence in either the police or criminal justice system within republican or loyalist communities, albeit for different reasons. The prospect of a radical shift in support for the organs of the state is unlikely in the short term under changes resulting from the parallel reviews – Patten on policing and the Criminal Justice Review. Nationalist and republicans are wary of any dilution to the changes suggested by Patten for the RUC/PSNI. These discussions are inextricably linked to the wider political debate within the re-established devolved administration. In the meantime, communities are caught up in this cycle of crime and violence with only the paramilitaries to turn to, either by choice or force of circumstance. Figures 4.1 and 4.2 show the clustering of 'punishment' attacks in the

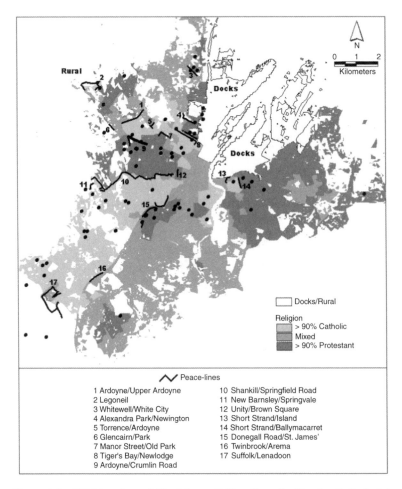

Figure 4.1 GIS Mapping of 'Punishment' Shootings in Greater Belfast, July 1998–June 2000

Greater Belfast area and highlight their concentration within single identity communities. The politicians unanimously oppose 'punishment' attacks, although those parties linked to paramilitary groups[34] argue that they 'understand why such attacks come about and why the paramilitaries are involved in them' (interview with John White, Ulster Democratic Party, September 1999). The police claim that their investigations are impeded by the fact that most of the victims will not identify the perpetrators even though they may know their identity. On the other

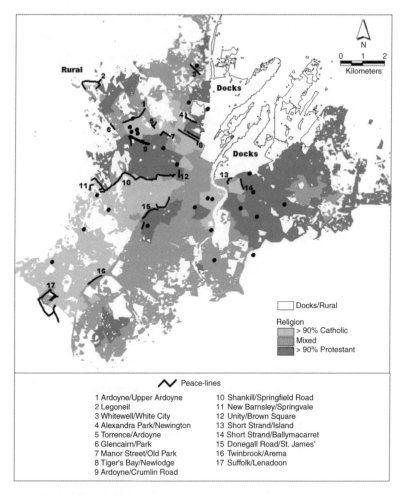

Figure 4.2   GIS Mapping of 'Punishment' Beatings in Greater Belfast, July 1998–June 2000

hand, the Criminal Justice Review highlights the fact that victims do not get the level of support and assistance they require. Throughout the criminal justice process, the Review suggests 'there was an undercurrent of fear about possible retaliation by the offender... an implication that the balance in the system was too much in favour of offenders at the expense of the victim' (Criminal Justice Review Group, 2000a: 321).

The police recognise, however, that it isn't simply about investigating these attacks but 'trying to create a situation where people have trust in us to report the crime and finding alternative ways to deal with them' (interview with Chief Superintendent, December 1998). The RUC/PSNI is however critical of the role played by political parties. As one senior police officer suggested: 'I have no doubt in my mind that the politicians linked to these paramilitaries know exactly what is going on in their areas and could take action to have it stopped' citing evidence (noted in Chapter 2) of the complete cessation of attacks during the American presidential visits to Northern Ireland and during the Mitchell review process (RUC/PSNI Chief Superintendent Brian McCargo speaking on Channel 4 News, 21 May 2000). Those within communities who wish to see the stranglehold of paramilitaries loosen have few alternatives. To raise one's head above the parapet runs the risk of crossing the hard men of violence. This has become increasingly hazardous as paramilitaries in cease-fire circumstances, particularly in loyalist communities, diversify further into drugs, racketeering and extortion.

Community response to crime in South Africa

Prior to the peace process in South Africa, the police and criminal justice system were viewed by large sections of the population as being both illegitimate and tools of the repressive apartheid state. The police were involved in policing the apartheid laws, crushing resistance, recruiting informers and supporting vigilante groups, rather than combating crime. In addition, the courts were busy enforcing apartheid legislation, instead of trying alleged criminals and incarcerating those found guilty of crimes such as rape and murder. Thus the townships in many areas were devoid of a police presence, and a dispute settlement/policing vacuum emerged. Subsequently township inhabitants developed informal criminal justice mechanisms for dealing with crime in their community, as described in Chapter 2. These mechanisms evolved, in part, from traditional rural practices such as the *lekgotla*, which emphasised the restoration of harmony and the re-integration of offenders into the community. Sentences handed down to those found guilty included fines, corporal punishment and community service. Neighbourhood patrols and street committees were also established in an attempt to deal with 'normal' crime, for instance, robbery, theft and rape. With the emergence of the politicised youth or 'comrades', people's courts developed within the townships and residents were encouraged to take their problems to the 'comrades'. These courts were seen as part of the political struggle against apartheid as they represented an alternative to the state structure and dealt with both 'normal' and 'political' crime. They advocated discipline, accountability and promoted a culture which emphasised that crime against one's own community was both damaging and counter-productive (see Chapter 2). These courts handed down punishments ranging from community service to sjambokking but emphasised that wrong doers could be dealt with as part of a community infrastructure which encouraged reintegration rather than exclusion. As people's courts grew in number, they began to acquire the reputation of 'kangaroo courts' (Brogden and Shearing, 1993; Minnaar, 1995) not least because the accused tended to be assumed guilty for which instant redress was administered including, on occasions, the death sentence. Those accused of being collaborators and informers, for example, could be 'necklaced' for their alleged crime. Not everyone within the townships supported the anti-apartheid struggle and by the mid-1980s, organised and often violent, vigilante groups emerged in opposition to the 'comrades' and supportive of the apartheid state. These groups received varying degrees of support from the police, businessman and urban gangsters (Haysom, 1986; Murray, 1994). They only responded to 'political' crime, which was defined broadly as any action against the apartheid state.

The various mechanisms developed by the township inhabitants to counter crime within their areas received mixed community backing and acknowledged legitimacy. Like the *makgotla* before them, the people's courts of the 'comrades' lost support when their methods and punishments became more arbitrary and violent. As Brogden and Shearing noted, 'township ordering processes could only work effectively as long as they were regarded as legitimate by all those who appeared before them – or dared not resort to the state system' (Brogden and Shearing, 1993: 164). With the ending of apartheid and the negotiation of a political settlement, the question arose as to whether community responses to crime would remain the same in the 'new' South Africa.

In the years leading up to South Africa's first multi-racial democratic elections the country experienced both an increase in overt political violence and a dramatic rise in 'normal' crime. As noted in Chapter 2, crime statistics for the transition years of 1990 to 1994 showed a 7 per cent decrease in the murder rate but increases in rape (42 per cent), robbery (40 per cent), vehicle theft (34 per cent) and burglary (20 per cent) (Shaw, 1996). In the same period, people's courts continued to hear cases and hand down punishment. For example, in Nyanga (near Cape Town) two men were given a hundred lashes for stealing a pair of shoes

(South African Press Association, 1991), while in Mamelodi (near Pretoria) a newspaper reporter was sentenced to 500 lashes for writing about the township's informal courts (Cembi, 1991). Anti-crime committees were also set up within a number of townships with varying degrees of success (Minnaar, 1995). Furthermore, non-violent community courts have also been established. These courts, or forums as they are frequently known, operate a restorative justice philosophy echoing the practices of the *makgotla* and seek to involve the community directly in the resolution of disputes and problems. Punishments are non-physical and incorporate an element of shaming. A community forum co-ordinator explains how this is done to those found guilty:

> We educate them so that they respect the community, ... it's not a punishment where people are sjambokked, it's education where people get themselves embarrassed. [W]hen people come from work, they want to see the people who have been punished by the court ... So people like to see them ... [and] if they see you there they will laugh at you. Everybody will know he was a thief, or whatever. (Interview with Sipho Citabatwa, Guguletu, March 1999)

The democratic elections of 1994 saw the formation of a new government, one that was finally recognised by the majority of the population of South Africa as being the legitimate government of the people. This (new) government inherited its predecessor's structures of law and order. Subsequently it has attempted to address the problems of illegitimacy and accountability within the criminal justice system. In 1995, the South African Police Service Act was passed. This Act not only renamed the police but also envisaged their transformation into a public service provider. It allowed for greater civilian oversight and community co-operation with the police through the creation of Community Police Forums. Within the magistrates' court system, lay assessors drawn from the community have been introduced thereby giving the community a greater say in the sentencing of those found guilty of crime. More recently the South African Law Commission (1999) has begun to explore the possibility of not only recognising the informal community court structures which operate a restorative justice approach in the townships, but also incorporating them into the formal system (this will be looked at in detail in Chapter 6). It should be noted that these reforms have not resulted in the eradication of informal justice in the townships. Indeed, there has been a growth in extra-state mechanisms of law and order, together with a declining confidence in the state to provide a safe and secure environment. High crime rates, perceived police ineffectiveness and alleged corruption within the criminal justice system have all contributed to the continued existence of retributive informal justice. To those who can afford it, the private security industry now provides safety and security for a fee. It is estimated that the private security industry is worth more than R9 bn (approximately US$1.145 bn) and that the ratio of private security personnel to uniformed police officers is 4 : 1 (Schönteich, 1999). Those communities who cannot afford this alternative protection have to rely on their own initiatives. The 'comrades' are no longer involved in anti-crime activities, rather new groups have emerged, that include Peninsula Anti-Crime Agency (PEACA) in the Western Cape, *Mapogo-a-Mathamaga* in the Northern Province and the willingness of taxi associations in some townships to become involved in crime solving for a fee (detailed in Chapter 2). Furthermore, in some cases spontaneous mobs form to mete out justice to alleged criminals. All of these groups stand accused of using corporal punishment and violence in responding to crime.

Vigilantes and the community

To the inhabitants of the townships, the kangaroo courts of the taxi associations or justice of the mob are the only effective source of crime control and justice available to them. The police and criminal justice system, although accepted as legitimate, are perceived as ineffective, cumbersome, and in some instances corrupt. The anti-crime activities of the taxi-drivers in Guguletu (Cape Town) and PEACA (based in Khayelitsha) are seen by many residents as an effective crime control measure; not only are goods and monies retrieved and the alleged criminal dealt with, but the actions of the taxi-drivers were viewed as a deterrent to other criminals in the area. Crime figures cited in the *Cape Times* for the first month of the taxi-drivers' actions show a decrease in theft (21 per cent), murder (56 per cent), and housebreaking (24 per cent) in the area (Ntabazalila and Mokwena, 1998). Superintendent Conradie, head of crime prevention at Guguletu Police Station, while condemning the taxi-drivers' methods, acknowledged that crime had risen since their anti-crime activities had stopped: 'After these people of the taxis were arrested, immediately there was an enormous lot of robberies especially with firearms and the taxi people really made a difference' (interview, Guguletu, November 1999). Community endorsement and support for the taxi-drivers are outlined by two interviewees:

> You have just bought a new microwave, a new fridge and so on. Perhaps you go to work, the kids go to school, you come back later during the day and everything is gone and it's quite a difficult situation. You have seen the taxi people working. They were able to catch the thief, bring back the stolen goods. So you are obviously driven towards the taxi people to ask for help. Immediately they have picked up the individual and the individual has dished out the necessary information in terms of where the goods are. The taxi people go beyond that to the extent of perhaps killing the person, and that leaves the community spirit crushed.
>
> People go to the taxis because they are looking for a quick fix, because the police is a long road that can take years. The taxis, you go now and you get your stuff in the afternoon, and the case is solved, everything. (Focus Group interviews, Guguletu, November 1999)

In some instances it is not the direct victim of crime that informs the vigilantes. For example, a victim of an armed robbery in Guguletu reported the matter to the police but members of the community involved the taxi drivers:

> I told everyone I had gone to the police station. I don't know why we have to have this taxi thing happening. They [local residents] said 'no, you don't go to the police, they're useless'. Every person I spoke to in the community told me 'you're wasting your time, don't go, they won't do anything, the taxi drivers are the only people the gangsters will listen to'. (Interview, Cape Town, November 1999)

In terms of *Mapogo*, members pay a subscription fee ranging from R100 to R10 000 depending on their status or the size of their businesses. Paid-up members on becoming a victim of crime contact *Mapogo* and recount the incident, often naming suspects. The alleged offender is then tracked down by *Mapogo* and subjected to an interrogation as to the whereabouts of stolen goods, often involving physical punishment.

Vigilantes, like paramilitaries, claim to be responding to a public demand for them to do something about crime in the townships. Subsequently, they mete out violent 'punishments' to alleged offenders. These are often carried out without an investigation and in some cases, rely solely on the word of the victim. Thus, the rights of the accused to a fair trial and to be considered innocent until proven guilty are ignored. The visible nature of vigilante actions serves as a deterrent to other potential offenders in the community. Individuals witnessing a vigilante attack may also be subject to vigilante attention if they question the attack. As one interviewee explains after taxi drivers had brought one of the attackers to her for identification:

> I had this heroic idea of pulling the guy out of the car and keeping inside and telling everyone to go away, but the way they were psyched up and ready for the punishment, I don't know. I thought maybe they would do something to me because I tried to stop them. (Interview with a victim of an armed robbery in Guguletu, November 1999)

The existence of fear of the vigilantes by onlookers or by-standers is often cited as a reason for the persistence of vigilantism in communities. This fear is generated and maintained through the very public nature of vigilante actions. Subsequently, the police find it difficult to locate witnesses after a vigilante attack.

In addition to developments in the black townships, the organised vigilante group, People Against Gangsterism and Drugs (PAGAD), has emerged from within the coloured and predominantly Muslim community living in the Western Cape (detailed in Chapter 2). PAGAD has followed a dual policy of holding overt large-scale public meetings and protests and conducting covert operations such as drive-by shootings, petrol and pipe-bombings against individuals it claims are involved in drugs and gang-related crime. Initially PAGAD received significant backing from the Muslim community, however, more recently original supporters including individuals and Muslim groups have begun to distance themselves from the organisation. The then Safety and Security Minister, Steve Tshwete, regarded PAGAD as 'terrorists, pure and simple'. The state has advocated a much harsher response to their activities and has proposed a new Anti-Terrorism Bill that would allow for the detention of suspects for 14 days and the banning of organisations like PAGAD.

In discussing community responses to crime it is important to remember that the recourse to violent action outside the formal institutions of the state is a well-established principle in South Africa. Indeed a 'culture of violence' can be said to exist in which society endorses and accepts violence as an acceptable and legitimate means to resolve not only problems but also to achieve goals (Hamber and Lewis, 1997). The Reverend Frank Chikane wrote in 1987 that 'the most tragic reflection of [the] war situation in which South Africa finds itself is that it faces the years to come with children who have been socialised to find violence completely acceptable and human life cheap' (quoted in Mehlwana, 1996: 31). In the period before the un-banning of the ANC and the lifting of the state of emergency (February 1990), much of the conflict and violence was driven by township residents' opposition to apartheid and their attempts to make the townships ungovernable. This included rent, services and consumer boycotts, worker stayaways, protest marches and mass mobilisation. The state responded by imposing a state of emergency and clamped down on overt political activity thus leading to confrontation between township residents and the security forces. The period leading up to democracy (1990–94) was characterised by both inter and intra-community violence facilitated by the deregulation of the repressive state security forces and the legitimisation of violence by all political groupings prior to the 1990s (Hamber, 1998a). In the democratic South Africa violence is endemic and can be found in almost all parts of social life including attacks against illegal aliens and xenophobia, campus violence, domestic violence, minibus taxi 'wars' and violent crime (Minnaar *et al.*, 1998). Thus the sjambokking of 'skollies' (local hoodlums) by organised groups such as *Mapogo* or the coming together of concerned community members like taxi-drivers or ex-combatants has become common place in the townships in the 'new' South Africa.

Community condonation

In summary, communities argue that paramilitaries are involved in the informal justice system for three principal reasons. First, particularly in republican areas, there is an absence of an adequate policing service. The RUC/PSNI has no legitimacy among republicans, and their communities would not normally involve the police in dealing with crimes in their areas. Republicans claim that the PSNI are prepared to tolerate at best, or encourage at worst, crime in their communities as a way of undermining republicanism. Police are therefore willing to trade dropping charges for petty crime in return for low-level intelligence gathering. In loyalist areas where the RUC/PSNI, given its composition, was once seen as 'their' police force, things have changed. Political developments have eroded Protestants' monopoly grasp on the state and its organs, creating a real sense of alienation. Police tactics, for example, in upholding the rights of Catholic parents to walk to school through loyalist areas in North Belfast (the Holy Cross dispute[35]) have reinforced antagonism towards the police. Loyalists want to keep the PSNI out of communities where drug dealing, racketeering and illegal drinking dens and clubs are commonplace. Second, there is a rising level of 'anti-social behaviour' and petty crime, particularly in working-class areas. From police statistics the levels of recorded crime, of which common assault and criminal damage account for about one third, have been increasing (Police Authority, 2001: 53). In the absence, therefore, of a legitimate police force and/or because people are discouraged from seeking PSNI intervention, communities turn to the paramilitaries to secure a prompt, visible and, in their view, effective response to crime in their areas. Third, the formal criminal justice system within these communities is perceived as slow, ineffectual and soft on crime. In a society where violent conflict has been the norm for over 30 years, it isn't surprising that the time taken to process offenders, the necessary safeguards in the legal system, and the standard of proof required for conviction is seen as no match for summary justice meted out by paramilitaries.

Working-class communities in Northern Ireland that have been brutalised during the conflict have become desensitised to violent crime. Victims of crime reporting to paramilitaries almost certainly know the consequences of their actions for the alleged perpetrator. In a country which has witnessed over 3600 deaths and numerous serious injuries, the emphasis is more on revenge than justice (McKittrick, Kelters, Feeney and Thornton, 1999). The nature of the conflict and roles played by the key protagonists is important in understanding the response to community crime. As noted in Chapter 1, when the legitimacy of the state and effectiveness and impartiality of its organs (security forces and legal system) are integral to the conflict, this forecloses recourse to the normal channels by which communities seek to tackle crime (Ní Aoláin, 2000; Rolston, 2000). Hence communities develop their own responses to crime through informal justice mechanisms which will be significantly influenced by the violent environment within which they live. As one communitarian suggested 'if you have a gripe with someone, the way to resolve it is to hit them a dig on the gob (mouth), if it was bigger than that, pull the paramilitaries in' (interview with loyalist community worker, 2000). 'Punishing' mainly young people is therefore tacitly or explicitly supported by communities and in some cases endorsed by unlikely sources such as the aberrant clergyman, Father Pat Buckley who said:

> I have never come across a case where the victim of a 'punishment' squad was innocent. When I hear the names of those who have been

beaten up, I often recognise them as well-known criminals. I have no sympathy whatsoever for criminals and their families who squeal like pigs when they, the guilty, get a touch of the treatment they happily mete out to the innocent. (Buckley, 1995: 16)

All of this suggests that the meaning of violence in Northern Ireland and the community response to it is closely bound to the political milieu within which it takes place. Given this argument, it is obvious that attempts to tackle the informal criminal justice system have been politically derived. Similar community support/endorsement for informal 'justice' is also evident in South Africa.

Like Northern Ireland, a number of principal reasons are cited by communities for the continued existence of the informal criminal justice system in the 'new' South Africa. Firstly, although the South African Police Service (SAPS) is now regarded as the legitimate police service of the government, it is widely seen as being ineffective. According to recent research conducted by the Institute for Security Studies (cited in Meyer, 2001), 'crime pays in South Africa' as the majority of criminals never get caught and, of those who are arrested, a mere 8 per cent spend any time in jail. Of the 2.58 million cases that were reported to and/or recorded by the police in the year 2000, only 610 000 went to court and, of these only 210 000 ended in a conviction. Secondly, the formal criminal justice system is viewed as ineffectual, slow and soft on criminals. As one township resident explained: 'The law takes it very easy [on criminals] and the person gets out of jail easily' (community focus group participant, Khayelitsha, November 1999). Although mandatory minimum sentences for certain offences and tough bail laws have been introduced, this has not countered criticism levelled against the judiciary. Rape, for example, now carries a life sentence where the victim is raped more than once, is seriously assaulted, or is under the age of 16 years. Lesser sentences may be imposed if 'substantial and compelling' circumstances exist. In October 1999, Judge Foxcroft handed down a seven-year sentence to a man found guilty of raping his 14-year-old daughter. In his judgment, Foxcroft stated this was 'not one of the worst cases of rape' and that the man's 'sexual deviancy' was limited to the accused's own daughter (see Smith, 1999a and South African Press Association, 2001 for more details). Such sentencing rationale does not inspire confidence in those communities most affected by crime and sends a message to the community. As Bronwyn Pithey, a Rape Crisis legal adviser explains: 'One can empathise with people who take the law into their own hands. With the Foxcroft judgment it is no surprise that people are acting like this' (Abarber, 1999). In contrast, informal justice is quick and 'punishes' offenders immediately and in some cases stolen goods and moneys are returned to their rightful owner/s. More often, alleged suspects are killed or end up in hospital in a critical condition. In a recent incident in a township in Cape Town, a mob began stoning a suspect in full view of the police. The police fired warning shots into the air; however, the crowd refused to disperse and threatened the police and ambulance staff (Le May, 2001).

Commentators note 'as was the case with the conservative vigilantes of the apartheid era, it appears that those involved in vigilante action today are most unlikely to face legal consequences for their actions' (Bruce and Komane, 1999: 41). Victims of vigilante attacks are reluctant to lay charges against their attackers. For example, a 16-year-old youth suspected of housebreaking was assaulted by three men in Vredehoek (Cape Town), although the attackers were known to the police, the youth declined to make a complaint against them (Kemp, 2001). Since its inception, at least 20 people are thought to have been killed by *Mapogo*, although none of those initially charged has been convicted (Tromp and Gophe, 2001). Although 607 members of the group have been arrested between 1996 and 2000 and charged with a range of other offences including kidnapping, assault and attempted murder, only 14 members have been convicted of an offence (for more details see Sekhonyane, 2000). In August 2000, *Mapogo*'s leader Magolego and 11 other members were cleared of murder and assault charges because witnesses were too frightened to testify against them.

All of the above sets out the context within which communal crime takes place in both Northern Ireland and South Africa and the communities' response to it. It is too easy to frown upon their support for such violent retribution and fail to acknowledge how they are trapped in an environment where lawlessness and lack of police control is the norm. It is also difficult to appreciate the complexities of their relationship with their 'protectors' on whom they depend for informal justice but, at the same time, of whom they are both fearful and suspicious. We now consider how government and non-governmental agencies respond to both the causes of the informal justice system and its victims.

5
The Agencies' Response

'Joined-up' government

The growing recognition that social problems are multi-faceted and need to be tackled in ways which cut across traditional departmental boundaries has heralded the advent of 'joined-up' government. Yet this new emphasis does not appear to have permeated the provision of public services in Northern Ireland and South Africa in their response to the increasingly pervasive social problem of communal violence perpetrated by paramilitaries/vigilantes against those suspected of committing crime within their own communities. This chapter examines the response of governmental and non-governmental agencies to this issue and questions whether victims of paramilitary 'punishment' attacks or vigilante actions could benefit from a multi-agency approach. A deep suspicion and mistrust of the statutory authorities and the 'undeserving' character of victims currently militate against a 'joined-up' approach. Statutory bodies either minimise the problem of community violence or remain indifferent to it. The net result is a disjointed response at both the inter-sectoral and inter-agency levels. In South Africa, the response of governmental and non-governmental agencies has been somewhat lacking and the plight of victims of vigilantism has been ignored. This is, in part, linked to the financial squeeze being felt by non-governmental organisations (NGOs) in response to international funders seeing the South African conflict as one which is 'solved'.

Great Britain/Northern Ireland

It has now become fashionable to promote an integrated response to complex social issues in public services such as health, education and employment. Joining up, according to Bevir and Rhodes (2001), takes various forms such as area-based programmes linking central and local government, health authorities, the private sector and voluntary organisations, and group focused programmes targeting policies aimed at client groups. The state under New Labour 'is an enabling partner that joins and steers flexible networks ... the task is to build bridges between the organisations involved in designing policies and delivering services' (Bevir and Rhodes, 2001: 127). The philosophy behind such an approach is that resources are being wasted because of insufficient collaboration between agencies and a new emphasis is needed to 'promote more holistic and preventative approaches to social policy problems' (Painter, 1999: 109). This approach is rooted in the government's agenda of 'renewal and reform' heralded in *Modernising Government*, which promotes inclusiveness and integration in policy making and programmes (Cabinet Office, 1999a: 10). In order to modernise government, therefore, it is seen as necessary to ensure that policies are forward-looking, inclusive, fair and delivered in a joined-up way, regardless of organisational structures.[36] The government acknowledges that issues like crime and social exclusion cannot be tackled on a departmental basis and is experimenting with different ways of organising work around crosscutting issues. In a Cabinet Office report 'the successful cross-cutting review of the criminal justice system in the comprehensive spending review' is cited as an exemplar, out of which emerged 'a common set of overarching aims and objectives for the various criminal justice departments and agencies' (Cabinet Office, 2000: 59).

The current crime reduction programme is also an example which relies on co-ordinated working across central and local government, drawing on their expertise in policy development, implementation and research to identify and deliver measures for reducing crime. Under this programme the government has launched an integrated approach to tackling violence against women (*Living without Fear*, 1999). It recognises that volunteers, community organisations, probation officers, police, social workers and others have been working to help and support women who experience violence. But government argues 'help is still not comprehensive enough or easily accessible. In some cases women are sent to up to ten different places before they get the help they need. And often how they are treated is entirely a matter of where they live' (Cabinet Office, 1999b: 6). The government's goal therefore is to see effective partnerships operating throughout England and Wales to tackle this problem within five years.

A similar programme aimed at ensuring Better Government for Older People is ongoing in which integrated inter-agency strategies set out innovative ways of delivering services in a co-ordinated and user friendly way. Evaluators of this programme highlighted how relationships between the different tiers of state government are changing, partly in response to the government's drive to modernise and join-up governance and public services. 'Multi-level and citizen-centred governance implies not only closer integration within and between the different tiers of the state, but also engagement with the informal community governance structures and processes within civil society' (Hayden and Benington, 2000: 27). This is a particularly important conclusion when considering how and why the informal criminal justice system operates within communities in Northern Ireland. Hayden and Benington (2000: 28) conclude that 'new patterns of joined-up citizen-centred multi-level governance cannot be contained within traditional metaphors of organisational pyramids, but have to be pictured in terms of inter-organisational networks, complex three-dimensional webs, and cross-cutting lattices'.

Allied to this idea of collaborative working are attempts to incorporate the output of the voluntary sector into public programmes. The government has acknowledged the contribution made by the sector to social, economic, environmental and cultural life and sought to establish partnership arrangements through a 'compact' which sets out their complementary roles in the development and delivery of public policy (Morison, 2000; Voluntary Activity Unit, 1998). This is very much in line with the Labour government's efforts to find a 'Third Way' between state intervention and *laissez-faire* which emphasises partnerships between government and civil associations (Blair, 1998; Giddens, 1998; Tonkiss and Passey, 1999).

Joined-up government has, however, an intuitive political appeal. Who could disagree with a holistic approach to service delivery? Moreover, it could imply that joined-up government is an operational reality rather than, as critics would argue, part of the untested political agenda of New Labour. One critique suggests that 'it is legitimate to speculate that joined-up government is a code for increasing the power of Number 10 over ministers' (Kavanagh and Richards, 2001: 13). In other words, it has more to do with tackling competing power centres based on strong departments *within* government and reasserting the political will over a civil service concerned with protecting their vested departmental interests. Kavanagh and Richards (2001: 17) conclude that 'joined-up government relies on prime ministerial authority rather than a well-established institutional base and new cultural values'.

What is perhaps surprising about this new emphasis on joined-up government is that so little of it appears to have permeated the thinking of public services in Northern Ireland. In a wide-ranging review of the structure, management and resourcing of the criminal justice system emanating from the Belfast Agreement 1998, there is no more than a passing reference to working 'co-operatively to reduce crime' (Criminal Justice Review Group, 2000a: 35). Yet the problems of violent crime, particularly the ongoing role of paramilitaries in cease-fire circumstances, exercises several statutory and voluntary agencies. The informal criminal justice system operates whereby paramilitaries, largely immune from the law, exert often violent control over people living in their local areas. Such is the level of this activity that it has been described as 'a flourishing culture of gangsterism' and a 'Mafia state' in which paramilitaries 'perpetrate mutilations, beatings, shootings, intimidation and exiling under the guise of maintaining law and order within their communities' (Salter, 1999: 383).

South Africa

In the 'new' South Africa, integrated responses to the country's social and economic problems have emerged. This is in contrast to previous approaches adopted during the apartheid regime, which by design and default privileged the minority and failed to meet the needs of the majority. In an attempt to address this, the ANC-led alliance developed the Reconstruction and Development Programme (RDP) in consultation with other mass movements, trade unions, civic organisations, NGOs and research organisations. The RDP represents an important shift in the processes of planning and development in South Africa. Major structural weaknesses were identified in terms of policy making and service delivery linked to the previous regime. Such weaknesses include excessive departmentalism resulting in unco-ordinated and sometimes contradictory decision-making by various state agencies, the exclusion of the general public from participation in decision-making, the failure of bureaucrats to consult with stakeholders, decision-making lacking in accountability and transparency, and projects which were fragmented and isolated (ANC, 1994). The RDP is therefore guided by six basic principles: '[It is] an integrated programme, based on people, that provides peace and security for all and builds the nation, links reconstruction and development and deepens democracy' (ANC, 1994: 1.3.8). Moreover, the RDP is the embodiment of a combined macro socio-economic reform policy, which recognises the inter-connectedness of South Africa's problems (i.e. violence, crime, unemployment, inadequate housing) and proposes an integrated planning approach involving the government and civil society to address these problems simultaneously. As noted in Chapter 1, the RDP contains five major policy programmes that are inter-linked. These are (a) meeting basic needs (e.g. jobs, land, housing, water and electricity); (b) developing human resources (e.g. education, training, literacy and youth development); (c) building the economy; (d) democratising the state and society, and (e) implementing the RDP.

The RDP also allowed for the creation of the National Growth and Development Strategy (GDS). The GDS identified six pillars including safety and security. As Mbeki (1995: 4) explains:

> We can already define the six pillars of our Growth and Development Strategy. They are not new. In fact, they have emerged by clustering the key areas identified in departmental and provincial policies and plans. Their power is their simplicity. Although not every issue of importance to every department is covered explicitly, these pillars aim to encompass and crystallise all our work.

The key areas for growth and development are as follows:

- Investing in people as the productive and creative core of the economy, especially the poor majority.
- Creating employment on a massive scale, while building a powerful competitive South African and Southern African economy.
- Investment in household and economic infrastructure, both to facilitate growth and to improve the quality of life for the poor.
- A national crime prevention strategy to protect the livelihood of our people, secure the wealth of the country and promote investment.
- Building efficient and effective government as a responsive instrument of delivery and empowerment, able to serve all South Africans while directing government resources primarily to meet the needs of the poor majority.
- Welfare safety nets which aim to draw the poorest and most vulnerable groups progressively into the mainstream of the economy and society.

Thus, a national crime prevention strategy was not only recognised as one of the key national priorities but also included in an economic development strategy. According to Rauch, 'the contextualisation of crime prevention with the six pillars of the GDS made links between crime and the economic development of the country and its people, which had not been seen before in government policy' (Rauch, 2001: 2).

Although the government later abandoned the GDS, the initiative to develop a National Crime Prevention Strategy (NCPS) began in 1995. Observers note that the evolution of the NCPS was 'a slow and painful process, reflecting a universal lack of experience in crime prevention and a lack of experience in working co-operatively in an interdepartmental style' (Simpson and Rauch, 1999: 296). The NCPS will be discussed in more detail later in this chapter.

The extent to which the first democratic government of South Africa met or delivered the RDP's mandate[37] through the implementation of national government policies, laws and performance is questionable. An 'RDP Audit' conducted by researchers associated with the University of Witwatersrand Graduate School of Public and Development Management and the Human Sciences Research Council in 1998–99, covering some 36 areas of sectoral policy, legislation and implementation concluded:

> Whatever the reason, some directives did, and some did not, become policy; some policies did, and some did not, have the necessary legislative codification; and some policies and laws were implemented well, and others were not. Because of the subjectivities involved, however, no final judgment can be made by the researchers involved – as to the overall success of South Africa's first democratic government in adopting, legislating and implementing RDP policy directives, that judgment belonged to the voters on June 2, 1999, and will be made by the new ministers and officials who can now better assess their inheritance. (Bond and Khosa, 1999: 62)

Joined-up responses in criminal justice

Great Britain/Northern Ireland

A joined-up approach in the field of criminal justice preceded the current focus on holistic government stimulated, in part, by Home Office circulars *Partnership in Crime Prevention* (1990), *Partnership in Dealing with Offenders in the Community: A Decision Document* (1992) and *Inter-agency Co-ordination to Tackle Domestic Violence* (1995). Researchers in the area have observed that the integrated approach 'has increasingly come to be seen as a panacea for recurring crises within criminal justice' (Crawford and Jones, 1995: 17). Its application, however, has not been without problems. In examining the relevance of an integrated approach to domestic violence, for example, Hague and Malos (1998) and Hague (1998) evaluated collaborative forums comprising local authorities (housing and social services departments), the police, probation, local refuges and support services, along with other voluntary sector organisations. They concluded that such an approach can move beyond basic single agency service provision and result in co-ordination, preventative and educative work. They qualified their remarks, however, by adding that 'we need to be aware of the way in which a supposed commitment to inter-agency co-ordination can allow governments and authorities to "save face" by appearing to take on the issue of domestic violence while actually doing almost nothing' (Hague and Malos, 1998: 385).

On a similar theme, Mama's study (1989) of domestic violence against black women in Greater London, based on first-hand accounts of their experiences in dealing with statutory and voluntary agencies, painted a picture of individuals caught in a complex and often alienating web of state bureaucracies. While Mama highlighted the importance of integrated responses to the problem, she cautioned against such an approach multiplying the pain and suffering that abused women and their children experience. She found evidence that for black women this is what often happens: 'The case material indicates that public services can quite easily become coercive rather than supportive, particularly with the linking up between the police state (police forces, immigration service) and the welfare state (housing, social services, healthcare)' (Mama, 1989: 135).

Phillips and Sampson (1998) reported research on an integrated approach to reduce repeat racial victimisation of Bengali and Somali residents on a local authority housing estate in east London. What emerged was a 'negative interaction' between victims and the statutory agencies in the study – in particular the housing department and the police. Victims were reluctant to report incidents to the authorities because their prior experience suggested that little if anything was done; the statutory bodies claimed they could do nothing until incidents were reported. The researchers concluded that 'the project would have been more successful if it had been accepted that agencies with a history of difficult working relationships are unlikely to work productively in an inter-agency setting' (Phillips and Sampson, 1998: 141).

Crawford and Jones (1995) critique the work of Pearson *et al.* (1992) who suggest two dominant perspectives in assessing integrated or joined-up approaches to crime – a 'benevolent' and 'conspiracy' approach. In the former Pearson *et al.* suggest an unproblematic consensus within and between the local state and communities and therefore see the approach as 'a good thing'. In the latter, the coercive nature of the local state causes conflict in interagency relations and is therefore 'a bad thing'. Crawford and Jones claim this dichotomous assessment is over-simplistic in that 'it fails to give due significance to the fact that competing perspectives are premised upon very different understandings of the complex structures, relationships, and interactive exchanges within and between state agencies, communities and the market' (Crawford and Jones, 1995: 19).

In the context of Northern Ireland, Garrett's (1999) study evaluated the response of state agencies through a joint working initiative between police and social workers to child abuse and domestic violence. He concluded that the role of the agencies and their operational practices could only be understood if the abnormality of the Northern Ireland state(let) was recognised. Because the political and moral legitimacy of the state has been routinely contested, he argued, 'this has also inescapably impinged on, constrained, even determined, the nature and extent of interventions by the police and social workers' (Garrett, 1999: 32).

South Africa

According to Dullah Omar (1998), the former Minister for Justice, there are two fundamental principles to successful crime prevention: a) the involvement of the community and b) a multi-agency approach, both of which are deeply rooted in the National Crime Prevention Strategy (NCPS) issued by the government in May 1996. The NCPS states,

> No organised or systematic approach to the prevention of crime has existed in South Africa. No single agency or level of government has had responsibility for crime prevention in its broadest sense, and there is currently no special structure to plan, manage and co-ordinate crime prevention policy and activities...The traditional responses to crime by the police, the judiciary, the government, the private sector and the non-governmental community have not been coordinated. This has often resulted in competition for, and poor utilisation of, scarce resources. (Department of Safety and Security, 1996: 7)

The NCPS was designed to address this lack of co-ordination in an organised and systematic way. Thus, it represents a prime example of an integrated response to the social problem of crime in South Africa. The ultimate aim of the NCPS is to reduce the levels of crime by:

- Establishing a comprehensive policy framework to guide the various government departments (national, provincial and local), community-based organisations, NGOs and the private sector in areas that impact on crime.

- Generating a shared understanding of the concept of crime prevention.
- Integrating the policy objectives of a range of central government departments while providing guidelines to provincial and local governments, NGOs and the private sector on programmes to be adopted.
- Providing a basis for the development of a common vision around crime prevention and maximising community participation.
- Setting out a programme that identifies priority areas for action.

The NCPS marked a shift in emphasis towards crime prevention rather than short-term reactive law enforcement measures, which had characterised previous approaches in South Africa. The NCPS also called for the development of long-term co-ordinated strategies involving a range of participants beyond those of the traditional criminal justice system.

As a policy, the NCPS prioritises victims. This is due to a number of reasons, including the belief that victim aid and empowerment provide a proactive intervention in cyclical patterns of crime and violence. The lack of effective victim empowerment within the formal criminal justice system is seen as a contributory factor in the resort to informal justice or vigilantism. Subsequently, one of the priority programmes identified within the NCPS was the Victim Empowerment Programme (VEP). This is a multi-faceted and inter-sectoral programme comprising the core NCPS departments of Justice, Welfare, Safety and Security and Correctional Services, and the South African Police Service. The VEP is tasked with addressing and acknowledging the lack of sufficient recognition and services for the victims of crime in South Africa. As Camerer and Kotze note,

> The programme's point of departure is not that there are no services available to victims, but rather that the fragmentation of services to victims should be addressed. The focus is therefore on co-ordinated action, the consolidation of existing models, the testing of new practices and the expansion and strengthening of existing services. (Camerer and Kotze, 1998: 2)

In light of this, the South African government has published a draft consultative Victims' Charter (August 2001). The draft attempts to address the needs and experiences of victims/survivors of crime and outlines a number of victims' rights including the right to: be treated with fairness and with respect; compensation; restitution; and protection.

At a provincial level, governments are also promoting a multi-agency approach on issues of safety and security. For example, the Guateng Provincial Government is active in the Johannesburg Inner City Development Forum (ICDF). The ICDF involves representatives from the community, business, local and provincial governments and has developed an integrated strategy to the issue of reviving Johannesburg's city centre. Thus, the ICDF's public environment team is tasked with addressing a broad range of issues including homelessness, street hawkers (informal traders), lighting, street cleaning, refuse removal and crime. Further to this, the provincial government has been promoting (in conjunction with the ICDF) the 'Safety Lung' concept, a multi-dimensional approach designed to establish 'an attractive, safe and secure environment, in the Central Business District of Johannesburg'. The project intends to do this by establishing partnerships between businesses in the same streets and through the introduction of 'sector policing'. 'Sector policing' involves police foot and motorcycle patrols as opposed to vehicles patrols thereby increasing police visibility and accessibility (for more details see Bruce, 1997).

The NCPS also provided for a local government role in the fight against crime, namely to co-ordinate and promote inter-agency crime prevention work within local boundaries. While the NCPS has suggested that local government has a key role to play in crime prevention, it does not, however, provide any details as to what this involvement should look like. Furthermore, the White Paper on Safety and Security 'In Service of Safety' (September 1998) explicitly calls upon local government to take responsibility for the implementation and co-ordination of social crime prevention programmes within its jurisdiction. It argues that 'local government, the level of government which is closest to the citizenry, is uniquely placed to actively participate in social crime prevention initiatives and to redirect the provision of services to facilitate crime prevention'. Shaw (1998) notes that this new desire for local government involvement in crime prevention is based on a number of reasons:

Primarily, much of the ordinary daily activities of local government involve issues of local level management and governance. Thus, many crime functions are inherent to the ordinary operations of local government. Crime also varies from area to area across the country, as do the causal factors for offending. These factors imply that different strategies and approaches may need to prioritise different problems in different areas. In turn, both a local implementing agency as well as a mechanism in which needs of particular communities can be determined, are required. Representative local government fulfils both these functions. (Shaw, 1998: 9)

Subsequently, a number of metropolitan councils including Johannesburg, Cape Town and Pretoria have established Safer City programmes. These programmes seek to prioritise, co-ordinate and implement crime prevention at local government level. The research that has been conducted on their application suggests they are not without problems including funding, capacity, political support and the need for experimentation or 'learning by doing' (for more details see Shaw, 1998).

The NCPS advocates a multi-agency approach incorporating all government departments and civil society. Although the NCPS has successfully built government–civil society partnerships, its ability to create partnerships between various governmental departments has been less effective. According to Simpson and Rauch,

> Cross-cutting policies and programmes demand horizontal lines of accounting across departments, whereas government is grappling with just sustaining vertical lines of authority. Most obvious in this regard is the key institutionalised problem of competition between departments for scarce budgetary resources. This actively inhibits any co-operative and co-ordinated ventures. (Simpson and Rauch, 1999: 301)

The NCPS's approach assumed that co-operation between various government departments would occur naturally and spontaneously but this has not been the case (Rauch, 2001). Furthermore, the core criminal justice ministries such as Justice, Safety and Security and Correctional Services possess dissimilar and conflicting objectives. For example, the Justice Department's call for the automatic denial of bail to certain offenders will have repercussions for Correctional Services whose facilities are filled to capacity (Singh, 1999).

Studies in allied areas and attempts by government in both the UK and South Africa to co-ordinate the response of public agencies in tackling crime therefore appear to suggest three things. First, that an integrated or joined-up approach *can* offer the potential for an improved response to victims of violence, although there are circumstances which could exacerbate their plight. Second, the nature of the pre-existing relationships between the agencies (in particular the statutory bodies) and the client group is an important determinant of its likely success.

Third, and as a direct consequence, effective inter-agency approaches to crime may be both context and issue-specific. There is some evidence, for example, that because Northern Ireland is 'abnormal', the involvement of state bodies curtails their potential effectiveness in tackling crime problems compared to other parts of the UK (Garrett, 1999). Research from South Africa highlights significant differences between geographical areas in terms of the nature and causes of crime and a governance structure with responsibilities which isn't directly comparable to Northern Ireland (particularly the role of local government). However, the common existence of informal justice systems in both countries warrants some consideration of the roles played by statutory and voluntary organisations in relation to this type of criminal activity.

The response of governmental and non-governmental agencies

Northern Ireland – minimisation and indifference

Two key responses were discernible across the range of statutory and non-statutory organisations to the problem of 'punishment' beatings and shootings by the paramilitaries. The first of these, most characteristic of statutory organisations, has been minimisation of, and indifference to, the problem, or what Conway describes as 'reactive containment' (Conway, 1994: 99). Paramilitary 'punishment' beatings and shootings are but one component of what has become known in Northern Ireland as 'an acceptable level of violence'. This response is informed by a number of factors. Those subjected to beatings and shootings tend not to engender sympathy from both the police and, more often, the communities within which they reside. In the case of the former, the RUC/PSNI claim that those attacked will usually have been involved in 'anti-social behaviour' (car theft, joyriding, burglary, drug dealing etc.), may have a criminal record and are therefore reluctant to report the crime lest they are investigated. There is also fear of reprisal from paramilitaries should they co-operate with the police. As one senior police officer pointed out 'we are unfortunately in a Catch 22 situation … if they refuse to make a witness statement, then in fact the RUC is at a loss in many regards, unless we have the forensic evidence or unless they're caught in the act' (interview with RUC Chief Superintendent, December 2000). Communities, on the other hand, feel they have little option but to tacitly or explicitly support the actions of paramilitaries. They are unwilling and/or reluctant to go to the RUC/PSNI, feel threatened or terrorised by crimes perpetrated in their areas and respond accordingly. 'People want instant justice. They are not prepared to wait on the rules of evidence, on long processes of the court – they feel "we are the victims and we want something done about it now". The paramilitaries respond to this' (community Focus Group respondent, November 1999). In sum, the RUC/PSNI feel limited in their response, communities demand protection from crime in their areas and those attacked are fearful of paramilitary reprisal. The police therefore acquiesce in the *status quo*.

This indifference is confirmed, and in some cases compounded, by the response of other statutory agencies. The Police Authority (PANI – replaced by the new Policing Board in September 2001) for example, receive information from the RUC/PSNI on the number of 'punishment' beatings and shootings but cannot disaggregate data on detection rates from reported 'violence against the person' statistics. This is rather surprising given that the Authority meets with the Chief Constable on a monthly basis and paramilitary beatings, attacks and shootings 'always feature very prominently in the monthly report' (interview with Police Authority member, January 2000). If, as the PANI suspects, the detection rate is 'relatively low' and this does not include other means of paramilitary control such as exiling individuals from an area or imposing curfews, then the scale of illegal activity is likely to be significantly higher than official statistics suggest. One way of minimising the problem from the statutory authorities' perspective is to deal only in recorded figures and, in so doing, ignore the full extent of the problem. A PANI representative put this more diplomatically:

> There may not be a specific reference to paramilitary assaults, partly because of the Authority's determination not to depart from its stand that these amount to criminal assaults, violence against the person. I think, at one level, whilst we do look at them under separate headings, at another level we don't want to give them a special legitimacy by singling them out. There's that kind of ... not double standards approach, but there's that kind of schizophrenic approach to them. (Interview with Police Authority member, January 2000)

The RUC/PSNI, in turn, is accused by republicans of demoralising communities by manipulating those involved in 'anti-social behaviour' and thus undermining the 'republican struggle'. 'It has employed anti-social elements as informers in return for immunity from prosecution. This has allowed anti-social activity to escalate' (McGuinness, 1999: 16).

The Northern Ireland Office's response is to see 'punishment' beatings and shootings more within a general framework of crime prevention and community safety which seek to address the causes of 'anti-social behaviour'. They do not commit resources directly to the problem and didn't think they had made any impact upon it (interview with NIO official, February 2000). Their interest in the issue appeared to peak, perhaps predictably, when it became inextricably linked with the political agenda of the day.

Disjointed approach

The second key response by agencies could be described as a disjointed approach to the problem. There are several manifestations of this. At the inter-sectoral level, for example, there is no obvious collaboration and development between the statutory, voluntary, community and support sectors. The Probation Board is an executive non-departmental public body (a quango) within the Northern Ireland Office which also grant-aids three voluntary organisations in the criminal justice field: the Northern Ireland Association for the Care and Resettlement of Offenders (NIACRO), the Extern Organisation and Victim Support (NI),[38] all of which have direct or indirect involvement with those who have been subjected to beatings and shootings. The Probation Board sees its contribution being in the area of funding community development groups to work in schemes with 'difficult young people ... who are causing damage or sometimes an extreme nuisance ... so that the community wouldn't feel obliged to take unacceptable action against them' (interview with senior Probation Board official, May 2000). NIACRO provides a crisis intervention service for individuals who are under paramilitary threat through an organisation known as BASE 2. This can range from checking the authenticity of the threat, trying to mediate for its removal and, in the last event if the person threatened is exiled, assisting them with the necessary arrangements. Extern provides programmes of intensive support for young people (Time Out and Youth Support) through referrals from the Social Services. Although these programmes are not aimed specifically at those subject to paramilitary threat, there are cases where this applies. Victim Support (NI) offers a listening service and practical advice on forms of help available to those who have been hurt by crime or their family members.

What is clear from the services provided by this range of organisations is that collaboration between these agencies, all of which are funded from the one source, is *ad hoc*, non-existent or personality dependent. Aside from Base 2, those subjected to paramilitary attacks are seen as part of a general client portfolio within which their specific needs are neither identified nor addressed. There is little or no understanding of the impact of the services they are providing on paramilitary beatings and shootings. Indeed in some cases there is an open admission that the effectiveness of their services is marginal to the needs of those that have been shot and beaten. One respondent suggested his organisation had 'very little impact for two reasons ... first, we have been developing our responses over the past five years ... and second, we have been working in a climate whereby there has been a perception that regardless of how hard anyone argues against it, physical punishment works' (interview with Chief Executive, June 2000 – agency name withheld to protect identity). There is also evidence of disagreement between the provider agencies about giving financial support to organisations such as BASE 2 whose work was described by a government minister as 'being seen to implement a social exclusion policy for paramilitaries' (cited from interview with NIACRO official, June 2000). Some statutories have also been unwilling to work with voluntary organisations which refuse to recognise the police.

The second manifestation of a disjointed approach is at the interagency level. Three of the most important agencies for those who have been beaten or shot by paramilitaries are the Social Security Agency, the Northern Ireland Housing Executive, and the Compensation Agency.[39] None of these agencies records separate data on applicants that present with injuries resulting from paramilitary attacks; all are dealt with under their existing client classification schemes. The Social Security Agency was, for example, 'unaware of public criticism' that had been levelled at the amount of benefit to which a father of three who had lost both his legs in a shotgun paramilitary shooting was entitled. The same organisation was the subject of a recommendation from the Northern Ireland Victims' Commissioner's Report that in dealing with victims, they should 'be sensitive and understanding in their approach' (Bloomfield, 1998: 50). The Housing Executive 'hadn't come across' situations where a member of a family was subjected to paramilitary intimidation and felt they had to move rather than break up the family. Both of these admissions point to either a denial of the problem and/or a failure to respond to those who had been attacked, shot or intimidated. The Compensation Agency, on the other hand, suggested these cases 'need careful handling' because they are expensive to settle (interviews with officials in the respective agencies). The agency is required by legislation to compensate '*innocent* victims of violent crime' (our emphasis). In so doing, it must take into account 'the character and way of life' of the applicant as evidenced by their criminal record. Those, who by their own activities, were judged to have contributed to the violence inflicted upon them, could have their compensation claim rejected or reduced. This necessarily involves co-operating with the police, but the agency never sees the applicant. The agencies presented a picture of a disjointed and less than sympathetic approach to those subjected to this kind of attack. As one official suggested, 'we don't assume with every other applicant that they're going to have a lengthy criminal record but with a 'punishment' attack I think we maybe do have a predisposition to think "there'll be a criminal record here"' (interview with Compensation Agency Official, December 2000).

The third manifestation of a disjointed approach is the emergence and operation of victim support groups. The status of victims in general assumed greater importance with the early release of paramilitary prisoners under the terms of the Belfast Agreement. As a consequence, victim support voluntary groups, some of whom offer services to those who had been subjected to paramilitary 'punishment' attacks and shootings, burgeoned. Not only has this resulted in overlap, duplication and confusion in terms of the services which are provided, but because the legitimacy of victim status has been challenged, there are organisations claiming to exclusively represent 'innocent victims' (Knox, 2001). Hence support groups set up to deal with victims of 'state violence', such as families of the IRA members shot dead in Loughgall by the SAS in 1987, found themselves in conflict with 'deserving' victim groups. In these terms, the status of those who have been beaten and shot by paramilitaries is similarly ambiguous, with communities in some cases endorsing 'punishment'. The plethora of organisations offering some kind of victim support such as the WAVE Trauma Centre, Families Acting for Innocent Relatives, Victim Support, Institute of Counselling and Personal Development, Survivors of Trauma, Shankill Stress Centre, and the Family Trauma Centre therefore struggle to find a distinctive role. Their attempt to provide a range of services simply adds to the disjointed nature of provision. They compete to survive on short-term funding in an area where the long-term needs of the 'punished' are not being addressed.

South Africa – condemnation and toleration

Like Northern Ireland, a number of key responses were discernible across the range of statutory agencies and NGOs to the problem of vigilante attacks. Firstly, there is condemnation of vigilante attacks by government ministers, politicians, NGOs and public prosecutors. For example, the former Minister for Safety and Security, Steve Tshwete stated 'we cannot and will not condone any action by vigilante groups as this can only contribute to crime. Merely resorting to vigilantism is not only unscrupulous, but an abdication of responsibility. Criminals don't stay on Mars, but in our communities' (Leggett, 1999: 8). This view is echoed by police personnel in areas where vigilante groups operate and/or mob justice has occurred. In the Western Cape, which has seen seven suspected criminals killed by mobs in townships in and around Cape Town, the Provincial Police Commissioner Lennit Max, has issued a lengthy public statement saying that vigilantes will 'face the full brunt of the law'. The second response identified was that of toleration. On the ground, pockets of toleration and in some cases support for vigilantism were found within the ranks of the South African Police Service (SAPS). Bruce (2001) argues,

> Many rank and file members of the SAPS tacitly support vigilante justice, while some of them may even overtly encourage it. It is frequently the case that, when the police hear a report that an alleged criminal has been apprehended and is being assaulted by members of the public, they deliberately delay their arrival on the scene. Sometimes this is because they wish to avoid the risky task of confronting an angry mob. At other times it is because they wish to allow the mob an opportunity to 'deal with the suspect' first. (Bruce, 2001: 1)

Research undertaken by researchers from the Criminal Justice Policy Unit at the Centre for the Study of Violence and Reconciliation (a Johannesburg based NGO) involving interviews with police personnel working in Pretoria, Durban and Cape Town, found that some officers were tolerant of vigilantism (Bruce and Komane, 1999). This toleration included non-intervention in a situation where an alleged criminal was being attacked, expressing support for vigilante action and failing to take action against individuals involved in vigilantism. The reasons given for non-intervention were three-fold; firstly, some officers expressed sympathy with the original victim of crime. Secondly, intervention may have placed the officer in danger of being physically assaulted or vulnerable to intimidation. For example, many officers relied on the taxi industry for transportation to and from their homes, and cases involving taxi drivers meting out 'justice' placed them in an exposed position as the taxi drivers may be aware of their home address. Thirdly, some officers expressed a lack of confidence in the criminal justice system – a view not confined to community members. Community members also perceive that there is police support for vigilante actions.

In Khayelitsha (Cape Town) it was suggested that 'PEACA [the local vigilante group] and the police are in cahoots. What they do in Khayelitsha, also involves the police' (Community Focus Group participant, Khayelitsha, November 1999). Other interviewees suggested that police officers were taking cases to PEACA to be dealt with, although an Inspector at the Khayelitsha Police Station denied this. However, he did acknowledge that PEACA had provided accurate information concerning stolen vehicles in the area.

Indifference and a disjointed approach

Vigilantism in South Africa also generates an indifferent and disjointed response from the key agencies. Historically, the government has largely neglected victims of political violence and indeed, crime. The work of the Truth and Reconciliation Commission was an attempt to address the plight of victims of political violence by piecing together a comprehensive picture of the human rights abuses of the apartheid era. Discussions about what should be done for victims of crime, which in theory would include victims of vigilante attacks, continue. A conference convened in Kimberley in June 1998, organised by the Department of Welfare and the Northern Cape Department of Environmental Affairs, Developmental Social Welfare and Health was solely concerned with victim empowerment. The Minister for Welfare and Population Development, Geraldine Fraser-Moleketi stated:

> Attempts to assist victims have been *ad hoc* and short-lived due to a lack of resources. Until recently, very little attention has been paid to victims by the government. The formation of partnerships between government and NGOs, as is happening at present, could ensure a better quality of service to victims. (Fraser-Moleketi, 1998: 6)

Unlike the United Kingdom, systematic victim support services do not exist in South Africa. Moreover, there is very little financial support available to victims of crime in the form of benefits from the Department of Welfare. According to the South African Constitution (1996) 'Everyone has the right to have access to social security, including, if they are unable to support themselves and their dependants, appropriate social assistance' (section 27(1)(c) of the Constitution). In practical terms, social security in South Africa is divided into two types, social assistance and social insurance. Social assistance is a means tested, needs based and non-contributory payment and is divided into three main categories: support for the elderly, persons living with disabilities and child and family support. In terms of the disability grant, only persons aged of 18 years are eligible for consideration and a medical officer must confirm that the person is unfit to provide for his/her maintenance due to a physical or mental disability. Such a disability may be permanent or temporary. The maximum amount payable is R520 (approximately £52) a month and is also dependent on a means test. If the person is not married and earns over R13 324 per year or R1110 per month they are not eligible. If the person is married, the spouse's income is taken into consideration. Thus, if the combined income is more than or equal to R24 884 per year or R2074 per month, then again they are not eligible. If the individual is aged between one and 18 years of age and requires and receives permanent home care owing to either severe mental or physical disability then the parent or foster parent of the child may qualify for a Care-Dependency Grant of R520. Again this is subject to the annual combined family income being less than R48 000. In some circumstances, a grant may be awarded for 'social relief of distress', these are available for persons in need of temporary material assistance who are awaiting permanent aid or are medically unfit to work for a period of less than six months. The maximum period of payment is three months, although, in certain cases, it may be approved for an additional three-month period. As Liebenberg and Tilley (1998) note the award of 'social relief of distress' is not at all common, its award is discretionary and thus is not guaranteed.

The second type of social security is social insurance. In order to receive benefits, individuals need to have worked and paid money into the scheme for a minimum period of time. The main form of social insurance is the Unemployment Insurance Fund and benefits are calculated at 45 per cent of the wages earned by the individual prior to becoming unemployed. In addition, the Fund can only be claimed for a maximum 26 weeks within a period of a year (for more details see Liebenberg and Tilley). Social security benefits are open to all South African citizens who meet the eligibility criteria but are very limited in terms of financial assistance and the types of benefit offered. Thus, if you are a person aged of 18 who has never worked, there is no social security provision to which you are entitled. Furthermore, victims of crime, including vigilante attacks, are not eligible for any special grants or awards and can only apply for those grants already offered. At present, no compensation fund exists for victims of crime.

Unlike Northern Ireland, there is no statutory duty to provide housing in South Africa: 'There is no provision which requires you to be housed by anybody' (interview with a representative from Black Sash,[40]

November 1999). Thus, if a person's house or shack is burnt down as a result of a vigilante attack, then there is no state safety net provision. This was the case for the mother of an alleged rapist and murderer, whose home was burnt down following an attack on her son:

> I had to move because my house was burned down…I was never alone like that period in my life. I was all alone with my kids, with nothing, because all of my things were burned down. I got help from no one…Not a single person came from the Democratic Party, not the National Party, not anyone gave me a blanket to sleep with. I had to buy blankets. I bought second-hand blankets. We never received nothing. You go to my house and we don't have carpets, you walk on concrete. (Interview, Cape Town, November 1999)

In the above case, the woman was in employment and was able to move to another township and rent a house. Other victims of vigilante attacks are not in such a fortunate position and are made homeless as a result of their home being torched.

Some NGOs are beginning to offer services to victims of crime. Those subjected to vigilante attacks are, in theory, incorporated into the general client portfolio. It is difficult to ascertain from a number of NGOs if any victims of vigilante attacks had ever availed of the services on offer or if they had, what sort of numbers were involved. For example, the Trauma Centre for Victims of Violence and Torture based in Cape Town 'provides holistic mental health services to individuals, families and communities affected by political and organised violence'. Thus, the primary clientele groups of the centre would include ex-political prisoners, returned exiles, refugees, victims of urban violence (e.g. taxi and gang violence, sexual violence and abuse) and victims of rural violence. Indeed, the Centre's own research into trauma in the Western Cape, *Apartheid's Violent Legacy* (1998) found that respondents in the township of Crossroads were unaware of the existence of the Trauma Centre and that counselling and therapy were viewed with deep suspicion. The Centre primarily offers counselling to victims and training to other professionals who may come in contact with a traumatised person, for example, health care workers, the police and other NGOs such as Rape Crisis. The largest area of work for the Centre comes from victims of criminal violence, predominantly car hijackings and armed robberies. Although the Centre has no specific policy for dealing with victims of vigilante attacks, that is not to say that they would not offer their services to them if they were requested. This is also the case with NICRO's

Community Victim Support Project,[41] which offers victim support services at police stations, at magistrates courts, at community centres and at NICRO offices. There are currently 46 victim support centres throughout South Africa, which are mainly staffed by volunteers trained by NICRO. In terms of access to such services, they are in theory open to 'any victim' but given the perceived 'deserving' nature of their victim-hood, it is plausible to suggest that victims of mob justice or vigilante attacks may not avail of the services offered. Community members from the same community as their attackers will be delivering the services. Furthermore, given that some members of the police tacitly support vig-ilantism, it may be the case that the existence of victim support services are not made known to victims of vigilante attacks.

NGOs rely, in part, on donations from domestic and international donors in order to carry out their work. Many have found that since the establishment of a democratically elected government, international governments and funders have donated money directly to government departments. As a result, NGOs have felt a financial squeeze and this has affected their ability to run programmes, offer services and address issues. This was summed up by a representative from NICRO:

> Some of our funders that we still maintain, have had a history with us for years so they continue to fund us but also what funders want to see nowadays is how are you going to sustain it. They cannot fund you forever! So it's also finding creative ways of remaining in exis-tence. Crime is a hot topic. But you're right, they are channelling money through state departments and that's how we access it now. What happens is the state departments put projects out to tender. So we are like anybody else. (Interview with NICRO official, Cape Town, March 2001)

Thus, organisations offering support services to victims of crime add to the disjointed nature of such service provision. Given the precarious nature of NGO funding, the long-term needs of victims of crime, including those who have been attacked by vigilantes, are not being addressed. It is hoped that the consultation process surrounding the draft Victims' Charter will attend to the needs and experiences of all victims of crime and result in meaningful policy decisions and service provision.

This review of the agencies' response to the problem of community crime and the victims of informal justice in Northern Ireland and South Africa suggests several things. There are significant differences in the governance arrangements in both countries which make comparison difficult. The level and type of social welfare available to victims in South Africa is either non-existent or much less generous than in the UK/Northern Ireland. This is a systemic difference rather than one relating specifically to victims of informal justice. Infrastructure arrangements and lack of public service provision clearly highlight the major disparities which gave rise to the collapse of the apartheid state. This level of discrimination, injustice and absence of public services did not apply to the same extent for the minority community in Northern Ireland as the majority community in South Africa. That said, there are a number points of comparison. In both countries the increasing status of victims in general is emerging as an important focus for government policy with a greater emphasis on victim empowerment. In South Africa, through the National Crime Prevention Strategy, there is recognition that tackling the deep-rooted problem of crime demands a multi-agency and multi-tier approach. While these trends are discernible at the general level, the specific plight of victims of the informal justice system is somewhat different. In both countries there is evidence of indifference to the problem. This is fuelled both by a lack of sympathy (*a priori* assumption of guilt of those subject to violent attacks from paramilitaries/vigilantes) and suggestions of complicity or collusion on the part of the police in Northern Ireland and South Africa. This is compounded by a disjointed response from the public and voluntary sectors in Northern Ireland and withdrawal of direct funding for NGOs in South Africa. The net result is that there is either explicit support for, or implicit acquiescence in, the *status quo*. In short, despite the nature and extent of violence associated with the informal justice system in both countries and the needs of its victims, public agencies (both government and non-government) show limited interest in or willingness to tackle this problem head-on.

6
Community-Based Alternatives

Restorative justice

Restorative justice projects have emerged in Northern Ireland (in both republican and loyalist areas) and South Africa. These projects seek to (a) meet the needs of victims; (b) make the offender accountable for their actions and offer a pathway back into the community; and (c) give communities a sense of ownership and responsibility over dealing with crime in their areas. Two restorative justice projects currently operate in Northern Ireland; these are the Greater Shankill Alternatives and Community Restorative Justice. Both projects offer a non-violent community-owned alternative to paramilitary 'punishments' in the area of petty crime and/or 'anti-social behaviour' and are based on the principles of restorative justice. In contrast, in the townships of South Africa, restorative justice projects are nothing new and have been operating for a number of years. Their exact format varies slightly from township to township. This chapter will examine these non-violent community-based alternatives to existing informal justice practices.

Restorative justice in Northern Ireland

Alternatives to the formal justice system (both violent and non-violent) existed in Ireland as far back as the eighteenth century when revolutionary agrarian organisations challenged British rule and justice. These challenges included alternative arbitration tribunals and more violent acts of injuring caretaker farmers who replaced those evicted from their holdings. The contemporary debate however is directly linked to the outbreak of 'the Troubles'. At the outset this involved tactics such as tarring and feathering young women who consorted with British soldiers, public humiliation of offenders by ordering them to wear placards (for example, 'I am a housebreaker') and 'breeze-blocking' – inflicting punishment by dropping blocks on to the limbs of the accused. As the conflict developed, so too did the informal justice system, detailed in Chapter 2. Paramilitary groups, particularly in republican areas of Northern Ireland, became less tolerant of those whom they perceived as undermining 'the republican struggle' by their 'anti-social behaviour' and turned their weaponry on them. Loyalist groups engaged in similar tactics but for different reasons. Beatings and shootings were used to maintain internal discipline within and between the more heterogeneous loyalist factional groups.

A number of things changed however, which resulted in a radical rethink on the use of punitive sanctions. First, the political environment altered radically. The multi-party talks, chaired by Senator Mitchell, committed the political parties, including those with paramilitary links (the Ulster Democratic Party, the Progressive Unionist Party and Sinn Féin), to 'democratic and exclusively peaceful means of resolving political issues'. All participating parties signed up to six fundamental principles of democracy and non-violence, one of which urged that 'punishment' killings and beatings stop and parties take effective steps to prevent such actions. Second, external pressure was exerted by the Dublin and American administrations, both of which had political clout with the British Government, on political parties linked to paramilitaries to end their involvement or endorsement of this kind of violence. The case was made at that stage that the Belfast Agreement and pledged reforms of the RUC and criminal justice system would obviate the need for informal justice administered through paramilitaries. Third, working-class communities felt increasingly repressed by what they perceived as violent control exercised by paramilitaries, particularly in loyalist areas where in cease-fire circumstances, they have diversified further into drugs, racketeering and extortion. There was however a muted community reaction, through fear of reprisal, to the 'brutalisation of their young men'. In transitional circumstances where a new policing service and criminal justice system were promised, recorded crime was increasing, and the *raison d'être* for paramilitary groups during a time of 'peace' questioned, an alternative to punitive sanctions emerged in the form of restorative justice programmes in both loyalist and republican areas. We consider two of the most prominent – the Greater Shankill Alternatives Programme on the loyalist side and the republican Community Restorative Justice Scheme.

The Greater Shankill Alternatives Programme

The genesis of the programme in the loyalist community is rooted in a research project undertaken during 1996 by an ex-political prisoner in the Greater Shankill District of Belfast (Winston, 1997). The research was initiated in both communities by the Northern Ireland Association for the Care and Resettlement of Offenders[42] (NIACRO) and funded by a private American donor (widely reported to be Charles 'Chuck' Feeney). The position of NIACRO is an interesting one, in that most of its core funding comes via the Northern Ireland Office who were very sensitive about any direct linkage with this work, lest it be construed as encouraging or endorsing parallel justice systems. The research was designed to explore, with a range of community activists (including loyalist paramilitaries), the potential for an alternative strategy to 'punishment' beatings and shootings. The analysis categorised punitive sanctions carried out by loyalist paramilitaries into three broad categories: internal disciplinary matters within their own membership; those involved in 'anti-social behaviour' (ranging from vandalism, burglary and fighting); and feuds between paramilitary groupings involved in the sale of drugs. 'Anti-social behaviour' did not extend to more serious violent acts such as sexual assaults on women, children and the elderly, where any proposals for mediation and negotiation with offenders were considered inappropriate. The parameters for intervention were restricted to *one* category – 'anti-social behaviour'. A three-part programme was suggested based upon investigation of the complaint and follow-up offender/victim mediation; community-service work for the individuals under threat; and intensive training and discussion/ peer education groups focused on behavioural problems. Importantly the research highlighted legal difficulties in negotiating and working on a scheme with paramilitaries groups who legitimised an extra-state system that engaged in illegal violent acts with little due process. It also recognised that such a scheme would have limited enforcement powers without the weight of law but perhaps the overriding sanction that paramilitaries would step in to 'deal with' programme 'drop-outs'. The principles of restorative justice did not feature in the model or inform the scheme until later. The project manager described it as follows:

> When the initial research was carried out, no one knew anything about restorative justice. We thought we were doing something new. Then a project officer joined the team who had worked on a restorative justice programme in America for four years and was quite excited about the approach we were taking. So that gave us a handle

on it and then it was just a matter of trying to refine it and come up with a programme that everyone would be happy with. (Interview with Tom Winston, Alternatives, May 2000)

This work provided the context for the Greater Shankill Alternatives Programme which began in September 1998 with the endorsement of the paramilitary groups the Ulster Volunteer Force (UVF) and the Red Hand Commandos, but not the Ulster Defence Association (UDA). This, in itself, is significant and demonstrates the factionalism within loyalist areas. The rationale for the approach adopted is based on the perceived failings of the formal criminal justice system where crime is treated as a violation of the law which elicits retribution – hence equating punishment with justice. This scheme treats crime as a breakdown in human relationships and the focus is on healing and repairing the harm caused by crime. The Alternatives Programme receives referrals from Social Services, the Probation Board, victims, and the families of offenders and paramilitaries. An 'investigation' is carried out to establish the facts and veracity of the victim's claim. When complete, the needs of the victim are determined and a contract is drawn up with the offender to fulfil those needs. To assist in this process, a trained community mediator facilitates a face-to-face meeting between victim and offender. The outcome is an agreed determination, endorsed by a community panel of local volunteers, between the victim and offender as to the appropriate form of 'justice'. This may, for example, be restitution for damage caused, an apology and/or an agreed period of volunteer work in the community, linked in some way to the original 'anti-social behaviour'. Victims may decide not to meet offenders but their views are incorporated into the process in a way which is not provided for within the formal criminal justice system. Hall (2000) outlines the distinction between the two approaches as follows:

Retributive	Restorative
Crime violates laws set by government	Crime violates relationships between people
Focus on placing guilt	Focus on needs and responsibilities
State is central to the process	Victim and offender are central to the process
Rules are key	Assumption of responsibility is key
Victim plays minimal role	Victim's participation vital
Offender takes mostly passive role	Offender required to be active in the process

(Contd.)

Retributive	Restorative
Offender marginalised from the community	Offender marginalisation decreased
Directed and led by professionals	Community and voluntary involvement
Focus on the past	Focus on the future
Low percentage of restitution	High percentage of restitution

The project manager for Alternatives described the role of the scheme as dealing with petty crime and 'anti-social behaviour' that hitherto led to 'punishment' attacks. He pointed out:

> We don't get involved with anything of a sexual nature, a violent crime or on a sliding scale upwards – it's pretty low level stuff. The type of crime that we deal with is vandalism, petty theft, burglary, and joyriding. The clear-up rate for this type of crime in the area is ten per cent. The remainder is being dealt with by paramilitaries, or not at all. This is a major indictment of the community in which I live and work. The police have either turned a blind eye to this or their priority is fighting terrorism. People approach the paramilitaries as defenders of the community to deal with this. Paramilitaries supporting this project now refer people on to us. They don't want to be involved any longer in this role. Those knockers who suggest that paramilitaries want to continue in this way to have some sort of control have got it wrong. Everyone knows who the paramilitaries are and they don't need to be beating up young people to have that kind of control. (Interview with Tom Winston, Alternatives, May 2000)

The project claims good relations with the major statutory agencies for the work they do, although the position of the police is rather ambiguous. There appears to be support from local police (Tennent Street Police Station) where Alternatives is seen as a useful collaborative model but there is suspicion among the higher ranks. In part, this has to do with the police's long-standing monopoly on tackling crime, compounded by their role in policing terrorism within the very areas where they are now expected to work in partnership with communities. There are also some difficulties for the RUC/PSNI in moving from the specific circumstances of Alternatives to a general endorsement of restorative justice schemes. Police involved in the Shankill scheme claim that the approach adopted there is unlikely to work in middle-class communities and hence attempts to develop a generic model of restorative justice for Northern Ireland simply cannot work in practice. Moreover, they point out that for the RUC/PSNI to endorse the Alternatives programme might create political pressure for them to support restorative justice programmes in republican areas where the police, by design, are not involved. It is to the republican scheme that we now turn.

The Community Restorative Justice scheme

The republican Community Restorative Justice (CRJ) scheme had similar origins. With private donor backing, NIACRO approached Sinn Féin to explore ways in which non-violent alternatives might be found to tackle community crime. This resulted in a series of seminars, organised by NIACRO, on crime and justice issues, which looked at topics such as policing in an international context, the nature of offending and juvenile delinquency. This was followed by a weekend residential, out of which came a publication entitled 'Designing a System of Restorative Justice in Northern Ireland' (1997), referred to as the 'blue book' representing the agreed views of republicans who participated in the process. The model that emerged contained the following key elements. A community liaison team would be established made up of trained volunteers with wide respect in the community. This team would receive and investigate complaints of 'anti-social behaviour' from the community, engage in informal mediation, issue informal cautions or refer more complex cases to the mediation service (a group of trained voluntary mediators) to reach an agreed solution. As a last resort, contested cases would be referred to a community forum, which has the 'power' to impose an outcome. Typically this could include a mediated agreement, work with families, restitution, payment of damages, referral to a programme or statutory agency and community service. As one project worker remarked:

> Restorative justice isn't about punishment and we don't punish people. If restorative justice was about punishing people then getting a young fellow to dig a garden isn't going to stop them joyriding. If shooting them in the arms and legs doesn't stop them, them painting out a bit of graffiti isn't going to stop them either. (Interview with Jim Auld, Community Restorative Justice, May 2000)

The ultimate sanction envisaged by the forum was a community boycott or 'the right of the community to refuse to have persons living in its midst who consistently and seriously flout the norms of tolerable behaviour as codified in a community charter' (Auld *et al.*, 1997: 27–33). Anticipating criticism that the proposed model would attract, specifically because of its refusal to involve the police, its exponents argued that it should not be seen as an alternative police service (or 'Provo police force' as its detractors suggested). Instead, they argued that the creation of a legitimate and fully accepted formal policing and criminal justice system, pledged in the Belfast Agreement, would be both problematic and time consuming. This would unnecessarily delay 'the creation of an effective non-violent alternative to violent punishments indefinitely' (Auld *et al.*, 1997: 40). Moreover, republicans point to different models of restorative justice ranging from police-run and controlled schemes through to community led initiatives which give total ownership and empowerment to local people. Their preference is clearly the latter, conceived of as a community development approach, which has local support. They have sought to elicit this support through public meetings, open-door access to CRJ offices, leaflet campaigns, newsletters and education projects. Their founding philosophy is that they should neither be seen as elitists trying to do work on their own with preconceived solutions, nor do they wish to be an alternative police force.

In January 1999 Community Restorative Justice, with the backing of Sinn Féin, launched five pilot projects in Derry and Belfast aimed at addressing 'anti-social behaviour'.[43] This has grown to more than 14 projects throughout Northern Ireland involving some 300 volunteers working within the scheme, and demand is still growing from communities for participation. Reports from project workers suggest that about two-thirds of their workload is with adults and the remainder largely young males under the age of 25, the target group for victims of 'punishment' beatings. They point out that many of their cases involve disputes between neighbours and within families. This appears at first sight to suggest a move away from intervention over the issue of 'punishment' attacks. However, project workers claim that domestic or neighbour disputes have the potential to develop with consequent violent paramilitary intervention. If rows escalate between neighbours, for example, physical assaults, broken windows, and damage to cars may ensue. One or other party may appeal to paramilitaries to become involved on its behalf and the end result can be a 'punishment' beating or shooting. As one project worker explained:

We have coined the term 'M&M', milk and murder, because we have dealt with people who have been accused of stealing milk from the door and cases involving murder. The milk thing is self-explanatory and we don't deal with people who have been accused of murder, but the families of a murderer and the victim still live in these communities. The hostility between the families after a murder is intense and nobody deals with that. We are finding that a lot of cases that we're dealing with are cases that wouldn't normally be referred to a police service or would only be referred to them as a last resort. (Interview with Jim Auld, Community Restorative Justice, May 2000)

Sinn Féin advice centres now refer dispute cases directly to restorative schemes who, in turn, co-operate with a range of statutory and voluntary organisations when they do not have the expertise to deal with particular cases/issues such as alcohol and drugs problems. Republican schemes have experienced problems in collaborating with statutory organisations. Senior managers 'because of political interference from the Northern Ireland Office' officially object to working with Community Restorative Justice but middle management co-operate in a pragmatic way. Project workers extol the merits of restorative justice as a major tool in influencing offenders to reintegrate, empowering victims and restoring their confidence through community support. It is, they argue, up to the statutory bodies, in particular the police, to come to terms with the fact that vibrant republican communities exist and they should be working with and developing new models of best practice through monitoring standards and ongoing support.

Reactions to restorative justice

Reactions to the emergence of restorative justice projects in Northern Ireland have been mixed. There is obvious anxiety in the police and the Northern Ireland Office and their official position is quite explicit. In the case of the former, they see merit in the concept of restorative justice but 'cannot give legitimacy to schemes where there is not an interface with the police' (interview with Herb Wallace, Vice-Chair of the Police Authority for Northern Ireland, January 1999). The RUC/PSNI is currently piloting its own schemes in two areas in Northern Ireland[44] based on a model developed by the Thames Valley Constabulary which involves a restorative caution system – offenders agreeing to co-operate in a restorative scheme who would otherwise be prosecuted. Both projects are part of the formal criminal justice process. The police argue that while restorative justice has emerged as a way of dealing with 'punishment' attacks, this is somewhat limiting. They would like to see the concept broadened as a mechanism for dealing with youth crime, and fear that because it has become synonymous with paramilitary attacks, failure to impact on this crime will emasculate restorative justice generally.

The Northern Ireland Office's position is outlined in three official papers on: restorative justice; a community partnership approach to crime; and a protocol outlining the principles which must inform community responses to crime (NIO, 1998a, 1998b, 1998c). Therein they welcome innovative ideas aimed at empowering communities, in partnership with public agencies, to improve social cohesion, promote social inclusion, resolve disputes and address the problem of crime and fear of crime. Community empowerment however, according to the Northern Ireland Office, 'must be subject to certain ground rules'. These are articulated in the protocol and include the following:

- Schemes must recognise that statutory responsibility for the investigation of crime rests with the police and that the only forum which can determine guilt or innocence, where this is at issue, is a court of law.
- There should be a clear understanding that the initial response to crime is to notify the police. It would, however, be open to the police and other criminal justice agencies to be flexible in their response and to work with a community-based group in dealing with offenders, whether after adjudication in court or as part of a diversionary or restorative approach.
- In the event that a community-based group wishes itself to address certain types of minor offending/offenders or nuisance type behaviour, it would only do so on a consensual basis (involving agreement between community and local police) with the freely given agreement of all parties including victims, those responsible for the behaviour in question, parents and others who might be affected.
- In the event that an individual fails to follow a course of action previously agreed with any community-based organisation, the individual cannot be compelled or coerced to do so and there can be no sanction against the person.
- All criminal behaviour remains liable to investigation and appropriate action by the police. This means that any group or structures organised by the community should include provision for full co-operation and communication with the police.

Republican communities found this protocol totally unacceptable. The role of the police was central to reporting, investigating and applying sanctions at the community level. For republicans this was simply unworkable. The police, on the other hand, argue that they need to know the nature of the crime, who the offender is and that he/she is being dealt with by the scheme. If not, the offender is left open to double jeopardy because the scheme is promising restoration, and a development plan yet, at the same time, the police are likely to investigate the crime, may prove the offender guilty and prosecute. If the police are made aware of the crime, they can then exercise discretion through the restorative programme. The police also point to sensitivities around the name 'community justice' which they find loaded in an exclusionary way and indicative of republican thinking that what they are really interested in is an 'alternative' system of justice in which there would be no role for the police. The republican response is that these crimes are unlikely to be reported to the police in the first instance.

Acutely aware, however, of the need to satisfy standards by which its schemes should operate, CRJ developed its own code of practice (Community Restorative Justice, 1999) setting standards pertaining to participants, the community and outlining fundamental concepts of restorative justice and values of practice. No reference to the RUC/PSNI appears in its documentation. Loyalists also developed 'principles of good practice' for the Greater Shankill Alternatives Programme. Therein they commit 'to working in partnership with the formal justice system and with the statutory, voluntary and private sectors' although they highlight that 'there are issues around the scope and limits of confidentiality and disclosure that are viewed differently by the Greater Shankill Alternatives and the police, which need to be resolved' (Greater Shankill Alternatives, 1999). Republicans claim that the extent to which there is genuine co-operation between the police and the Greater Shankill Alternatives Programme is much exaggerated and cynically exploited to criticise their own work (interview with Jimmy Gray, Community Restorative Justice, November 1999).

In the review of the criminal justice system, resulting from the Belfast Agreement, restorative justice was examined both as potentially forming part of the formal justice process and the emerging community schemes. The report recommended that restorative justice should become a central part of the formal justice process for juveniles, driven by the courts, based in law, and subject to the full range of human rights protections (Criminal Justice Review Group, 2000a). In considering community restorative justice schemes however, the review 'could not support schemes which act outside the criminal justice system, which are not linked to the criminal justice system, and yet which say they deal with criminal activity' (Criminal Justice Review Group, 2000b: 17). The Review saw a role for community restorative schemes in dealing with low-level crime *only* when they received referrals from a statutory justice agency, rather than from within the community (the police must be told of all such referrals); are accredited by and subject to standards laid down by government (for example, training, human rights, fairness issues and complaints procedure); are regularly inspected by the Criminal Justice Inspectorate; and have no role in deciding on the guilt or innocence of alleged offenders. Restorative schemes should therefore only deal with those individuals referred by a criminal justice agency who have said that they do not wish to deny guilt and where there is real evidence of guilt (Criminal Justice Review Group, 2000a). These recommendations, in essence, undermine the *raison d'être* of CRJ and the Greater Shankill Alternatives programme.

The criminal justice review drew heavily on a research report by Dignan and Lowey (2000) which criticised the republican approach to restorative justice contained in the 'blue book'. Dignan and Lowey argued that the model proposed therein differed from most restorative justice initiatives in a number of important respects. First, the process of mediation operates in the context of a self-contained community justice system without any of the judicial safeguards that would normally act as a guarantee of due process and safeguard against abuse of power. Second, the community liaison team has the power to receive and investigate complaints of 'anti-social behaviour', to organise community patrols and oversee the implementation of either agreed or imposed solutions decided by a community forum or mediation service. Third, the model operates on the basis of communitarianism which is exclusionary and authoritarian through the ultimate sanction of community boycotting. Dignan and Lowey conclude:

> As such, the system that is proposed combines many of the attributes associated with the conventional retributive criminal justice system, including its coercive and exclusionary sanctions, but without its procedural safeguards. The only aspect that bears any resemblance to a restorative approach is mediation. However, the overall context in which this is expected to operate is likely to be influenced by a particular notion of 'communitarianism' which is fundamentally incompatible with the concept of restorative justice. (Dignan and Lowey, 2000: 18)

Interestingly, Dignan and Lowey (2000: 18) argue that this form of communitarianism can be used as a façade for vigilantism and community despotism, and compare it to people's courts in South Africa which they suggest are 'vulnerable to powerful personalities and cliques, and are associated with a tendency towards the increased use of violence and summary justice'. At the very least, they argue, the South African experience raises concerns about whether systems based on the notion of popular justice can be combined with respect for individual human rights.

Those supporting restorative projects point out that the phenomena of 'punishment' beatings emerged because of a failure to achieve consensual policing in many working-class communities (Wall, 1999). While paramilitary organisations have taken advantage of this for their own ends, many of the practices of the police, for example in the use of young vulnerable people as informers, and focusing on anti-terrorist crime at the expense of 'ordinary' crime, have damaged police–community relations. In the absence of an effective justice system and a police service acceptable to the whole community, there is a need to support non-violent community-based alternatives when the only feasible option is punitive sanctions administered through paramilitaries. Because consensual policing is still an aspiration rather than a reality, restorative justice offers the medium-term option for reducing the involvement of paramilitaries in dealing with community crime. This requires boldness on the part of the RUC/PSNI to work with communities. As a voluntary worker with Greater Shankill scheme put it:

> The Greater Shankill Alternatives is a genuine community response to failings of formal and informal attempts at dealing with anti-social activities. We are not the long arm of the police or paramilitaries. 'Alternatives' is in no way trying to undermine the police or create two-tier policing. We would, however, like to remind some who continually ask communities to trust the police, that trust is a two-way process and it is time they showed some trust in the community when we try constructive and positive initiatives to solve our own problems. (Drummond, 1998: 9)

The role played by the police has formed part of a wider political reaction to restorative justice both in Westminster and the devolved Stormont Assembly in Northern Ireland. An MP in the House of Commons, for example, posed the following question to the former Northern Ireland Security Minister, Adam Ingram: 'does the Minister appreciate that many people in Northern Ireland feel the principles of restorative justice would be more firmly founded if those officers of the RUC who issued death threats to Rosemary Nelson were prosecuted and if there was an international enquiry into her murder?' (McDonnell, 2000: 264). In a debate on 'punishment' beatings in Stormont the issue became similarly politicised. The Democratic Unionist Party (DUP) brought forward a motion 'deploring and condemning' the government's inadequate response to a research report (Knox and Monaghan, 2000) presented to the Assembly on the informal criminal justice system which accused the Northern Ireland Office of turning a blind eye to the issue in the interests of political expediency. The DUP demanded measures to ensure those responsible were made amenable to the law. Sinn Féin proposed an amendment which called on the government to address the issue 'through the creation of an accountable policing service that has the support of all communities'. Sinn Féin outlined its support for restorative justice:

> I would like to pay tribute to those in the community who are working to tackle crime through non-violent means. These people recognise that the RUC and the formal justice system have failed our communities. Restorative justice projects, such as Community Restorative Justice (CRJ) and others, have demonstrated a real commitment to tackling these problems. We need to see a greater commitment from Government to increase resources for these initiatives. (Gildernew, 2001: 356–69)

The debate became an issue on the merits and demerits of the Belfast Agreement. In the former, Assembly members argued that the Agreement was the only way to ensure the long-term eradication of violence, of which 'punishment' attacks were but one manifestation. Anti-Agreement members claimed that the continuation of paramilitary assaults served to demonstrate how the Belfast Agreement had failed.

Impact on the informal 'justice' system?

What impact, if any, has the emergence of restorative justice had on paramilitary assaults – 'punishment' beatings and shootings? Views range from 'it is too early to assess', through to 'the experiment in restorative justice has been a significant success'. McEvoy (quoted in Nicholls, 2000: 4), for example, one of the co-authors of the 'blue book' argued: 'I think you have got to give the scheme time to work. It is very early days and there is no question that the CRJ schemes were designed to achieve long-term objectives'. Jim Auld (quoted in Trainor, 1999: 2), Project Director for Community Restorative Justice Ireland, claimed 'there is a direct correlation between the scheme and the decline in "punishment" attacks'. He subsequently argued that from their own research evidence 'around 90 per cent of victims and offenders were satisfied with the outcomes of the restorative process and some 80 per cent do not re-offend' (interview with Jim Auld, Community Restorative Justice, May 2000). Tom Winston, Project Manager in the Greater

Shankill Alternatives Programme reports similar successes. 'Three years ago there were 15–20 "punishment" attacks each year, now you're lucky if there's one or two in this area. There might be more elsewhere but we can only deal with what we have here. So that's a vast improvement' (interview with Tom Winston, Alternatives, May 2000).

Feedback from those involved in the schemes, however, illustrates the problems in measuring impact. While ultimately the projects aim to eradicate 'punishment' attacks, there are intermediate goals which need to be achieved before this can happen. They must, for example, engage in an awareness and education programme to inform communities what their role is, and to convince them of the merits of restorative justice as a mechanism to deal with community crime. This, in itself, is a major task. There is clearly suspicion about the motives of those involved and a natural misgiving that restorative justice represents a soft option. In the case of the former, communities see 'ex-combatants' now centrally involved in restorative justice programmes and question the veracity of their claims to act impartially on their behalf[45] – the poacher turned gamekeeper accusation. In terms of the latter, communities, which over a period of 30 years have demanded and witnessed 'rough justice' through physical violence against perpetrators of petty crime, are unlikely to immediately embrace apologies, reparation and community service as an effective alternative. Other intermediate objectives could, for example, consider the number and nature of referrals to the schemes. If political parties and paramilitary groups increasingly refer complainants to restorative justice projects, their endorsement can be taken a measure of its effectiveness in dealing with problems they would otherwise become involved with. Similarly, unsolicited approaches to restorative schemes are not only a measure of community awareness but, if effective, an indicator of community confidence in non-violent alternatives.

Looking at the RUC/PSNI statistics for recorded beatings and shootings, several points can be made.[46] The cease-fires of August and October 1994 witnessed a significant decrease in the number of shootings to the lowest recorded level, a total of five in 1995. Since then, aside from a slight drop in 1998 and 1999 within loyalist and republican areas respectively, shootings are on the increase to levels higher or similar to pre-cease-fire levels. As shootings decreased following the cease-fires, beatings simultaneously increased in 1995/96 to their highest recorded levels – a technical cop-out for the paramilitaries who could claim they were not breaking the conditions of a cease-fire. Beatings dropped in both communities during 1997 but continue at levels significantly in excess of pre-cease-fire levels. Considering the intervention of restorative

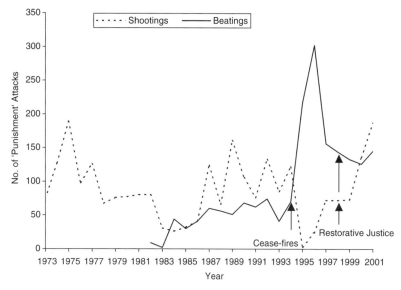

Figure 6.1 'Punishment' Attacks
Source: RUC/PSNI.

justice programmes from January 1999 onwards, loyalist shootings have increased to their highest recorded level and beatings remained roughly the same. Republican shootings and beatings dropped in 1999 but subsequently increased. The total number of paramilitary attacks (shootings and beatings) actually increased to its highest level in the two years following the cease-fires. While the numbers dropped significantly in 1997, they are now increasing and remain at levels higher than the pre-cease-fire era. Looking crudely at the figures therefore would suggest that restorative justice schemes have had little or no impact on the overall trend in 'punishment' attacks. This is particularly true of the loyalist community where shootings and beatings exceed those in republican areas.

There are clearly deficiencies in assessing impact through these statistics, not least because of our inability to isolate cause and effect variables in the restorative justice schemes and establish the counterfactual position – in the absence of programmes the beatings and shootings could have been a lot higher. The level of 'punishment' attacks may have little to do with what happens within these programmes but subject to extraneous factors over which they have no control. The loyalist turf feud between factional groups in the Shankill in 2000, for example, probably resulted in a number of 'housekeeping' attacks by paramilitaries. Developments in the wider political landscape such as police reforms and changes in the criminal justice system will impact on the continuance or otherwise of 'punishment' attacks. Exponents of community restorative justice argue that it must be seen as a long-term project addressing the root causes of 'anti-social' behaviour rather than its symptoms. A restorative justice project manager in the Creggan (Derry), pointed out:

> At the bottom of all this lies an absence of neighbourliness which manifests itself in a lack of respect for others: a lack of respect that has its roots in inequality and alienation, where many young people feel excluded from mainstream society. This exclusion begins with our schooling system, which separates winners from losers at the 11+ stage. It is reinforced by the lack of job opportunities for those leaving school. If we are to turn things around and create conditions where our children feel welcome anywhere in Derry, then we must begin by bringing a sense of neighbourliness back to our communities, turning housing estates into neighbourhoods. It is too serious to leave solely to the politicians. (Quinn, 2000: 10)

It is unrealistic to expect restorative justice projects of themselves to tackle systemic causes of 'anti-social behaviour' but they do operate within a wider social, economic and political milieu which influences participants in their programmes. The prospect for their continuation, however, looks bleak. First Minister Trimble claimed that some of the restorative justice schemes operating in Northern Ireland could be accurately described as 'alternative justice schemes'. He asked for guarantees from the Security Minister that legislation would be introduced ensuring that only those remain which 'have a clear legal basis, are integrated into the legal system, fully respect the rights of those involved and comply wholly with the letter and the spirit of the European Convention on Human Rights' (Trimble, 2000: 263). This was a veiled reference to the Greater Shankill Alternatives Programme and Community Restorative Justice. The tenor of the Criminal Justice Review would suggest that they may well be legislated out of existence and/or allowed, through a process of financial starvation and limited co-operation from other statutories, to wither on the vine.

Restorative justice in South Africa

Informal justice has a long history in South Africa. Before colonisation, the indigenous African population had developed their own set of laws, customs and institutions. These processes emphasised the reconciliation of disputing parties and the restoration of harmony within the community. If an offending party was found guilty, they were shamed and then re-integrated into the community. The re-emergence of *lekgotla*-like practices during the apartheid years can be viewed as attempts to revive this restorative justice tradition and develop mechanisms that met the needs of the people. With the ending of apartheid and the establishment of a legitimate democratically elected government, one of the main priorities of the state was/is to make justice accessible to all by transforming the justice system. The South African Law Commission identified two challenges to this transformation process: i) a justice system that is acceptable and accessible to all and ii) a system that incorporates the concept of restorative justice as one closer to indigenous approaches to dispute resolution (South African Law Commission, 1999). The Commission noted that,

> The present system of justice is based predominately on one approach of resolving disputes, namely the adjudicative approach ... there is another approach where parties resolve their own disputes through a process of reconciling their different interests ... It is about constructing resolutions to disputes which allow the interests of both parties to be met as opposed to deciding the dispute on the basis of one of the parties winning and the other losing. (South African Law Commission, 1999: 10)

The current debate is therefore focused on what type/s of alternative community-based dispute resolution structures should be endorsed by the state and what sort of relationship should exist between the formal courts and these informal structures. We consider two programmes that resemble the structures advocated by the Commission in their discussion paper 'Community Dispute Resolution Structures' (1999).

Community Peace Programme

The origins of the Community Peace Programme (CPP) can be traced to a previous organisation, the Community Peace Foundation (CPF). The CPF was established by Clifford Shearing (a South African-born, Canadian-based academic) at the behest of the ANC in the early 1990s. The CPF was primarily a policy think tank concerned with issues of crime and policing but which also offered practical training in 'community policing'. For example, at the time of the first elections in 1994, it trained local people as election marshals. Drawing upon the work of

John Braithwaite from Australia and David Bailey from the United States, the CPP established its first pilot project in Zwelethemba, a black township near Worcester in the Western Cape in 1997. The CPP aimed to build a model of community-based conflict resolution in co-operation with local people and was designed to achieve two principal purposes. First, the mobilisation of local knowledge and capacity to promote safety and security in poor communities, and second the networking of this knowledge and capacity with the knowledge and capacity of others, for example, criminal justice professionals, the police and social workers. In practice, this involves establishing a Peace Committee comprised of local people who may volunteer their services, be elected or recommended by other community members. At least half of the Peace Committee must be female with membership lasting for six months in the first instance and subject to renewal. Once established and trained in facilitation, the Peace Committee offers its dispute resolution services to community members.

Referrals can come directly from individual/s party to a dispute, from police officers at the local station level (before charges are laid) and, in some cases, from assistant magistrates. No distinction is made between civil and criminal cases and the CPP believes 'that, in principle, there is no offence that could not be brought to a Peace Committee to facilitate its resolution' (interview with John Cartwright, Community Peace Programme, February 2001). Although in practice there are constraints as to the type of dispute or problem that Peace Committees can deal with – for example, cases involving murder fall outside the jurisdiction of the Committees. Furthermore, they are unable to become involved in disputes that are already being dealt with by the police. The community also limit Peace Committees in the types of disputes they deem appropriate for their remit: 'They don't have any authority other than the authority which is given to them by the people who come to those gatherings. They are not judges, they are not police, they are not prosecutors, they are there to facilitate and help other people come to conclusions' (interview with John Cartwright, Community Peace Programme, February 2001). Peace Committees thus deal with a range of cases involving assault, domestic violence, theft, trespass and unpaid loans. They also deal with matters that do not fall into the normal ambit of justice or policing, such as insults between neighbours. Such incidents in the townships have the potential to escalate from irritation to assault through to shack burning.

On receipt of a referral, Peace Committee members first interview individuals involved in the dispute or problem to see if they are willing to attend a meeting (also known as a gathering). At these pre-gathering meetings the Peace Committee tries to ascertain the facts of the case and discover who else could be invited to the gathering to assist in finding a peaceful and practical solution. A minimum of two Peace Committee members need to be present for a gathering to take place – one to act as the facilitator and the other as secretary. Those directly involved in the dispute/problem are given the opportunity to tell their version of events, which is recorded by the secretary. The notes are then read back to the disputants, allowing for any additions or modifications of the notes to be made. Any other persons who believe they have been affected by the dispute/problem are also given the opportunity to speak about their feelings of what happened and how it has affected their lives. After everyone has told their story, the facilitator then encourages those present at the gathering to think about a plan of action that will make things better, thereby shifting the focus of attention from what happened in the past to what can be done in the future. Peace Committees do not take sides in disputes nor apportion blame. As the Project Co-ordinator explains,

> We don't actually use the term 'justice' much … It's not that we think justice is not being done but there are so many different definitions, aren't there? Rather it's about community building, it's about peace building, establishing the basis for community in a way which is based on meaningful negotiation, changing things that are being obstructive and turning them into something positive. (Interview with John Cartwright, Community Peace Programme, February 2001)

The gathering is concluded when those present agree upon a resolution and an individual is nominated to monitor the agreement. Outcomes vary and may include the payment of expenses to the injured party/ies, the return of goods/moneys and/or an apology. According to the CPP more than 90 per cent of gatherings held in Zwelethemba (site of the pilot project) reached a resolution of the dispute or problem under discussion. If, however, no agreement is made then the matter may be taken to the police. At no point in the process is coercion exerted either physical or otherwise. The stated aim of Peace Committees is 'to heal, not to hurt'. To this end, a Code of Practice has been developed outlining operational guidelines for Peace Committee members.

There are currently 18 Peace Committees in operation and a further seven were expected to be operational by end of 2001. Peace Committees receive a payment of R100 (equivalent to £10) for each gathering that they convene from the CPP who in turn receive funding from the Finnish government and some local councils in South Africa. The CPP is keen to stress that these payments are not handouts but moneys earned by the Peace Committees for their conflict resolution services. Each gathering usually deals with one case and there have been approximately 700 gatherings since 1997. This R100 payment is divided into four funds:

- peace making – the payment of Committee members who are present at a gathering (R30),
- peace building – actions designed to alleviate some of the generic problems in the community such as lack of infrastructure e.g. the provision of a playground in an informal settlement (R30),
- micro-loans – investment in the community (R30),
- administration costs – such as transport etc. (R10).

Peace Committees can be viewed, in part, as an organic response to community conflict, given that they are set up by local community members who request the assistance of the CPP. Although the initial model was proposed by the CPP, it has been subsequently adapted and refined by the experiences of the Peace Committees:

> They are not part of the state structure. They operate entirely within the law and with, as the saying goes, entirely transparent guidelines, frameworks, procedures, but one of the strengths of peace committees is that they do not replicate the hierarchical, state based, authoritarian system of justice at all. They're intended to be opening a door for communities to find their own path, deal with their own problems as far as possible, but within very clear and fully negotiated guidelines on what is acceptable. (Interview with John Cartwright, Community Peace Programme, February 2001)

In terms of accountability, Peace Committees are accountable to both the CPP and the communities in which they operate. The CPP requires each Peace Committee to submit on a regular basis reports on all gatherings for processing and feedback. This process ensures that the activities of the Peace Committees are transparent. Furthermore, Peace Committees undertake regular surveys within the communities in which they operate to assess the nature of the problems facing them and the steps that individuals will take in order to resolve them. The Peace Committee is also answerable to the community – if the community is not happy with its operation and handling of disputes then people will refrain from taking their problems or disputes to them. Peace Committees are not the only non-violent restorative justice schemes operating in the townships of the Western Cape, an alternative scheme involving adjudication is also operating and it is to this scheme which we now turn.

Guguletu Community Forum

The Guguletu[47] Community Forum, previously known as the Guguletu Community Court was officially launched on 17 May 1998. Guguletu has a history of community-based mechanisms of ordering and conflict resolution such as street committees. Street committees have long provided channels through which local disputes between neighbours can be addressed and have also taken responsibility for facilitating the maintenance of order e.g. the provision of patrols. In 1993–94 the Community Peace Foundation provided community-policing training for members of the South African National Civic Organisation (SANCO) street committee in Guguletu. The training involved 32 activists and lasted three weekends. Topics discussed included human rights, conflict resolution, problem solving, and the functioning of state agencies, such as the police and the courts. These training sessions resulted in drafting guidelines for the operation of street committees in Guguletu. As the trainers explain,

> The training programme managed to enhance the working capacity of existing structures operating in the community. We aimed not to change them, but to provide additional skills that could contribute to the culture of problem solving in this community. (Mncadi and Nina, 1994: 20)

Street committees were the first port of call for township residents who had a problem or a dispute with neighbours. If the street committee was unable to deal with the matter, it would be referred to an area committee and thereafter to the branch committee until it reached the executive committee of the township. The executive committee represented the whole community and it is from this hierarchical structure that the Guguletu Community Forum emerged.

The Forum has approximately 20 members who are elected by the local community. Forum sessions take place on a weekly basis on a Sunday at a local community centre (the Uluntu centre). These sessions are open to anyone who wishes to attend, thereby ensuring transparency.

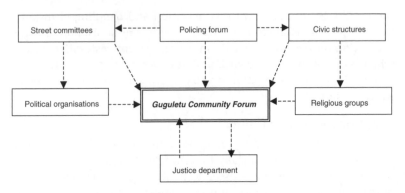

Figure 6.2 Relationship of the Guguletu Community Forum to Other Township Structures

Referrals can come from a variety of sources including self-referral from individuals who have a problem/dispute or from persons (complainants and defendants) who are in the process of going through the formal criminal justice system. Furthermore, Forum members may become aware of a dispute and offer their services to those involved. A number of cases come directly from the police either before a charge is laid or after a complaint is made. Senior prosecutors at the local magistrate's courts also refer cases and suspend the charge from the court roll until such time as the case is either resolved by the Forum or passed back to the prosecution services.

In terms of the type of cases dealt with, the Forum considers both big and small problems including disputes over money, house break-ins, domestic violence, malicious damage to property, assaults, theft and arguments concerned with the rightful ownership of property. The Forum does not, however, deal with cases of rape, murder or armed robbery. On taking on a case, Forum members investigate the matter and call upon all those involved in the dispute or problem to attend the Forum. Attendance is purely voluntary and no one to date has refused to attend a Forum meeting: 'When we have called people, they come' (interview with Sipho Citabatwa, Guguletu Community Forum, March 1999). Parties to the dispute can call witnesses and present their version of events. The Forum aims to help those in conflict arrive at a remedy that restores the parties to a situation as close as possible to where they were before the conflict arose. This involves the victim or complainant in a process in which the offender takes responsibility for their actions and allows for the repairing of relations between the two. The Forum allows for mediation, offers solutions to correct an injustice and supervises the implementation of the decision. In most cases a negotiated settlement is reached between the parties but the Forum is also able to adjudicate and pass judgement. Outcomes vary from an apology, the payment of compensation or expenses such as medical costs or lost income, the return of goods or moneys and/or the undertaking of community service. Community service involves an element of re-integrative shaming whereby the community can observe an individual making good on his/her past deeds. Service orders are usually very visual and have included cleaning the community centre and work on the brick-making project. The brick-making project not only allows for the 'punishing' of offenders but also provides the individual with a new skill.

The following example of a case brought to the attention of the Forum illustrates the workings of the Forum. An elderly man had his bicycle stolen by a group of youths. During the incident the man was injured and required medical treatment. The theft and assault were reported to the police and a charge was laid. Two members of the group were arrested but the rest of the youths were not charged. The grandmother of one of the accused asked the Forum to deal with the case. The magistrate's court was approached and the case was passed to the Forum. All the youths that had been involved in the incident were called to the Forum along with their parents and asked to give their version of events. The youths admitted their involvement and the matter was resolved by the Forum whereby the victim of the theft received reimbursement for the loss of the bicycle, medical costs, lost earnings and the youths involved undertook community service (interview with Bukelwa Sontshatsha, Community Dispute Resolution Trust and Guguletu resident, March 1999).

In 80 per cent of the 200 cases dealt with by the Forum in its first ten months of operation, a resolution was found. The remaining 20 per cent were either referred back to the formal criminal justice system or passed to other structures to deal with. For example, a dispute between a church congregation and its minister was passed to the relevant church council (interview with Sipho Citabatwa, Guguletu Community Forum, March 1999). The Forum receives no funding from the state or from non-governmental organisations (NGOs) and relies on its members giving their time voluntarily and on the community centre to donate a room free of charge. The Forum's acceptability and authority is derived from the support it receives from the community.

Reactions to restorative justice

Reactions to community-based dispute resolution structures have been positive at both national and grass-roots level. The Minister of Justice in 1995 extended the mandate of the Assessors' Co-ordinating Committee to include drafting proposals on community justice. Their discussion paper supported the establishment of community courts and suggested a pilot project aimed at establishing community court structures as a second tier to the existing formal court adjudication structure (Twigg and van der Merwe, 1996).

The South African Law Commission is also a strong advocate of such structures and has been engaged in an investigation into alternative dispute resolution since 1996. The Commission undertook extensive consultation on the issue of community dispute resolution structures and held workshops in each of the nine provinces with a further two held in Soweto and Pretoria. Written responses to the issue papers on alternative dispute resolution and the simplification of the criminal justice system were invited. Those who responded included NGOs such as Lawyers for Human Rights and the Centre for the Study of Violence and Reconciliation, government departments, lawyers and members of the judicial system. The Commission published its findings in 1999 and recognised the advantages of such informal justice mechanisms. As participation in such structures is of a voluntary nature they are more likely to result in the resolution of the problem or dispute. They are cheap and accessible to those who use them. Meetings are usually held in the locality at the weekends or in the evenings. Legal representation is not required thereby dispensing with legal fees. The language used is understood within the community. Such structures create the opportunity of relieving the criminal justice system of certain disputes and are based on restorative justice with its holistic approach to problem solving. They are sensitive to local community values and background conditions, there are fewer delays, and they offer a swift and a less formal system of justice that helps in the knitting of the social fabric (South African Law Commission, 1997).

The Commission also highlighted a number of disadvantages including the vulnerability of members to political pressure, a lack of investigative capacity and representation, their current parallel status with the formal system thereby signalling that they are a second-class system, and their inability to involve people if there is no voluntary participation. Despite these potential problems, the Commission concluded that they 'serve a useful purpose in meeting the needs of the majority of the South African population for accessible justice' and that 'these structures must now be recognised and supported by law' (South African Law Commission, 1999: iv). The Commission made a number of recommendations that include the following:

- Reference to these structures as 'community courts' is misleading and they should be called community forums. Community forums should not be considered to be 'courts' but dispute resolution and peace-making structures which provide 'first aid' justice for local communities.
- Attendance at any community forum should be entirely voluntary.
- Decisions of a community forum are binding on the parties only if they have agreed beforehand to be bound by such decisions. Certain levels of community forum should not have decision-making powers at all, their task being mainly to facilitate between the disputants.
- Recognition of community structures should be based on an Act of Parliament setting out their status, role, function, jurisdiction and procedure. Care must be taken to ensure community forums remain informal and flexible in their procedures, inexpensive in their operations, accessible, non-alienating and responsive to the needs of the communities in which they operate.
- Community forums shall function at all times within the laws and the Constitution of the Republic of South Africa.
- Training in various aspects of leadership, mediation and the ideas of restorative justice must be given to the individuals who operate community forums in order to empower them.

In terms of structures, the Commission proposed two levels of forum operating within any community. The first level would offer 'first aid' dispute resolution and peace-making within the community along the lines of the Peace Committees already outlined. Peace Committee members would act as facilitators and solutions to disputes would come from those persons present at the meeting. The second level forum is more in keeping with the Guguletu Community Forum in which Forum members can adjudicate and take sides in a dispute.

Both the national government and provincial government of Guateng have given their support to community-based dispute resolution mechanisms. Dullah Omar (1998), the then Minister of Justice and Mathole Motshekga, the Premier of Guateng pledged their support for community courts/forums in 1998, albeit for different reasons. The Minister of Justice supported community courts/forums on the grounds that they would ensure community participation and access to justice. Motshekga (1998) argued that they would allow for the empowerment of victims, the community would witness the application of justice, and restitution would be paid to the victim and the community at large.

Given the absence of any legislation to date on community-based dispute resolution mechanisms, a number of issues remain unresolved. Firstly, should community forums have criminal jurisdiction? Currently community forums do not distinguish between civil and criminal jurisdiction. This is seen as a positive attribute in that they focus on the relationship between the disputants, and the effects of the dispute on their relationship and to the peaceful co-existence of the community. The removal of criminal matters from community forums might result in a loss of legitimacy in the eyes of the community if their role in deterring criminal behaviour is restricted in any way.

Secondly, to what extent should the state administer and regulate community forums? If community forums become regulated by the state and forum personnel become employees as opposed to volunteers, a number of problems may arise. The basis upon which these community-based dispute resolution structures receive their support and legitimacy from the community will change. In addition, the presence of forum employees in areas of high unemployment will cause conflict. Increasing bureaucratisation and paperwork would affect the forum's ability to be responsive to community needs and the potential would exist for communities to form new structures that meet their needs, parallel to the ones now enjoying state support (Schärf, 1997). State regulation would, however, ensure a unitary justice system, accountability of officials, enforceable judgments and ease in referrals and cross-referrals between different elements of the justice system.

Thirdly, are community forums merely poor people's justice for black people? During the apartheid years dual systems of justice – informal and formal – existed. Indeed within the formal system Commissioners' Courts administered an inferior system of justice to township residents (Brogden and Shearing, 1993). These courts were designed to provide a simple and inexpensive apparatus for setting disputes between blacks, and experts in indigenous law and custom would hear cases. However, this was not the case and Commissioners' Courts created 'poor law for poor people' (Brogden and Shearing, 1993: 138). Within the 'new' South Africa, blacks are still being denied access to justice (Omar, 1996) and the state's recognition of community forums merely reinforces this rather than addresses it. Alternatively it can be argued that the recognition of community forums by the state represents not only an attempt to regulate all forms of justice systems in the country, but also to move towards a unitary system that will be more effective. This would make the justice system more accessible and user-friendly, while at the same time bringing justice closer to the people.

Despite the absence of formal state recognition at the grass-roots level, informal arrangements have been made between community-based dispute resolution mechanisms and the formal justice system. In the case of the Guguletu Community Forum, a working relationship with the local magistrate's courts has been established. The Co-ordinator of the Forum would approach the senior prosecutor at the magistrate's court and ask for particular cases to be handed to the Forum. The senior prosecutor would also offer defendants the option of their case being passed to the Forum. Furthermore, individuals who were due in court could request diversion to the Forum. According to the Senior Prosecutor at Wynberg Magistrate's Court, the Forum is a mutually beneficial operation in that it allows people to deal with their own minor problems and reduces the burden on the formal courts:

> The African person has his/her own way, historically and tradition-ally, of dealing with certain matters and these type of community courts give him/her a foothold into solving some problems that they maybe can solve … If you talk about community courts and restora-tive justice, they [the people who use them] are quite happy. All they want is for their window to be replaced again or their hi-fi set that was stolen to be brought back again, or to be placed in a position where they can buy another. It is a very simple way of meting out justice. (Interview with Lindsey Louther, Wynberg Magistrate's Court, Cape Town, November 1999)

Community organisations in the townships such as civic associations have also been supportive of local dispute resolution mechanisms. Indeed, the Eastern Cape South African National Civic Organisation (SANCO) proposed guidelines aimed at creating a uniform system in the province. In Guguletu, SANCO is firmly behind the Community Forum. As noted previously, such structures are dependent on community members making use of their services and they receive their legitimacy from the community. If they were not seen as acceptable mechanisms for dispute resolution then community members would not use them and alternative structures would emerge.

Impact on the informal 'justice' system?

What impact, if any, has the emergence of restorative justice had on the punitive sanctions meted out by agents of informal justice, namely vigilantes? This is a difficult question to answer for a variety of reasons. Firstly, unlike Northern Ireland, no statistics are kept by the South African Police Service on assaults or killings perpetrated by vigilantes. Even in areas where community forums are said to be operating well, incidents of vigilantism continue. For example, in Guguletu, residents turned to a local taxi association to deal with alleged criminals. The methods used by the taxi association were often brutal and suspects were beaten or whipped until they revealed the location of stolen goods and moneys. Not only were their anti-crime methods seen as effective by those who went to them but they also acted as a deterrent to criminals in the area. Even residents who disagreed with the actions of the taxi-drivers conceded that the township had become 'peaceful', women could wear their jewellery without fear of robbery and people could go out at night: 'those taxi-drivers, yes they did abuse their power but it contributed also in eliminating this thuggery that was taking place in the township' (interview with Danile Landingwe, Guguletu Community Police Forum, November 1999). Indeed, at the time of the taxi association's anti-crime activities the Community Forum was operating simultaneously. In the neighbouring township of Khayelitsha, the Community Peace Programme has been approached by the local vigilante group, PEACA (Peninsula Anti-Crime Agency) which is keen to move away from punitive sanctions. It should be remembered that community-based dispute resolution mechanisms were not established with the explicit aim of ending vigilantism but rather to offer township residents mechanisms by which to resolve disputes. The types of disputes that such mechanisms deal with are limited in nature and do not usually constitute violent crime. Thus it is difficult to assess whether they have reduced the incidence of vigilantism. In terms of the future it is likely that vigilantism will persist given the combination of high crime rates and low levels of township community confidence in the state to maintain law and order. Community forums will be recognised by the state but the precise details of their jurisdiction and relationship to the justice system will be the subject of forthcoming legislation.

In summary, the description of restorative justice schemes in Northern Ireland and South Africa serves to illustrate their very different historical antecedents and operational detail. The question posed as to whether such schemes have affected the violent system of punitive sanctions perpetrated by paramilitaries in Northern Ireland or vigilantes in South Africa remains difficult to answer definitively. The absence of crime statistics in the latter, and capacity to screen out extraneous variables which may impact on crime in the former, means that we have to rely on qualitative responses from those involved. Often views expressed are tendentious because of the vested interests of the stakeholders involved such as police and communitarians. Both countries seem receptive to the integration of restorative justice programmes within their formal justice systems but this must involve recognition of, and collaboration with, the organs of the state. For ideological reasons and/or lack of confidence in the effectiveness of the state's formal justice system, this may not be possible for some communities currently supportive of grass-roots restorative justice initiatives. Moreover, to expect restorative justice programmes to deal with (often violent) crime which has been the preserve of paramilitaries or vigilantes is to demand too much of them. This dumbing down of expectations has been realised in South Africa but not yet in Northern Ireland where the introduction of restorative programmes is hailed as the panacea for 'punishment' beatings by paramilitaries. The South African experience would suggest that there is an important role for restorative justice schemes but one which runs in parallel with, rather than substitutes for, the formal (or indeed informal) retributive system. Vigilantism continues in South Africa and paramilitary involvement in community crime persists in Northern Ireland.

The lessons of South Africa for Northern Ireland are clear. Restorative justice schemes do offer an effective mechanism for resolution of disputes and petty crime, but they cannot survive as alternative justice systems that attempt to work outside the rubric of the state under the auspices of paramilitaries who see themselves as administering the ultimate sanction for the less compliant. In Northern Ireland and South Africa there is still strong support for summary justice, a legacy of years of violent struggle. There are several similarities in both countries' transition to a post-conflict scenario. Constitutional settlements have been no guarantee of a reduction in 'normal' crime and the statistics would suggest an inverse relationship. There is an obvious time lag in moving from transitional status where the formal justice system remains ineffectual and politically tainted, to one which can command the credibility and trust of the community(ies). The nature of the conflict has caused those most affected to look inwards for protection, not outwards to the state. With the move to new political dispensations there have been attempts at 'regulatory capture' of community-based restorative justice schemes by the state, ostensibly in the interests of human rights protection and securing due process for those accused. This has resulted in a hiatus. The transition to acceptable and effective policing and criminal justice systems inevitably is taking longer than envisaged which provides justification for paramilitaries and vigilantes to tackle violent crime. Meanwhile restorative justice schemes operating outwith the state system are criticised as alternative justice systems. Those integral to the formal system are increasingly regulated to the extent that they as seen by communities as little more that minor dispute centres with limited clout and even less jurisdiction in the area of violent crime. It should be borne in mind that the legitimacy of local restorative justice programmes comes from the community who must recognise their value and support their *modus operandi*. If this community ownership is wrested from them and they become part of the formal justice system, then they may not be seen in the same light.

South Africa also provides some insights into the future direction of informal 'justice' in Northern Ireland. The 'comrades' in South Africa, post-settlement, no longer wanted to be involved in vigilante-type activity aimed at tackling community crime. They have been displaced by professionalised mobs running crime prevention scams. The paramilitaries in Northern Ireland now publicly eschew involvement in community crime. In practice, however, 'punishment' gangs are likely to have direct links with paramilitaries. Racketeering and 'protection' money is part of their core funding. Similarly in Northern Ireland a two-tier system is developing. Community restorative projects deal with minor disputes and petty crime but more serious issues are dealt with by paramilitaries and the inexorable lust for summary 'justice' has resulted in more brutal consequences: respectively necklacing and six packs (shots to the knees, ankles and elbows). While the formal policing and justice systems in both countries struggle to achieve legitimacy and effectiveness, restorative justice schemes are perceived as 'first-aid clinics' for minor disputes and petty crime. Beyond that, there remain the hard men of violence still wedded to punitive measures and seemingly untouched by attempts to reform the formal system.

One salient issue in considering alternatives for the informal justice system is what protection, if any, are victims of these attacks afforded under the law? It would appear that paramilitaries and vigilantes violate the human rights of their victims in at least three ways: the right not to be tortured or subjected to cruel, inhuman or degrading treatment or punishment; the right to liberty and security of the person; and the right to a fair trial. The question is whether the perpetrators can be held to account under international laws on human rights and, if not, whether national law and institutions can protect those subject to such attacks. This forms the basis of the next chapter written by the Northern Ireland Human Rights Commissioner.

7
Legal Alternatives: the Protection of Human Rights

Brice Dickson
Northern Ireland Human Rights Commissioner

Background

Traditionally – some would even say inevitably – the delivery of justice, like the guarantee of security, is seen as one of the primary functions of any government. However differently they might define justice, one of the ideas which links such disparate thinkers as Hobbes (1651), Rousseau (1762) and Paine (1790) is that the obligation to ensure its provision rests upon those who are in authority in society. They all view the settling of disputes and the protection of the safety of citizens as fundamental duties of such authorities. In more modern times, most political scientists and legal theorists share this view. Rawls (1971), for example, despite resorting to abstractions such as 'the original position', simply takes it for granted that the purpose of developing a theory of justice is so that state governments can put it into practice. The debate is about how society should organise itself in order to ensure that, in the full range of situations needing to be dealt with, coherent and consistent standards can be applied.

To be acceptable to people in the street, however, grand theories of justice must relate to their everyday lives. The standards of justice being applied must be ones which typical men and women recognise as ones they themselves would apply in their own affairs, all else being equal. Concepts such as honesty, impartiality and non-violence are among those which they would strive to maintain on a personal basis and which they would expect to see mirrored at a societal level. At the same time, they would no doubt acknowledge, on reflection, that when a large organisation is drawing up rules of conduct for its members it often has to adopt a position that is less flexible, less tolerant of individualised circumstances, than their own position might be if they were confronted with a particular situation in their private lives. It is one thing for an individual man or woman to be inconsistent or hypocritical; it is entirely another for a whole society to be riddled with such characteristics.

With the rise of the nation-state in the nineteenth century, the autonomy of rulers within their own states, or when dealing with other states, grew ever greater. A multiplicity of approaches to the delivery of justice therefore developed, although the formation of various colonial empires meant that in large areas of the world very similar standards and delivery mechanisms were deployed. There was, however, no universalised system of justice at the global level. Of course the culmination of this nationalistic approach to justice was the aggressive *Lebensraum* policy of the German government in the 1930s and the Second World War which it precipitated. That conflict began because a democratically elected government decided not only to liquidate systematically large sections of its own population but also to extend this philosophy to neighbouring territories. The result was the Holocaust.

The development of international human rights standards

Out of the horror of the Second World War[48] one hugely important principle emerged, namely that never again must nation-states, even those with democratically elected governments, be allowed *carte blanche* to treat their citizens in whatever way they wished. Instead they must agree to adhere to common standards which, if breached, would justify international opprobrium and, if necessary, intervention. These standards were designated as human rights and were most eloquently encapsulated, first in an attenuated form in the Charter of the United Nations signed in San Francisco on 24 October 1945 and then more fully in the Universal Declaration of Human Rights signed in New York on 10 December 1948. The Charter, in its Preamble, says that the peoples of the United Nations are determined 'to reaffirm faith in fundamental human rights, in the dignity and worth of the human person [and] ... to establish conditions under which justice ... can be maintained', all of this for the purpose, among other things, of ensuring that, 'by the acceptance of principles and the institution of methods, armed force shall not be used, save in the common interest'. While Article 2(7) of the Charter says that nothing in the Charter authorises the United Nations to intervene in matters which are essentially within the domestic jurisdiction of any state, Chapter VII of the Charter goes on to permit measures not involving the use of armed force (Article 41) and, if the Security Council considers those measures to be inadequate, 'such action by air, sea, or land forces as may be necessary to maintain or restore international peace and security' (Article 42). Moreover, by Article 51, nothing in the Charter impairs the inherent right of individual or collective self-defence if an armed attack occurs against a Member of the United Nations, until the Security Council has taken measures necessary to maintain international peace and security.

The 1948 Declaration, in its Preamble, says that recognition of the inherent dignity and the equal and inalienable rights of all members of the human family is the foundation of freedom, justice and peace in the world, and it goes on to proclaim that the Declaration is a common standard of achievement for all peoples and all nations, 'to the end that every individual and every organ of society, keeping this Declaration constantly in mind, shall strive by teaching and education to promote respect for these rights and freedoms and by progressive measures, national and international, to secure their universal and effective recognition and observance'.

The task of monitoring the implementation of the Universal Declaration, and of developing further standards based on that foundation, was allocated to the United Nations itself. Since then there has been a proliferation of human rights treaties, some quite general, others more specific, and an explosion in the mechanisms devised to monitor them. While the United Nations has been to the fore in this regard, other regional inter-governmental bodies have been active too, most notably the Council of Europe, the European Union (as it is now called), the Organisation of American States and the Organisation of African Unity. When the so-called Helsinki process led in 1990 to the agreement of a Charter of Paris for a New Europe (embracing what was then the USSR), the state parties began by affirming that 'Human rights and fundamental freedoms are the birthright of all human beings, are inalienable and are guaranteed by law. Their protection and promotion is the first responsibility of government. Respect for them is an essential safeguard against an over-mighty State. Their observance and full exercise are the foundation of freedom, justice and peace'. In the Vienna Declaration and Programme for Action resulting out of the 1995 World Conference on Human Right, we see the same sentiments repeated.[49] In Article 17, moreover, this Declaration unequivocally condemns terrorism for what it is: 'The acts, methods and practices of terrorism in all its forms and manifestations as well as linkage in some countries to drug trafficking are activities aimed at the destruction of human rights, fundamental freedoms and democracy...'. Article 27 focuses on the need for a proper legal system in each country: 'Every State should provide an effective framework of remedies to redress human rights grievances or violations. The administration of justice, including law enforcement and prosecutorial agencies and, especially, an independent judiciary and legal profession...are essential to the full and non-discriminatory realization of human rights...'.

Today the two most significant human rights systems on the world stage are, first, the Council of Europe's Convention on Human Rights and Fundamental Freedoms, which was agreed in 1950 and is enforced by the European Court of Human Rights in Strasbourg, France, and, second, the UN's International Covenant on Civil and Political Rights, which was agreed in 1966 and is enforced by the UN's Human Rights Committee sitting in New York and Geneva, Switzerland. At the regional level, the African Charter on Human and Peoples' Rights, which was agreed in 1981 and came into force in 1986, is also of significance to our study. At present a commission within the Organisation of African Unity (the African Commission on Human and Peoples' Rights) is tasked with promoting and safeguarding the rights contained within the African Charter on Human and Peoples' Rights. A Protocol on the Establishment of an African Court on Human and Peoples' Rights has been passed (1998) but the Court has yet to be set up. There are now whole books which are compilations of international human rights standards. The number of people engaged in teaching, training, monitoring, researching and enforcing human rights has risen enormously. The concept has become an almost iconic phrase which is wafted around at every level of society, from international diplomacy to local sporting arrangements.

Do the standards apply to 'private' relationships?

The development of international human rights law marked an important shift in prior thinking about international law, which held that it was a system of law designed to deal with disputes between nation states. After 1945 the orthodox view became that international law was also relevant *within* states: governments were under an obligation not just to avoid treating other governments badly but also to respect the human rights of their own citizens. In more recent years a further question has naturally come to be asked, namely whether, *within* states, the standards agreed internationally are of relevance only to dealings between citizens and representatives of the state or also to dealings between citizens and other citizens.

As is the case with many good questions, the answer to this one is both affirmative and negative. It is affirmative in the sense that the international standards are of course founded on the idea that each individual is entitled to his or her dignity and well-being. Once these are taken away, the loss to the individual is the same regardless of whether the person responsible for the loss is or is not a state representative. There may of course be additional 'injury to feelings' if the person responsible is a state representative, because such persons are supposedly acting in the name of the state and one expects a state to act lawfully and with respect, but the actual deprivation suffered by the victim is no greater than where it has been caused by another citizen. However, the answer to the question is also negative, in the sense that the international standards, by definition, are ones which have been agreed only by states, not by private organisations. Some commentators therefore hold that it is inappropriate to describe private organisations as having breached those standards – they never agreed to abide by them in the first place. On this view it is the role of criminal law, whether national or international, to deal with non-state abuses (Meron, 1990).

Even if it is appropriate to say that the victims of wrongdoing by 'private' organisations can justifiably claim to have had their human rights breached, this still leaves open the questions, who is to be held responsible for the breach and what kind of remedy should be made available? In most legal systems it is the private organisation, or its representative(s), who are held responsible; the only 'remedy' available is that the organisation and/or those persons is/are 'punished', usually through being fined or sometimes, in the case of individuals, imprisoned. In more developed legal systems two other mechanisms may be employed. First, if the organisation or person responsible is solvent, and is identified, the victim may bring a civil claim seeking compensation for his or her loss and suffering. In the Anglo-American legal world such civil claims are called tortious claims (*tort* is still the French word for 'wrong') and they will succeed if certain preconditions are satisfied, such as that damage has been caused and the required standard of care has not been exercised. The standard of proof needed to be reached by such claimants is 'on the balance of probabilities', that is, more than 50 per cent likely. Second, if the organisation or person responsible cannot be identified, or, although identified is for some reason not convicted (perhaps because he or she has a valid defence, such as extreme youthfulness or insanity), the state may itself step in to provide compensation to the victim. States differ greatly as to the sophistication of the system they have in place for making such compensation available (Greer, 1996).

If it is appropriate to say that the victims of wrongdoing by 'private' organisations have had their human rights breached by that wrongdoing, it then becomes feasible to argue that the failure of the state to put in place any or all of the mechanisms just mentioned in the previous paragraph would qualify as a breach of those rights. This is made explicit in many of the international treaties on human rights. Article 13 of the European Convention on Human Rights, for instance, says that 'Everyone whose rights and freedoms as set forth in this Convention are violated shall have an effective remedy before a national authority ...'. Article 2 of the International Covenant on Civil and Political Rights also confers the right to an effective remedy but adds that each state must ensure that any person claiming such a remedy can have this right determined by competent judicial, administrative or legislative authorities. The case law on these Articles is relatively under-developed, although recently the European Court of Human Rights has held in relation to breaches of the right to life (protected by Article 2 of the Convention), that the fact that the family of the deceased is able to sue for compensation for the tort of negligence is not by itself an adequately effective remedy for the purposes of Article 13 (*Keenan* v. *UK*). In addition to conferring on individuals the specific right to a remedy, human rights treaties also impose duties on states to take positive measures to prevent breaches of rights occurring in the first place (Starmer, 2001). A notable example from the case law is *Osman* v. *UK* (1998), where the European Court of Human Rights held that the English common law (i.e. non-statutory law) was in breach of the right of access to justice conferred by Article 6(1) of the European Convention in so far as that common law prohibited victims of crimes, or the families of those victims, from suing the police for being negligent in not preventing the crime. As a result of this ruling by the European Court it is now possible to say that in English (and Northern Irish) law the police do owe a duty of care to potential victims of crime – including victims of crimes committed by paramilitary organisations.

The fact that national criminal and civil legal procedures have been in existence throughout the world for centuries, from a time which pre-dates by far the development of 'human rights' as the key concept in international legal proceedings, goes part of the way towards explaining why some human rights activists fail to acknowledge that the key concepts underlying national criminal and civil legal procedures are identical to those embedded in international human rights law; concepts such as respect for the individual's dignity and physical integrity, his or her property and reputation, and his or her personal characteristics. Criminal laws are in place to punish people in the name of society for the violations they have committed of another person's right to stay alive, right not to be physically assaulted, right to move around at will, right to have personal possessions, etc. Civil laws are in place to supplement the criminal laws by, in effect, allowing the victims of unacceptable behaviour (most crimes are also civil wrongs) to claim some kind of compensation from the perpetrator. The overall purpose of enforcing all of these laws is to counter anarchy and preserve liberty. It is therefore a distortion of language to say that the victims of wrongdoing by 'private' organisations or by individuals have not had their human rights breached by that wrongdoing. If the state fails to put in place any or all of the mechanisms mentioned above, this qualifies as an additional breach of human rights, but it does not take away from the fact that the wrong first suffered is in the same category.

Perhaps paradoxically (because 'purist' human rights activists do not like to be lumped together with those whom they would see as old-fashioned), people who adhere to the positivist school of legal philosophy tend to favour the negative answer to the question posed at the beginning of this section. In their eyes, if conduct is not presently designated by the law as a breach of human rights, it is not such a breach. It may be designated in the law as something else – such as a crime, a tort or a breach of trust – but that does not make it, on this view, a breach of human rights. Surely such a position is misguided? In the first place, 'human rights' is a portmanteau expression which enshrines a set of values. Those values have been singled out because they are fundamental. They are meant to underpin the whole of the justice system. They transcend the traditional legal categories of criminal or civil wrongs. In the second place, and rather obviously, just because certain forms of conduct are not at present labelled as breaches of human rights, this does not mean that they should not be so labelled in future. Rape within marriage was not made a crime in English law until just a few years ago, but that did not mean that in the years leading up to that reform it was wrong to say that it should have been a crime. Indeed, when someone was convicted for the first time of such a crime and then sought to challenge his conviction on the basis that a new law had been created retrospectively to criminalise behaviour which was not a crime at the time he indulged in it, he received short shrift from the European Court of Human Rights (*CR* v. *UK*). The Court held that to remove from a man who had forced a woman to have sexual intercourse with him the defence that he was married to that woman was not a breach of any of his human rights. If the flaw in English law had come to the European Court in a different way – through a wife who had been forced to have sexual intercourse bringing a claim based on her right not to be subjected to inhuman or degrading treatment under Article 3 of the European Convention and her right to an effective remedy under Article 13 – one imagines that she too would have been successful.

Which human rights are at stake?

Before developing the notion that, in the eyes of the law, human rights standards do and should pervade private relationships, it is important to identify the human rights standards which are at issue in this context. For the purposes of the present study, it is possible to highlight three particular rights which relate to the application of punishment within a justice system. Those rights are (1) the right not to be tortured or subjected to cruel, inhuman or degrading treatment or punishment, (2) the right to liberty and security of the person and (3) the right to a fair trial. Each of these will be considered in turn.

The right not to be tortured or subjected to cruel, inhuman or degrading treatment or punishment is guaranteed (with minor variations) by Article 5 of the Universal Declaration of Human Rights (1948), Article 3 of the European Convention on Human Rights (1950), Article 7 of the International Covenant on Civil and Political Rights (1966) and Article 5 of the African Charter on Human and Peoples' Rights (1981). It is, in addition, the focus of two separate sets of standards in the UN's Convention Against Torture and Other Cruel, Inhuman or Degrading Treatment or Punishment (1984) and the Council of Europe's Convention for the Prevention of Torture and Inhuman or Degrading Treatment or Punishment (1987). Article 2(1) of the UN's Convention unequivocally requires states to 'take effective legislative, administrative, judicial or other measures to prevent acts of torture'. In common with the other international instruments already listed, it makes it clear in the next paragraph that the right is an absolute one – one of very few such rights: 'No exceptional circumstances whatsoever, whether a state of war or a threat of war, internal political instability or any other public emergency, may be invoked as a justification of torture'. But it has to be conceded that the 1984 Convention – and in this regard it must be presumed to be following, or amplifying, the earlier treaties – specifies that 'torture' and 'other acts of cruel, inhuman or degrading treatment or punishment' are to be defined in terms of the actions of public officials or other persons acting in an official capacity. Article 1 reads:

> For the purposes of this Convention, the term 'torture' means any act by which severe pain or suffering, whether physical or mental, is intentionally inflicted on a person for such purposes as obtaining from him or a third person information or a confession, punishing him for an act he or a third person has committed or is suspected of having committed, or intimidating or coercing him or a third person, or for any reason based on discrimination of any kind, when such pain or suffering is inflicted by or at the instigation of or with the consent or acquiescence of a public official or other person acting in an official capacity.

It follows that the procedures laid down in the 1984 Convention for dealing with torture at the UN level can deal only with state-sponsored torture and other cruel, inhuman or degrading treatment or punishment. The procedures include the establishment of a Committee against Torture, with power to consider periodic reports from countries which have ratified the Convention and (in the case of countries which have declared that they recognise the competence of the Committee in this regard) power to receive and consider communications from or on behalf of individuals who claim to be victims of a violation by the state of the provisions of the Convention.

The Council of Europe's Convention for the Prevention of Torture etc. is not of much assistance in this context either. Its Preamble makes it clear that the rationale for the Convention is the conviction on the part of the states in the Council of Europe that 'the protection of persons *deprived of their liberty* [emphasis added] against torture and inhuman or degrading treatment or punishment could be strengthened by non-judicial means of a preventive character based on visits'. Article 2 then requires each state party to permit visits by the European Committee for the Prevention of Torture etc. to any place within its jurisdiction where persons are deprived of their liberty by a public authority. Thus, although the European Committee has been particularly active since its establishment (Evans and Morgan, 1998; Morgan and Evans, 1999), on none of its visits to European countries has it concerned itself with abuses by non-state agencies, even those which deprive their victims of their liberty before abusing them.

None of this means, of course, that it is wrong to describe what is done by people who are not public officials as torture or cruel, inhuman or degrading treatment or punishment. The fact that international human rights documents have apparently hived off those words to describe what some public officials do, cannot take away from the fact that in common parlance individuals and private organisations *are* often described as torturing their victims. Legal documents cannot alter the meaning of words in a non-legal context.

The right to liberty and security of the person is guaranteed by Article 3 of the Universal Declaration of Human Rights, Article 6 of the African Charter on Human and Peoples' Rights, Article 5(1) of the European Convention on Human Rights and Article 9(1) of the International Covenant on Civil and Political Rights. The last two provisions continue in a way which focuses on the right of individuals not to be arbitrarily deprived of their liberty, their right to be informed of the reason for any arrest and their right to challenge their detention in court. This suggests that kidnapping or falsely imprisoning someone would amount to a breach of the Articles 5 and 9 in question. But because the enforcement mechanisms for those treaties allow only states to be held accountable for breaching them, the provisions in question have been interpreted by the UN's Human Rights Committee and the European Court of Human Rights, respectively, not as permitting individuals to seek remedies against other individuals or organisations but as requiring state government to have laws in place which are aimed at protecting people against attacks on the security of their person by other individuals or private organisations. There is a duty on states, in other words, to have criminal laws to deal with such attacks. They must also enforce those laws by, for example, initiating prosecutions where appropriate. As already noted, the European Convention goes on to say in Article 13 that persons whose rights to security (or any other Convention rights) are breached must have an effective remedy before a national authority. Again, though, just because a state has good criminal laws and effective remedies in place, this does not mean that it is inappropriate to describe the wrongdoing committed by an individual or organisation as a breach of the fundamental human right to security of the person who is the victim of that wrongdoing.

The right to a fair trial is guaranteed by Article 10 of the Universal Declaration, Article 6 of the European Convention, Article 14 of the International Covenant and Article 7 of the African Charter on Human and Peoples' Rights. It is one of the most litigated of all human rights provisions and a vast jurisprudence has developed by way of explication

(Weissbrodt and Wolfrum, 1997). While the Articles in question focus on equality before the law and on fairness in relation to the determination of a person's rights and obligations in general, each of them specifically mentions the determination of criminal charges against an individual. Articles 6, 7 and 14 set out a list of protections which are to apply in that context. These include the right to be presumed innocent until proved guilty according to law, the right to be informed promptly and in comprehensible detail about the nature of the matter of which one has been accused, the right to have adequate time and facilities for the preparation of a defence, the right to communicate with legal advisers, the right to be tried and to defend oneself in person or through legal assistance, the right to examine, or have examined, witnesses and the right not to be compelled to testify against oneself or to confess guilt.

Other well-recognised rights deserve to be mentioned at this point, for they too might come into question if someone were to be the victim of a paramilitary 'punishment' in Northern Ireland or a vigilante attack in South Africa. First, and most obviously, a person's right to life could be at risk if an attack is particularly serious. Second, the right to a private and family life is interfered with if a person is abducted from his or her home or from the midst of associates in order to be assaulted elsewhere. Third, persons who are under 18 years of age have extra rights under treaties such as the UN's Convention on the Rights of the Child (1989) and the African Charter on the Rights and Welfare of the Child (1990). By Article 19 of the UN's Convention and Article 16 of the African Charter, for example, states must take all appropriate legislative, administrative, social and educational measures to protect children from all forms of physical or mental violence, injury or abuse, neglect or negligent treatment, maltreatment or exploitation, including sexual abuse, while they are in someone's care. Fourth, by various treaties dealing with social, economic and cultural rights everyone has the right to 'the enjoyment of the highest attainable standard of physical and mental health' (e.g. Article 12(1) of the UN's International Covenant on Economic, Social and Cultural Rights, 1966 and Article 16 of the African Charter on Human and Peoples' Rights, 1981).

Recent trends in international and national human rights law

While it is always dangerous to seek to identify trends in legal development at any particular time, few would deny today that in international human rights law there is a growing tendency to realise that the value-system which underpins the by now 'traditional' human rights treaties is one which can, and should, be transferred to a variety of other contexts, most notably that involving purely private relationships. In its work on humanitarian law, for example, the International Committee of the Red Cross has been trying to develop human rights standards which could apply to those participating in civil unrest which falls short of 'internal strife' (as defined by the Geneva Conventions of 1946 and the Protocols of 1977). The UN's Sub-Commission on the Promotion and Protection of Human Rights, at its 52nd session, in August 2000, decided to appoint one of its members to undertake a study of the issue of human rights and human responsibilities (Decision 2000/111) and at its 53rd session, in August 2001, it decided to continue a study of terrorism and human rights (Resolution 2001/18). The latter has brought to light the deep difference of opinion between states as to whether non-state actors can be guilty of human rights abuses. In her first progress report the Special Rapporteur stated:

> No State seems to be in doubt that terrorist acts are deserving of condemnation and that the perpetrators of terrorism need to be punished. However, a number of States do question whether this can or should be accomplished through the application of international human rights law. See, for instance, the different statements and explanations of vote recorded in the General Assembly and in the Commission on Human Rights during the adoption of their resolutions on human rights and terrorism. (Koufa, 1999)

Various national legal systems have initiated a process – usually by interpreting a home-grown Bill of Rights – of allowing international standards to infiltrate the national law. Indeed leading Commonwealth judges have been calling for years – ever since they first signed the so-called Bangalore Principles in 1988 – for national judges to make use of international standards when developing national law. With the ending of apartheid in South Africa, a new constitution (Act 108 of 1996) was drawn up and enacted containing a Bill of Rights. Accordingly this Bill of Rights was viewed as 'a cornerstone of democracy' enshrining the rights of all and affirming 'the democratic values of human dignity, equality and freedom' (Article 7(1)). Many of the rights outlined echo those contained in the Universal Declaration of Human Rights and the African Charter on Human and Peoples' Rights.

In the United Kingdom a great boost was given to the values underpinning international human rights standards when the Human Rights

Act was enacted in 1998, coming fully into force on 2 October 2000. The Act makes the European Convention on Human Rights part of the law of all parts of the United Kingdom. It does so by stating that, when faced with a claim that existing primary or subordinate legislation is incompatible with the rights set out in the European Convention, judges must, 'so far as it is possible to do so', give effect to the legislation in a way which makes it compatible. If the language of *primary* legislation is too clear to permit such an interpretation, a High Court judge can declare the legislation to be incompatible. Such a declaration does not invalidate the primary legislation – the Human Rights Act does not overturn the basic principle of the unwritten British constitution that judges cannot strike down Acts of the Westminster Parliament – but it sends a clear message to the government and Parliament that, unless the legislation is amended, successful claims could well be taken against the United Kingdom in the European Court of Human Rights.

To supplement this interpretative mechanism, the Human Rights Act permits judges to strike down *secondary* legislation if it is incompatible with the European Convention (section 4(2)), unless the primary legislation authorising the secondary legislation in question precludes this, and people who believe that their European Convention rights have been breached by a public authority have the right to bring court proceedings against that authority (section 7(1)). A court has a discretion to 'grant such relief or remedy, or make such order, within its powers as it considers just and appropriate' (section 8(1)). Intriguingly, the courts themselves are specifically listed as public authorities, so they too are under a separate duty to uphold the Convention rights in everything they do, which includes deciding cases (whether or not these involve any representatives of the state).

Within the first few months of the Human Rights Act coming into force it became clear that the UK courts were quite prepared to use their new powers liberally. Interestingly, it has been in the realm of private transactions that the Act has had the most profound effects. There have, for instance, been three high profile cases involving disputes between newspapers on the one hand and aggrieved private citizens on the other. In each of these cases the courts have come down on the side of the citizens, thereby emphasising that private organisations such as newspapers must adhere to the same human rights standards that public organisations must meet. In *Douglas* v. *Hello! Ltd* the Court of Appeal developed the common law on confidentiality so as to recognise, in effect, a right to damages for breach of privacy (*Hello!* Magazine had published pirated copies of photographs of Michael Douglas's wedding to Catherine Zeta-Jones). In *Venables* v. *News Group Newspapers Ltd* a judge imposed a life-time ban on the publication of the identity and whereabouts of the two boys who were convicted of the murder of Jamie Bulger. In *Ashdown* v. *Telegraph Group Ltd* the High Court again upheld the claim of a famous person (Paddy Ashdown, former leader of the Liberal Democrats) to the confidentiality of his diaries whenever a newspaper tried to publish extracts from them.

In only two cases has there been a declaration of incompatibility issued in respect of primary legislation. One concerned a provision in the Consumer Credit Act 1974 (*Wilson* v. *First County Trust Ltd*), another case involving a purely private transaction. The provision in question was held to have imposed a disproportionate penalty on the lender of money, thereby breaching the latter's right to a fair trial under Article 6 of the European Convention on Human Rights and the right to peaceful enjoyment of one's possessions under Article 1 of Protocol 1 to the Convention. The other case involved provisions in the Mental Health Act 1983, which were declared incompatible because they required a person who was detained on mental health grounds to show cause why his or her detention should not be continued, whereas Article 5 of the European Convention places the burden of justifying detention squarely on the shoulders of those who are doing the detaining (*Re H*). Although there is no 'private' dimension to this case, the outcome is worth noting for the emphasis the court placed on the liberty of the individual. There has to be objectively justifiable good cause if that liberty is to be curtailed.

Paramilitary associations and human rights

In so far as it is possible to attribute 'punishment' attacks in Northern Ireland to paramilitary organisations – and as they do not claim responsibility for the attacks it is hard to prove such attribution, even though 'the dogs in the street' may realise the connection – the chances of holding those organisations to account as human rights violators would be enhanced if the conflict in Northern Ireland could be portrayed as attaining a certain level of intensity. This is because there exist various sets of standards prescribing how paramilitary organisations must operate in such a conflict. In 1977 Protocol II to the Geneva Conventions of 1949 was agreed. It deals with internal armed conflict, that is, conflict 'which takes place in the territory of a High Contracting Party between its armed forces and dissident armed forces or other organised armed groups' (Article 1(1)). But to be applicable the Protocol presupposes that the dissident forces control part of the state's territory, conduct sustained military operations and detain prisoners. Even at the height of Northern Ireland's 'Troubles', in the first half of the 1970s, these conditions were not satisfied.

Another provision in the Geneva Conventions – Article 3, which is common to all four Conventions – applies to 'non-international armed conflicts', a phrase which is left undefined in the Conventions but which in the minds of those who drafted them probably connoted something much more systematic and serious than what Northern Ireland has experienced in the last 30 years or so. But it could be argued that the meaning of the phrase should change with the times. As today's non-international armed conflict is as liable to be characterised by relatively isolated acts of terrorism as by concerted military operations within a single state (the attack on the World Trade Centre and the Pentagon on 11 September 2001 are but the highest-profile examples of such acts), a case can be made for saying that such terrorist groups are themselves bound by Article 3. This would mean that they must adhere to certain minimum standards of behaviour, including the avoidance of violence to life and person, the taking of hostages, outrages upon personal dignity (in particular, humiliating and degrading treatment), the passing of sentences and the carrying out of executions without previous judgment pronounced by a regularly constituted court affording all the judicial guarantees that are recognised as indispensable by civilised peoples.

This is all fine and dandy if the terrorist organisation has its own (albeit twisted) 'rules of engagement' which it obliges members to follow on pain of punishment. But it is ludicrous to think that the kind of terrorist organisation which blew apart the World Trade Centre would ever think it could achieve its goals by limiting itself in the way prescribed by Common Article 3. In the face of suicide bombers the prospect of any legalistic approach to 'humanising' paramilitary organisations disappears completely. Not even the anthropologists, we imagine, could contend that there is still a system of order and value within such 'societies' (Harris, 1996). There is the additional problem that, if national or international law were to expect paramilitary organisations to adhere to specified standards of human rights protection, this would, at any rate in the eyes of the governments being attacked by the paramilitaries, confer an undesirable legitimacy on them. Yet even in times of inter-state war, where the dangers are much greater than in any terrorist campaign, each side is prepared to recognise the other's legitimacy by applying the Geneva Conventions. The downside of this is that combatants in the war are regarded as legitimate targets; everyone assumes that the killers cannot later be tried for murder.

Several attempts have recently been made to plug the gap in international human rights and humanitarian law (Meron, 1983; von Hehn, 2000). The most successful to date has been the initiative of a group of non-governmental experts meeting in Turku, Finland, in 1990 (Eide, Meron and Rosas, 1995). The Turku Declaration on Minimum Humanitarian Standards seeks to bind everyone at all times, but apart from referring to 'an irreducible core of humanitarian norms and human rights' it does not specify what the applicable minimum standards should be. The need to draw up such standards was endorsed by the UN's Commission on Human Rights in 1995 and the Secretary-General of the UN was mandated to report at subsequent Commission meetings on the progress being made with the task. Reports were duly submitted in 1998, 1999, 2000 and 2001. It seems that the production of 'Fundamental Standards of Humanity', as they are now to be known, may be imminent. The problem of how to ensure that paramilitary organisations and terrorist groups adhere to them will not, however, be any less difficult in the future than it has been up to now. The same would have to be said for an initiative of the International Committee of the Red Cross in this field, which is to compile a directory of *customary* international humanitarian law, that is, those standards which are *usually* adhered to by states and other groups and which have, over time, acquired a certain quasi-legal status.

Another way of approaching the problem of holding paramilitaries to account for their violent actions is to ensure that the ordinary criminal law is applied to them. In Anglo-American criminal justice systems there is a discretion vesting in prosecuting authorities as to when it would be appropriate to initiate criminal proceedings if a crime has been committed. Efforts made to get a court to order prosecuting authorities to initiate proceedings – or even to give reasons why they have or have not done so – are usually fruitless. Nor is there any relevant international standard available to serve as a guide in this matter, for even the UN's Guidelines on the Role of Prosecutors (1990) do not specify *when* proceedings should be started. The UN *is* concerned, however, about efforts to grant impunity to those who are suspected of having committed human rights abuses. Reports have been produced on impunity for the UN Commission on Human Rights, with regard not only to violations of civil and political rights but also to violations of economic, social and cultural rights (Joinet, 1997). Most recently, the Special Rapporteur on Terrorism and Human Rights has stated that she rejects any impunity for terrorist acts, whether perpetrated by state or non-state actors:

> Regrettably, impunity occurs, and in many guises. In the case of non-State actors, impunity can occur under the guise of selective prosecution or prosecutorial discretion. While this is occasionally valid, due to a realistic appraisal that existing evidence against persons accused of terrorist acts is unconvincing, in some situations there is sufficient evidence to prosecute but the State chooses to ignore it. In some States, victims of the alleged terrorist acts, or their survivors, may not have legal standing to compel a State to prosecute the perpetrators. These victims or their survivors may also be unable to bring a civil action for damages because of a wide array of judicial barriers. (Koufa, 2001)

It seems likely that when the Special Rapporteur submits her final report she will recommend that grants of impunity, whether *de jure* or *de facto*, are themselves breaches of the human rights of the victims involved. Translating this into a binding international human rights treaty will certainly take many years.

Vigilantism and human rights

Given the existence of a Bill of Rights within the South African Constitution, incidents of informal justice, whether they be carried out by organised groups such as *Mapogo-a-Mathamaga*, by hastily convened kangaroo courts or by spontaneous mobs comprising bystanders, constitute human rights violations. The South African Bill of Rights states that everyone has the right to dignity (Article 10), the right to life (Article 11) and the right to freedom and security of person (Article 12). To be stripped naked, made to walk through a township and subjected to violence either at the hands of an organised vigilante group or from a mob, as has been the case with alleged rapists, clearly violates Articles 10 through 12. The Constitution also contains further provisions relating to the rights of those arrested, detained or accused. Accordingly, everyone who is arrested for allegedly committing a criminal offence has the right to remain silent and the right not to be compelled to make any confession or admission that could be used in evidence against that person (Article 35(1)(a) and (c)). Furthermore, every accused person has the right to a fair trial, the right to have adequate time and facilities to prepare a defence, the right to be presumed innocent and the right to adduce and challenge evidence (Article 35(3)(b), (h) and (i)). Suspected criminals apprehended by vigilantes are denied all of these rights. They are presumed guilty and beaten until they confess to the crime and/or provide information relating to the location of stolen property or moneys. Even in circumstances where a trial is convened, the accused is not given the opportunity to defend his/herself, challenge evidence or appoint a legal counsel to represent them. A recent study by the Human Rights Committee into popular justice concluded that 'vigilante actions are not acceptable; their barbaric and inhuman methods, which include sjambokking, burning and killing, undermine our democracy and our collective human rights and need to be condemned by all' (Human Rights Committee, 1999: 81).

Developing national law and institutions

If international laws are not going to subject paramilitary, terrorist or vigilante groups to the opprobrium of being labelled violators of human rights or of humanitarian laws, the task has to fall to national legal systems. There are two strategies that states could pursue in this regard. One is to create special offences designed to highlight the barbarity of practices engaged in by these groups (with consequences for the punishments which can be imposed). The other is to adopt more proactive policies to help prevent the practices occurring in the first place. To be effective both strategies probably need to run in parallel. There are precedents as far as the first strategy is concerned: in many legal systems, including Northern Ireland's, special offences have been created to protect children and special laws have been enacted to combat racism and sectarianism and the incitement of hatred in general. As far as proactive policies are concerned, there are further precedents in that laws have been passed to indicate in general terms what the aims and objectives of organisations such as the police, the secret services and local authorities should be. These laws require the organisations in question to issue plans demonstrating how they will meet their stated aims and objectives. Failure to make adequate plans can lead to appropriate enforcement measures.

One of the objections to such a way of proceeding, however, is that it is anti-democratic. Some would suggest that if politicians are elected to office on a particular manifesto they should not be constrained in what they can do while in power by laws laid down by previous élites. If these laws are interpreted and applied by unelected judges, the anti-democratic nature of the regime can appear even more obvious.

But such an objection is ill-founded, so long as the laws in question are not immutable. Times do change, and so must the laws. However, the laws must not change too readily. The more basic the laws, the more difficult it should be to change them. That is the rationale for a country having a written Constitution, a document which provides the framework for basic rights and duties and the relationship between the state and its citizens as is the case in South Africa. In the United Kingdom, of course, there is no written Constitution, but in the constituent parts of the Kingdom the effect of devolution has been to create something very close to a written Constitution in the form of the Northern Ireland Act 1998, the Scotland Act 1998 and the Government of Wales Act 1998. In Northern Ireland this 'constitutional' document may well be supplemented in due course by a Bill of Rights (perhaps in the form of a Northern Ireland (Supplementary Rights) Act), advice on which is being prepared for the Secretary of State by the Northern Ireland Human Rights Commission (NIHRC, 2001a). The *preliminary* advice issued by the Commission leaves open the question whether these rights, additional to those in the European Convention, should be binding on non-state agencies as well as state agencies. The spirit of the document, however, is one that the Commission wishes to see percolating down through the legal system. In its proposals on social and economic rights the Commission recommends that the state take positive measures to progressively realise rights such as access to work, adequate housing and an adequate standard of living. If policies are directed in that manner there may be a consequential fall in the incidence of 'anti-social behaviour' and, in turn, a reduction in the rate of 'punishment' attacks, if not a complete cessation.

If law alone cannot be the route to the eradication of informal justice systems, perhaps an institutional approach should be adopted. This would mean the establishment of one or more institutions specifically tasked with examining and reducing the phenomenon. The Northern Ireland Affairs Committee of the House of Commons, in its recent report on intimidation, advocated the setting up of an Anti-Intimidation Unit, although it did not make it clear whether this was to be within a government department or a free-standing non-departmental public body. The Human Rights Commission has recently vowed to develop recommendations in this field after it has consulted with a broad range of voluntary, community, statutory and political groups (NIHRC, 2001b). The excellent work already being undertaken by some voluntary groups could be bolstered by the allocation of greater resources from the government, and inter-agency co-operation could certainly be facilitated by the intervention of a senior government minister prepared to engage, indirectly if necessary, with representatives of paramilitaries. The new Northern Ireland Policing Board, and even the International Commission on Decommissioning, could be given a role in this context also. Only by pulling together, sharing ideas, and interacting with members of the community at a grass-roots level, is progress likely to be made. Laws and institutions cannot make Northern Ireland into a perfect society but they have the potential to take us further down the road towards that goal than they have up to now.

8
Future Prospects

The future

Thus far we have traced the historical roots of the informal justice systems in Northern Ireland and South Africa and examined how both paramilitaries and vigilantes currently engage in summary punitive measures within their own communities. This has included insights into the different motivations behind, for example, loyalist and republican violence in Northern Ireland and the changing nature of community-based justice in post-apartheid South Africa. We have considered the victims of informal justice and the ambiguity surrounding victimhood status, posing questions as to who perceives themselves to be the true victims in this scenario – those subjected to paramilitary/vigilante violence or the community against which crimes are perpetrated. Importantly, within the context of increasing 'normal' crime and decreasing 'political' crime in two post-conflict countries, we have attempted to explore both the level of support for informal justice among the communities where it is most prevalent and understand their endorsement of a system which espouses violence as a means of retribution. We have also explored the response of statutory and other non-governmental agencies to the problem of informal justice, their indifference to, or at least minimisation of, both the extent and nature of the problem. Finally, we have looked at what the key alternatives are. Herein, we considered community-based restorative justice alternatives developing in Northern Ireland and South Africa, and the possibilities for using the law as a way of tackling the source of the violence perpetrated by paramilitaries and vigilantes, with a particular emphasis on addressing human rights abuses synonymous with summary justice. This final chapter will explore where we go from here. Given the ongoing experiences of both countries with informal justice we will, based on comparative learning, attempt to draw out any useful policy implications that emerge from the work so far. Such generalisations cannot ignore the very different political, social and economic circumstances of both countries referred to in Chapter 1. We do not suggest that there is, or indeed should be, a direct 'read-across' between Northern Ireland and South Africa – what works in one jurisdiction may not in the other. Notwithstanding these limitations, we conclude with a comparative overview intended as a means of reciprocal policy learning in tackling this pervasive problem in both countries.

It is perhaps useful at this point to refer back to our original conception of informal justice in Chapter 1 where we highlighted the problems associated with definition. Informal justice is considered as acts committed outside the boundaries of the formal criminal justice system and such acts usually involve collective violence and are often described as vigilantism. In turn, Abrahams' (1998: 9) definition of vigilantism as 'a form of self-help, with varying degrees of violence' which is activated as a result 'of the failure of the state machinery to meet the felt needs of those who resort to it' broadly aligns with our examination of informal justice in Northern Ireland and South Africa. It is, however, more nuanced. There is clearly a self-help agenda evident in both countries but this is inextricably linked to the wider political agenda, the focus of which is opposition to the very state machinery which generated the need for self-help. Hence, as Johnston (1996) argues, there are two modes of vigilantism, one focusing on crime control and the other concerned with social control or the maintenance of communal, ethnic or sectarian order and values. We would go further by arguing that this form of social control is used as a means of consolidating political opposition against the state. This is perhaps an obvious point to make *during* the conflicts in Northern Ireland and South Africa when the majority/unionist community or minority/white community respectively enjoyed a monopoly of power. What is less obvious in the post-conflict era is that both forms of vigilantism continue to exist. Informal justice is still utilised in the two countries as a means of crime control because of the failings in state police and legal systems, but despite constitutional settlements vigilantism/paramilitarism is also used as a means of securing or maintaining political support. Hence Sinn Féin, for example, encourages community dependency for safety and crime control that translates into political support which can be used in their pursuit of British withdrawal from Northern Ireland. Similarly in South Africa PAGAD is seen not just as a vigilante group set up to address criminal disorder, but politically motivated in their hostility to the ANC government which they perceive as primarily promoting black interests and not those of Coloured or Indians (Ero, 2000).

What makes for an interesting comparison between the two countries is the balance in these two forms of vigilantism, crime control and political opposition. There is now no political imperative for ANC supporters to engage in vigilantism, given their electoral mandate, but the need for self-help against increasing crime continues to exist. In Northern Ireland, particularly in republican communities, their ultimate political goal has not yet been fulfilled and hence paramilitary control exists for reasons of both self-help and as a way of consolidating their political base. In loyalist areas, paramilitary involvement is motivated more by the promotion of their own self-interests but also a means of what Johnston (1996) refers to above as social control in a bid to retain their ethnic identity. The Northern Ireland Secretary of State referred to Protestants as 'a community which feels its traditions, culture, and way of life are under threat from an alliance between the large vibrant Catholic minority within its boundaries, its larger neighbour to the South, and a spineless, ungrateful or even perfidious parent across the Irish sea' (Reid, 2001: 2). Paramilitary involvement in areas such as North Belfast which used to be a unionist stronghold and where Protestants now feel under threat as their numbers dwindle, is part of a wider battle for territorial stakeholding. Recognising and accepting the dual motives of self-help and political mobilisation/opposition is therefore important in policy terms, in that addressing the former through reforms to policing and the legal system will not, of itself, diminish the latter.

Punitive acts synonymous with informal justice systems for the purposes of self-help (or idealised political goals) can be rationalised by its exponents as legitimate violence – an oxymoron according to its critics. Guelke (1998: 21) suggests there is some ambiguity about vigilantism as a form of violence and it does not automatically carry the presumption of illegitimacy attached to other forms of violence. He argued that in stable liberal-democracies, action against criminals by vigilantes elicits an equivocal response 'though the degree of equivocation varies from country to country. In countries with effective criminal justice systems, sympathy for the vigilante is likely to be minimal'. By implication, those (reasonably) stable liberal democracies, such as Northern Ireland and South Africa, with less proficient justice systems are more sympathetic to paramilitary/vigilante activity. In South Africa, Roefs (1999: 34) draws a distinction between law-abiding anti-crime organisations (e.g. Women Against Violence and Business Against Crime) and vigilante organisations, although the line between them is thin. She argues that because 'communities blame the police service and courts for inefficiency, racism, corruption and unresponsiveness ... an anti-crime movement has developed'. In other words, the public is willing to resort to measures other than the criminal justice system in order to guarantee a protected and safe environment. The public is therefore sympathetic towards self-help measures but the difficulty arises as to where law-abiding anti-crime activities end and illegal vigilantism begins. Lack of confidence in the policing and justice system is also at the heart of support for paramilitary involvement in communal crime in Northern Ireland. Attempts to address this are contained in the Belfast Agreement as follows:

> The participants (to the Agreement) believe it is essential that polic-ing structures and arrangements are such that the police service is professional, effective and efficient, fair and impartial, free from par-tisan political control; accountable, both under the law for its actions and to the community it serves; representative of the society it polices, and operates within a coherent and co-operative criminal justice system, which conforms with human rights norms. The par-ticipants also believe that those structures and arrangements must be capable of maintaining law and order problems including respond-ing effectively to crime and to any terrorist threat and to public order problems. A police service which cannot do so will fail to win public confidence and acceptance. (Belfast Agreement, 1998: 22)

To what extent, therefore, has change taken place in policing and criminal justice in both countries to instil 'public confidence and acceptance' and, as a consequence, obviate the need for communities turning to paramilitaries or vigilantes?

Reforms to policing and criminal justice

In Northern Ireland police and criminal justice reforms were dealt with through an Independent Commission on Policing (chaired by Chris Patten) and a parallel review of criminal justice carried out by the British Government/Northern Ireland Office with an independent element. The Independent Commission on Policing reported in September 1999 and recommended, *inter alia*:

- A commitment via oath by all officers to uphold human rights.
- The creation of a new Policing Board (replacing the existing Police Authority) to hold the Chief Constable and police service publicly

to account. Its 19-member composition would include ten cross-party Assembly representatives and nine independents from the business, voluntary and community and legal sectors. The Policing Board would have the power to require the Chief Constable to report on any issue pertaining to the performance of his/her functions or those of the police service. The obligation to report would extend to explaining operational decisions.

• At the local level each district council would establish a District Policing Partnership Board with a majority elected membership and independents. The District Police Commander would meet with the Partnership Board, present reports and answer questions about community concerns and policing priorities. The local boards would have an additional community safety role with powers to purchase services on top of normal policing.

• A reduction in the size of the RUC's 13 000 officers to 7500 and a recruitment profile of 50/50 Protestant/Catholic over a 10-year period.

• A change of name from the Royal Ulster Constabulary to the Northern Ireland Police Service and the adoption of a new badge and symbols which were entirely free from any association with either the British or Irish States.

Unionists reacted to Patten's Report with hostility, accusing the Secretary of State of 'politicising the RUC, not only by taking away the good name, but also removing the independent Police Authority and placing a future police service under a Board controlled by politicians' (Taylor, 2000: 3). They saw the reform process as the symbolic cleansing of the RUC's association with the Crown and demanded a moratorium on police reform until the IRA moved on arms decommissioning. Nationalists, for their part, criticised the government for diluting Patten's proposals on police accountability in order to appease Ulster Unionists' concerns, ensure the survival of David Trimble and copper-fasten the UUP's commitment to power-sharing with Sinn Féin. Gerry Adams, in turn, pointed out that the legislation (Police (Northern Ireland) Act 2000 which enacted policing reforms) did not remove the Unionist ethos and emblems nor provide real democratic accountability. While the British government accepted the vision for policing contained in Patten, its recommendations were the subject of political negotiations.

The key changes which have been implemented are:

• The appointment of a new Policing Board (September 2001) to replace the Police Authority comprising 10 elected Assembly members chosen by the parties and nine independents appointed by the Secretary of State. The Board has wide-ranging powers and is responsible for holding the police to account and monitoring and evaluating the service provided.

- The RUC name changed in November 2001 to the Police Service of Northern Ireland (PSNI) for operational purposes.
- Applicants to the PSNI undergo testing (through an independent recruitment agency) to make it into a merit pool, to which 50/50 Catholic and non-Catholic recruitment procedures apply.
- An independent Police Ombudsman was appointed (November 2000) to deal with complaints about the police by the public. She can also instigate an investigation which has not been the subject of complaint but where she has reason to believe that there has been a criminal offence or breach of the police code of conduct.

A key setback to this 'new beginning for policing' (title of Patten's report) has been Sinn Féin's refusal to take its seats on the Policing Board because, they argue, Patten has not been fully implemented. The Chief Constable and the Police Ombudsman have also had a vitriolic public row over her investigations into the police's handling of the Omagh bomb incident (the largest single terrorist atrocity in Northern Ireland which killed 29 innocent people). As a result of her strong criticism of the role the police played in handling intelligence information before the bomb was placed and their subsequent enquiry, Sinn Féin has felt vindicated in their decision not to participate in the new Policing Board. The potential for policing reforms to restore confidence in the short term within alienated loyalist and republican communities seems limited. The medium to long-term prospect is more difficult to predict.

This has not been helped by recommendations coming out of the criminal justice review which reported in March 2000 and (at the time of writing) is in the form of a draft Justice (Northern Ireland) Bill, out for consultation until January 2002. Therein, the role of community restorative justice schemes in dealing with 'types of low-level crime that most commonly concerns local communities' is accepted in principle. In practice however, community restorative justice schemes can only receive referrals from a statutory agency, with the police informed of all referrals; they should be accredited by, and subject to, standards laid down by government;[50] they should be subject to regular inspection by the Criminal Justice Inspectorate; and should have no role in determining guilt or innocence. In a veiled reference to existing restorative justice programmes, the Northern Ireland Office point out 'schemes which set out to deal with criminal matters and which do not attain accreditation pose a serious threat to the human rights of those involved and risk undermining the rule of law' (Northern Ireland Office, 2001: 79). This is clearly a political and criminal justice response to existing schemes, about which there are legitimate fears for the rights of the accused and paramilitary involvement. It ignores, however, the legacy of community endorsement for summary justice and the reality of living in working-class areas controlled by paramilitaries. It is likely to legislate out of existence current restorative justice projects in republican areas which will not involve the police, and create problems for those struggling to gain official recognition and community support in loyalist communities.

In South Africa there have also been significant changes to policing and criminal justice through moves to create an integrated approach to tackling crime. The integrated justice system comprises four core departments: safety and security, central to which is the South African Police Service, Justice and Constitutional Development, Correctional Services and Social Development. The government claims progress in a number of areas. The National Prosecuting Authority (set up in 1998) established a number of specialised units to deal with organised crime and criminal gangs. It has also instituted reforms to improve prosecutions and reduce the huge backlog of cases. A victim empowerment programme is now in place to ensure victims are treated with respect and dignity and protected from secondary victimisation. New legislation has been enacted to allow government agencies to fight crime more effectively.[51] High priority pilot areas (in eight locations) where crime rates are linked with poverty and deprivation have been targeted to improve law enforcement, victim empowerment, economic regeneration and infra-structural investment. The South African Law Commission is working on a framework for restorative justice and community courts. Attempts are being made to reduce the number of firearms in public places and enable the policing of areas declared gun-free through new legislation. All police stations now have community police forums (formally established through legislation) although the government admits to tensions in some areas between them and community safety forums.

The Constitution (section 195(1)(i)) also requires that public administration be broadly representative of the South African people.[52] Subsequently, employment and personnel management practices must be based on ability, objectivity, fairness and the need to redress the imbalances of the past to achieve this representation. To this end, the

South African Police Service (SAPS) announced in November 1997 that it aimed to ensure that by the year 2000 more than half of the positions in the service would be occupied by blacks and that nearly a third of SAPS personnel would be female. By 2001, the racial composition of the service was as follows: African 53 per cent, white 26 per cent, coloured 18 per cent and Indian 3 per cent but only 12 per cent of sworn officers were female (SAPS, 2002).

Despite these efforts, little improvement can be detected as the crime wave intensifies. One of the key problems according to Grimond (2001: 7) is the quality of the police – 'some are corrupt, many are untrained, more are under-equipped and about a quarter are functionally illiterate'. Of particular interest to this study is the operation of the community police forums established as a partnership-approach to crime between the police and local residents, and the lynchpin of South Africa's community policing policy. The forums have three broad responsibilities: the improvement of police–community relations; the oversight of policing at local level; and the mobilisation of the community to take responsibility in the fight against crime. Pelser (1999) has argued that the response of the South Africa Police Service to the development of community policing policy has been largely symbolic. Reporting on pilot research which identified the challenges facing community policing, Pelser noted:

> The issue of trust remains the primary challenge faced by the majority of South Africa's police stations and the people represented on community police forums. Of importance is that in areas of low trust there is a real potential for the community police forum to be used as a platform for political interest groups.... The danger lies in the likelihood that, should a basic level of trust fail to be developed, the police will become increasingly marginalised through either the development of self-policing or its stronger form, vigilantism. (Pelser, 1999: 13)

The parallels with Northern Ireland are striking – new policing and criminal justice measures are designed to instil confidence and trust within alienated working-class republican and loyalist communities. If this does not happen the same prediction applies as in South Africa – people will continue to rely on paramilitaries as their guarantors for community safety. Government attempts in Northern Ireland to regulate community-based restorative justice initiatives through the legal reform process contrast with the situation in South Africa. In that context Schärf (2001) suggests that the South African state continues to flirt with private and community-based vigilantism simply because there is an overriding concern to 'do something' about the negative international reputation it has for crime. He warns of the dangers in this strategy if the government does not attempt to bring these organisations within a more law-abiding framework.

Comparative policy learning

Both case studies examined here generate wider thinking about the role of the state.[53] In pluralist theory the state is seen as a neutral arbiter among the competing groups and individuals in society. Its neutrality reflects the fact that the state acts in the interest of all citizens, and therefore represents the common good or public interest. This assumes however that power is widely and evenly dispersed and that the state is not biased in favour of any particular interest or group, and that it does not have an interest of its own that is separate from those of society (Heywood, 1997: 88). The conflicts in Northern Ireland and South Africa challenged this assumption in which unionist and white hegemony led to the abuse of power and privilege. Migdal (1998) has argued that justice can be delivered only by a democratic state that is strong and autonomous. State strength is a function of voluntary participation, compliance and legitimacy, and autonomy is derived from impartiality, non-partisanship, neutrality and functional independence.

In his later work Migdal (2001) challenges Weber's definition of the state as 'a human community that (successfully) claim the *monopoly of the legitimate use of physical force* within a given territory' (Weber, 1958: 82). He argues that the state's centralising and monopolising role in controlling behaviour minimises and trivialises the 'rich negotiation, interaction and resistance that occur in every human society among multiple systems of rules'. In his view this limits the possibilities for theorising 'about arenas of competing sets of rules, other than to cast these in the negative, as failures or weak states or even as non-states' (Migdal, 2001: 15). He offers instead an alternative 'state-in-control' definition in which the state is seen as a coherent controlling organisation in a territory which is a representation of the people bounded by that territory, and other groupings inside and outside the official state boundaries often promoting conflicting sets of rules with one another and with official law.

The research in the two case study countries would suggest two things. First, the reaction to restorative justice programmes has tended towards Weber's view of the role of the state in which the centre or formal criminal justice system wants to exercise monopoly control over community-based initiatives. Second, particularly in the circumstances of Northern Ireland, the strength and autonomy of the state remains in transitional status. Compliance and legitimacy are still conditional, best exemplified by Sinn Féin's refusal (at the time of writing) to join the new Policing Board. There are also signs of a reaction from the former hegemonists – unionists in Northern Ireland now claim to be 'out in the cold' and the white minority in South Africa claim abuses of power by the ANC government. The administration of justice and the role of the state therein still remain unresolved despite new political and constitutional arrangements in both countries.

What lessons can be learned from the post-conflict experiences of Northern Ireland and South Africa on informal justice? First, the implementation of reforms needs to involve a 'whole package' approach. The police reforms in South Africa have addressed the problem of police legitimacy but new problems of effectiveness and transparency have emerged. Marks (2000), for example, argues that changes in legislation and policy on their own are no guarantees for police transformation – the same is true in Northern Ireland. Assuming that the present difficulties of gaining political consensus about police reforms in Northern Ireland can be surmounted (hardly a foregone conclusion) there is, according to Reiner (1992), a need to change rank and file sub-culture and mechanisms for lower-level accountability. Both represent long-term challenges for policing in the Province. Wilson (2000) described it this way:

> For most Catholics to feel a genuine sense of ownership over the police, they need to believe that it will no longer be tarred with the *causes célèbres* of the past – requiring the investigations by Stalker, Stevens and so on – and that the 'canteen culture' will not be inhospitable to them. (Wilson, 2000: 4)

The 'new' police service in South Africa established in 1995 has inherited many of the personnel recruited during the apartheid years, some of whom are badly trained and educated. The service also suffers from a lack of resources, detective training and high absenteeism (Randall, 2000). The creation of Community Policing Forums and encouragement of community involvement also appears to be a rather superficial measure given the general lack of resources and, in some cases, police antagonism to civilian scrutiny. High community expectations of what could be achieved through these forums have not been met. The introduction of lay assessors at magistrate court level was designed to allow the community a greater say in matters of concern to them. Much confusion exists about the scheme and it appears to be haphazardly applied, working in some areas and not in others. The low levels of state aid to people without work, in addition to the high levels of unemployment, exacerbate the crime situation in the townships. For some, crime is the only option if they are to survive. Unless economic reforms are implemented to alleviate levels of poverty and deprivation then crime will continue to be a problem in the townships. Pelser (2001) refers to two goals identified by the National Crime Prevention Strategy approved by the South African Cabinet in 1996: (a) building the capacity of the justice system, and (b) fostering a real stake in society by rebuilding the torn social fabric and providing alternatives to the thrill and reward of deviance. He argues these societal aspects need to be addressed rather than an exclusive focus on the criminal justice system.

Second, on the issue of community restorative justice, the townships have a long history of such an approach and even in those townships where it is operating successfully, instances of retributive informal justice still occur. Community restorative justice projects are a relatively recent approach in Northern Ireland and there is no guarantee that they will work or result in a cessation of 'punishment' attacks. 'Normal' crime is increasing and the rationale for 'political' crime waning. Patten (1999) drew attention to the fear that crime levels may increase in the future – 'a perverse sort of peace dividend'. A more normal security environment, according to Patten, might lead to more 'normal' criminality (Patten, 1999: 76). The transition to 'peace' has exposed the activities of paramilitaries, especially in loyalist areas, as community oppressors rather than defenders of a cause which has been overtaken by political events. Yet it will take some time for the necessary changes in the policing and criminal justice system to be put in place, and even longer for the communities to have confidence in them. To whom do working-class people turn when faced with criminal activities that blight their lives? The apparent support by paramilitaries for community restorative justice schemes may be no more than a cynical response on their part to keep their political representatives involved in the democratic process. There is evidence that they can initiate and discontinue 'punishment' beatings and shootings at will. To cede responsibility for law and order to the formal criminal justice system would be to lose control within their communities where they have some social standing and exercise patronage (the 'hard men' image).

The dilemma facing communities in Northern Ireland is therefore stark. The government has opted to 'see no evil, hear no evil' in the case of 'punishment' beatings and attacks, given what is at stake in the wider political process. Because these acts of mutilation, torture and intimidation have become bound into the political equation there is a marked reluctance to view this phenomenon as anything other than politically motivated which demands a political response. Yet communities feel trapped in a web of criminal behaviour by paramilitaries over which they have little/no control and where much fear exists. The Ulster Unionist leader, David Trimble, described this as people who invested hope in the Belfast Agreement having a 'nightmare'. The nightmare is that the paramilitaries, rather than turning their backs on violence and crossing over into a democratic society, 'will come into the process and corrupt it, continue with their violence and continue the dominance and racketeering'. This, he argued, would not be confined to estates in certain parts of Northern Ireland but could be widespread. 'People have a nightmare that they will see the very heart of society become corrupted' (Trimble, 1999: 363).

The expectations of the communities, however, are also important here. Their experience is one of living in a conflict setting for 30 years where their major recourse to the 'law' was through the paramilitaries who administered 'justice' expeditiously and often through the use of violence. Brewer *et al.* (1998) have argued that civil unrest has, in fact, been a contributory factor to the survival of community structures – those under attack have been strengthened as a consequence. Their expectations of the formal system, even a reformed one, based on this experience will be difficult to fulfil. Brutalised communities have become tolerant of rough 'justice'. One commentator on South Africa remarked 'our high rates of criminal violence, road traffic deaths, domestic violence, rape and child abuse are all oblique expressions of the brutality that is embedded in this society' (Smith, 1999b: 3). The same is true in Northern Ireland. This questioning of the role now played by paramilitaries has not provided the communities with any obvious answers to tackling crime. As one interviewee put it:

> We've been brainwashed over the years. Whenever you heard of a 'punishment' shooting or beating the first thing came into your head was 'what did they do, they must have done something' because we placed so much faith and trust in the paramilitaries. Now I would put a question mark over these things but in our area the attitude is 'well it hasn't come to my door, I'm sorry for you but as long as they leave mine alone'. (Focus Group interview, Belfast, November 1999)

Experiences from South Africa on 'communal mechanisms of social ordering' are also instructive. People's courts existed in black South Africa townships for a long time but the period of political transition offered the opportunity to re-examine this form of popular justice. Van Zyl Smit (1999) notes the objective was both 'to improve the ability of a particular community to maintain order and to allow the community to relate on its own terms to the formal state agents of social control' (Van Zyl Smit, 1999: 203). Examples of this approach included training members of street committees in 'community safety', central to which was human rights issues, conflict resolution and the functioning of state agencies (police and courts). Treatment of juvenile offenders involved a process of reintegrative shaming within the context of restorative justice schemes (Braithwaite, 1989, 1993; Braithwaite and Mugford, 1994; Matthews, 1988; Foster, 1995). The parallels with Northern Ireland are striking. Van Zyl Smit argues this 'radical criminology with a strong commitment to communitarism is well entrenched in the sense that the centrality of community involvement in crime control has been established in virtually all policy debates about criminal justice in South Africa' (Van Zyl Smit, 1999: 211). He concludes, however, that South Africa is unlikely to be able to reform its system as a whole so that restorative justice operates in local communities with minimal outside interference:

> Recent criminological research has made us aware of the limits of the power of the modern state and the constraints on its ability to control crime effectively (Garland, 1996), but an efficient, uncorrupt and principled central criminal justice administration continues to be an important guarantor of individual freedom. (Van Zyl Smit, 1999: 213)

This concurs with Schärf's (2001) argument above on the need for state regulation of community self-help crime initiatives.

Third, in South Africa the police are now accepted as legitimate but a culture of violence persists. The 'comrades' may no longer 'police' the townships but other groupings have emerged who are willing to mete out their version of justice and/or retrieve stolen goods thus bypassing the formal criminal justice system. This has earned South Africa international notoriety through press coverage of the violence. In one recent account entitled 'guilty and innocent alike fall victim to necklace justice by South African mobs' the journalist reports as follows:

> Kinos Hlatshwayo lay bleeding and near death in the dust, the victim of a savage beating by vigilantes in Orange Farm, who said the

19-year-old had stolen jewellery from a woman at gun point. Then the mob in the shanty town near Johannesburg, rushed to fetch a tyre and petrol for his necklace, the fate of many a suspected informer during the apartheid era. (MacGregor, 2001: 3)

A senior researcher at the Institute for Security Studies (Makubetse Sekhonyane) commented on the violence:

> Vigilantism produces instant results. The police and courts often fail and, even when they do succeed, the results are harder to see. Vigilante groups are usually popular to start with. But, by nature, they are violent and lawless, and most spin out of control. Lots of innocent people have been killed. (MacGregor, *ibid.*)

A negotiated peace that results in the community accepting the formal system, does not necessarily mean that the utilisation of often 'success-ful' methods of retributive informal justice will be abandoned, as this press report demonstrates. This is particularly relevant in Northern Ireland where progress towards a post-conflict society is dependent on overcoming obstacles to police reform, demilitarisation and decommis-sioning of paramilitary arms. In circumstances where reform of the key organs of crime prevention, the police and criminal justice system, are inextricably bound to the (faltering) political process, then communities will continue to seek redress through the paramilitaries. A parliamentary scrutiny committee in Westminster (the Northern Ireland Affairs Committee) recently examined the whole area of paramilitary intimidation. Evidence provided by one organisation (the Maranatha Community[54]) highlighted the unwillingness of some people, in both Catholic and Protestant areas, to approach the police openly. It added that creating a state of fear was a key element used by paramilitaries in extending their control, and a resultant loss of empow-erment by community ensues. The report noted:

> If communities could be empowered to take responsibility for their areas again, then perhaps you would see what we would understand as effective policing, effective administration of law taking place. That is a feeling that people have, they do not have the ability to take back control of their own communities. This is across the board – Catholic and Protestant. (Northern Ireland Affairs Committee, 2001: xi)

For those in Northern Ireland and South Africa weaned on political violence, the promise of a robust and effective formal system of criminal justice seems a rather remote prospect. In the meantime, the alternative informal system continues, sustained by a demand from communities conditioned to violence who endorse, without necessarily agreeing, with its excesses. The key lesson for Northern Ireland is that political, constitutional and criminal justice reforms must operate in tandem to restore confidence in communities that real change is taking place. There must be an acceptance that such change will not happen overnight and the process is fragile and subject to scrutiny by those suspicious of its effectiveness. Any hint that the guarantors of change (e.g. Equality Commission, Human Rights Commission, and Police Ombudsman)[55] are being frustrated in their efforts, will simply reinforce community mistrust and reassert their reliance on paramilitaries.

The rather pessimistic conclusion is that vigilantism and paramilitary attacks are set to continue in South Africa and Northern Ireland. The cause of the violence is multi-faceted and a concentration on policing and criminal justice, while a necessary prerequisite, is not sufficient in addressing community crime. Communities still, under new constitutional arrangements, feel alienated and excluded from mainstream society, whether that is as a result of economic disparities and/or political opposition. That alienation is a legacy of bitter conflicts in both countries. Until their confidence can be secured and these communities feel empowered, paramilitaries and vigilantes will continue to exercise their own brutal form of justice and exert control. Both Northern Ireland and South Africa have some way to go in moving beyond 'an imperfect peace'.

Notes

1 Informal Justice in Context

1. South Africa Yearbook 2000/01: History – http://www.gov.za/yearbook/history.htm: 12.
2. The ANC achieved a 62.7 per cent majority, the National Party (NP) gained 20.4 per cent of the vote, Inkatha Freedom Party (IFP) received 10.5 per cent of the vote, the Freedom Front 2.2 per cent, Democratic Party 1.7 per cent, Pan-Africanist Congress 1.2 per cent and the African Christian Democracy Party 0.5 per cent. In terms of the Interim Constitution, the NP and IFP participated in a Government of National Unity until 1996 at which point the NP withdrew.
3. The ANC won 266 of the 400 seats in the National Assembly, falling short by one seat of the two-thirds majority which it would require if it sought to make constitutional changes. The Democratic Party, the heir to the country's long white liberal tradition, and perceived by most blacks as a party for rich whites, gained 38 seats to establish itself as the new official opposition. Third place went to Mangosuthu Buthelezi's Inkatha Freedom Party, which won 34 seats, most of them in its heartland of KwaZulu-Natal Province. The biggest loser was the New National Party, rump of the monolithic white party which governed under apartheid. Tainted by this legacy they lost much electoral support to the Democratic Party dropping from 82 seats in 1994 to 28 in 1999. Most of the remaining opposition benches are filled by the United Democratic Movement (14 seats) and the African Christian Democratic Party (6 seats). The ANC took all but two of the country's nine provinces (KwaZulu-Natal and the Western Cape).
4. Parties had to commit to: democratic and exclusively peaceful means of resolving political issues, the total disarmament of all paramilitary organisations, agree that such disarmament must be verifiable to the satisfaction of the independent commission, renounce for themselves, and to oppose any efforts by others, to use force, or threaten to use force, to influence the course or the outcome of all-party negotiations, agree to abide by the terms of any agreement reached in all-party negotiations and to resort to democratic and exclusively peaceful methods in trying to alter any aspect of that outcome with which they may disagree.
5. Based on the 1991 census details 38.5 per cent of the population are Catholics, 50 per cent Presbyterian, Church of Ireland, Methodist and other denominations, and 11 per cent 'no religion' or 'not stated' (figures rounded). Updated figures based on the 2001 census will not be available until December 2002.
6. GDP per head for the United Kingdom is $18 620.
7. The United Nations Development Programme publishes the Human Development Index (HDI) in recognition that GDPs were rather crude indicators given wide variations and fluctuations in exchange rates. The HDI ranked countries on a scale of 0–1 (1 being the most developed) from a small

number of carefully selected indicators – life expectancy, adult literacy, mean years of schooling and average income.

8. According to the Constitution, every person has the right to: be treated and protected equally by the law; freedom from discrimination; life; respect for protection of his/her dignity; freedom and security, including the right not to be detained without trail; not to be subjected to any torture; not to be forced to work against his/her will; personal privacy; freedom of conscience, religion, belief and opinion; freedom of speech and expression; freedom of assembly and to demonstrate peacefully and unarmed; freedom of association; freedom of movement; choose freely his/her place of residence; free political activity; a secret vote; have judicial disputes settled by a court; have access to all information held by the State, in order to exercise his/her rights; a fair trail; do business and to earn a living; fair labour practices; own property; a healthy environment; freedom of language and culture; a basic education; be taught wherever possible in the language of his/her choice.

9. The Victims' Liaison Unit was established in 1998 within the Northern Ireland Office to support the implementation of Sir Kenneth Bloomfield's report on victims *We Will Remember Them*. The devolved administration set up its own Victims' Unit within the Office of the Minister and Deputy First Minister in June 2000 in recognition that many victims' issues related to transferred (devolved) matters, and hence the need for a distinct unit.

10. The areas identified include Khayelitsha and Mitchells Plain in the Western Cape; KwaMashu and Inanda in KwaZulu-Natal; Mdantsane and Motherwell in the Eastern Cape; Alexandra Township in Gauteng; and Galeshewe in the Northern Cape.

2   Agents of Informal Justice

11. Although the English first invaded Ireland in 1172, their control and authority of the island was contested and incomplete. It is not until the reign of Henry VIII, that the monarch's authority was cemented with Henry becoming King of Ireland in 1541. Furthermore, Henry embarked upon a policy of conciliation and fusion of the Irish and English populations in Ireland and extended English law to the entire island.

12. Although 1652 is often cited as the date of the 'beginning of South Africa' with the establishment of a fort at Table Bay by the Dutch East Indian Company, colonial expansion and conquest by the British in the 1870s brought large areas of South Africa under imperial control.

13. In 1910 the South African colonies unified to become the Union of South Africa, and rural chiefs were brought under the control of the state at the lowest level of state adjudication.

14. These courts were established by the Black Administration Act of 1927, an Act which created separate systems of white courts and black African courts. Blacks were limited to submitting their disputes to the specially constituted courts located under the administration of the Department of Cooperation and Development, which handled black affairs, rather than the Department of Justice.

15. For more information see the Hoexter Enquiry which examined the structure and functioning of the Commissioners' Courts cited in Hund and Kotu-Rammopo (1983).
16. The Catholic Ex-Servicemen's Association (CEA) was established in 1971 following the introduction of internment and sought to protect Catholic areas from attacks by Protestants. The CEA was unarmed but its members had previous military training. At its peak in 1972 it claimed some 8000 members.
17. Sinn Féin's Gerry Kelly has denied the existence of Civil Administrators tasked with informal justice in a recent edition of the Channel 4 News, broadcast 21 May 2000.
18. In some cases paramilitaries have 'punished' the wrong person after assuming that the individual they are 'punishing' is the person they were seeking to beat or shoot. These instances are referred to as cases of mistaken identity.
19. The 'disappeared' is the term used to describe those individuals that the IRA abducted, executed and buried from 1972 to 1981.
20. In 1970 the IRA split into two factions the Official IRA and the Provisional IRA. For a detailed account of this split and the reasons for it see Smith, 1997. In May 1972, the Official IRA announced a cease-fire but reserved the right to act in self-defence and undertake defensive operations.
21. The Irish People's Liberation Organisation was formed as a result of a breakaway faction from the Irish National Liberation Army. A major internal feud was waged between rival groups in 1992.
22. The Irish National Liberation Army was established in 1975 with the aim of reunifying Ireland and the creation of a revolutionary socialist republic. Many of its early recruits came from the Official IRA. The group has been on cease-fire since 22 August 1998.
23. The Continuity IRA emerged in 1996 after it claimed responsibility for a number of attacks and attempted attacks in Northern Ireland. The group is opposed to the Belfast Agreement and has not declared a cease-fire.
24. The Ulster Volunteer Force is a loyalist paramilitary group formed in 1966 and adopted the name of the previous UVF, founded 1912 to oppose, by armed force, Home Rule in Ireland. The reformed UVF's aim is to ensure that Northern Ireland's constitutional position within the United Kingdom is secure. They have been responsible for a large number of assassinations, mostly innocent Catholics, in Northern Ireland. The UVF became part of the Combined Loyalist Military Command in 1991. In 1996 a number of disaffected 'maverick' members broke away to form the Loyalist Volunteer Force (LVF).

    The UDA was, and remains, the largest loyalist paramilitary group in Northern Ireland. It was formed in 1971 from a number of loyalist vigilante groups, many of which were called 'defence associations' – one such group was the Shankill Defence Association. Members of the UDA have, since 1973, used the cover name of the Ulster Freedom Fighters (UFF) to claim the responsibility for the killing of Catholics. The Ulster Democratic Party which earned a place at the multi-party talks following the Forum elections in May 1996 represented the UDA until November 2001 but has since dissolved as a political party over disagreements about the UDA's lack of support for the Belfast Agreement.

    The Red Hand Commandos (RHC) are a small loyalist paramilitary group closely associated with the UVF. They were formed in 1972 and have most

support in east Belfast and the Sandy Row area. The group was declared illegal in 1973. The RHC was part of the Combined Loyalist Military Command.
25. The Housing Executive is the regional housing authority responsible for the allocation and provision of public housing in Northern Ireland.
26. The result of specification includes measures such as early release prisoners associated with the UDA, UFF and LVF can now have their licences suspended and be returned to jail if they are believed to continue to support their organisation. Any UDA, UFF or LVF person found guilty of a scheduled offence that took place before the Belfast Agreement cannot qualify for early release provisions. The Real IRA, Continuity IRA, Red Hand Defenders and Orange Volunteers are already specified.

3 The Victims of Informal Justice

27. Under an early release scheme, set up in 1995, determinate sentence prisoners were entitled to automatic release at the half-way point of sentence. The Belfast Agreement allows automatic release at the one-third point and is implemented through a Sentence Review Body. Prisoners who qualify are released on licence and returned to prison if they engage in any further activity.
28. APLA was the military wing of the Pan African Congress, which was formed in 1959 under the presidency of Robert Sobukwe, with the slogan of 'Africa for the Africans'.
29. Amy Biehl was an American Fulbright scholar who was murdered in Guguletu, a township in Cape Town in August 1993.
30. Adopted in the *Declaration of Basic Principles of Justice for Victims of Crime and Abuse of Power*.
31. Violent crime includes offences against the person, robbery and sexual offences.
32. Criminal Injuries (Compensation) (Northern Ireland) Order 1988.
33. The former Conservative Leader, William Hague, in a Commons debate at which the Prime Minster announced a public inquiry into Bloody Sunday, said 'we are naturally sceptical about reopening an inquiry which was conducted 25 years ago, especially since previous governments have already examined new evidence submitted to them' (Hansard, 29 January 1998: 503).

4 The Community Response

34. The Ulster Democratic Party (now disbanded) is linked to the UDA, the Progressive Unionist Party to the UVF, and Sinn Fein to the Provisional IRA.
35. A picket was set up in June 2001 to protest against Catholic children, who attended the Holy Cross Primary School, walking through a Protestant estate in the Ardoyne area of Belfast. Ugly scenes of sectarian chants and taunts by Protestants aimed at the schoolchildren and their parents were broadcast around the world. North Belfast was once a unionist stronghold with a low-income Catholic minority. The demography has changed with the flight of middle-class unionists from the area. Protestants now see themselves

as a besieged minority and react with anger to what they perceive as increasing territorialism by Catholics.

5   The Agencies' Response

36. The three aims in modernising government are to:

   - Ensure that policy making is more joined up and strategic.
   - Make sure that public service users, not providers, are the focus, by matching services more closely to people's lives.
   - Deliver public services that are high quality and efficient.

37. The RDP Ministry has since closed (March 1996) and the RDP Fund returned to the Ministry of Finance.
38. In 1998–99 NIACRO, Extern and Victim Support (NI) received £303 000, £447 000 and £667 000 respectively from the Criminal Justice Directorate of the Northern Ireland Office (Department of Finance & Personnel and H.M. Treasury, 1999).
39. The Social Security Agency, the Compensation Agency and the Northern Ireland Housing Executive are located within the Department of Health and Social Services and Public Safety (formerly, the Department of Health and Social Services), the Northern Ireland Office, and the Department of Social Development (formerly the Department of the Environment) respectively.
40. Black Sash is a national NGO which monitors infringements of political and socio-economic rights, monitors how the rights of women are affected, engages in paralegal work which strengthens people's capacity to understand and claim their rights and campaigns for justice in legislation and state administration.
41. NICRO (National Institute for Crime Prevention and Reintegration of Offenders) is the only national non-governmental service provider for crime prevention services in South Africa and was originally established in 1910 as the South African Prisoners' Aid Association.

6   Community-Based Alternatives

42. NIACRO is a major charity working with prisoners, their families, ex-offenders and young people at risk of offending. It also works 'for a more humane and effective criminal justice system'.
43. Pilot projects were launched in Derry (Ballymagroarty) and north and west Belfast (Clonard, Beechmount, the New Lodge and Twinbrook).
44. Restorative justice schemes are being piloted by the police in Mountpottinger in Belfast and Ballymena as part of an inter-agency steering group involving the Northern Ireland Office Youth Justice Division, Probation Service and local community groups to tackle crime. The process involves conferences between the victim and the offender to decide how best to repair the harm caused. 'Solutions' are negotiated through trained facilitators. The Probation Service's Watershed Programme also has a restorative aspect.

45. Tom Winston (Alternatives) received a life prison sentence for his part in a UVF squad which murdered two Catholics in West Belfast. Harry Maguire (CRJ, Andersonstown) served 10 years for the murders of two army corporals and was released under the terms of the Belfast Agreement. Paddy O'Carroll (CRJ, Derry) was jailed for 18 years in 1979 for weapons and explosives offences and served ten years.
46. It should be borne in mind that these statistics are thought to under-represent by as much as 30–50 per cent the extent of paramilitary attacks many of which go unreported for fear of reprisal amongst victims.
47. Guguletu is a black township located on the outskirts of Cape Town in the Western Cape with an estimated population of more than 150 000.

7   Legal Alternatives: the Protection of Human Rights

48. The First World War had led to the establishment of the League of Nations in 1919, but the founding document of that body (its Charter) made no reference to the concept of human rights. The nearest it came to it was in Article 23, which required Members of the League to endeavour to secure and maintain fair and humane conditions of labour for men, women and children and to undertake to secure just treatment of the native inhabitants of territories under their control.
49. For example, Part of Article 1 reads: 'Human rights and fundamental freedoms are the birthright of all human beings; their protection and promotion is the first responsibility of Governments'.

8   Future Prospects

50. The standards laid down by government in respect of how they deal with criminal activity cover such issues as training staff, human rights protections, other due process and proportionality issues, and complaints mechanisms for both victims and offenders.
51. Examples include: Special Investigating Units and Special Tribunals Act 1996; International Co-operation in Criminal Matters Act 1996; Proceeds of Crime Act, 1996; Domestic Violence Act, 1998; Prevention of Organised Crime Act, 1998.
52. According to the 1996 Census the population of South Africa is as follows: African 77 per cent, white 11 per cent, coloured 9 per cent and Indian/Asian 3 per cent (Statistics South Africa, 1998). A more recent census was conducted in 2001 but results are not expected until 2003.
53. We are grateful to the external reader for providing useful references to this wider debate.
54. The Maranatha Community is a dispersed Christian community with 10 000 active members drawn from all the churches in the United Kingdom and beyond. The Community has been active in work for peace and reconciliation in Northern Ireland for 20 years. It has helped families caught up in 'the Troubles' and, in particular, has assisted those who have been expelled from their homes and settled in Britain.

55. The Equality Commission for Northern Ireland was set up on the 1 October 1999 and took over the functions of the Equal Opportunities Commission for Northern Ireland, the Commission for Racial Equality for Northern Ireland, the Fair Employment Commission and the Disability Council for Northern Ireland. It is responsible for enforcing the statutory duty on all public authorities in Northern Ireland to have due regard to the need to promote equality of opportunity across a range of areas including religion, political opinion, gender, race, age, marital status, sexual orientation, disability and those with or without dependants.

The Police Ombudsman was established by the Police (Northern Ireland) Act 1998 to exercise independent control of the police complaints system. Under the Act the Ombudsman must secure the efficiency, effectiveness and independence of the police complaints system; also the confidence of the public and of members of the police force in that system.

The Human Rights Commission was formally established by the Northern Ireland Act 1998 to promote and protect the human rights of everyone in Northern Ireland. One of the specific tasks given to it by the Act and the Belfast Agreement is preparation of advice for the British government on what rights could be added to the European Convention on Human Rights to form a Bill of Rights for Northern Ireland. The Commission is (at the time of writing) engaged in a consultation process on preparing a Bill of Rights.

References

Abarber, G. (1999) 'Rape fury surges into vigilante violence', *Cape Times* (Cape Town), 12 October.

Abrahams, R. (1998) *Vigilant Citizens*. Cambridge: Polity Press.

Adam, H. (1995) 'The politics of ethnic identity: comparing South Africa', *Ethnic and Racial Studies*, Vol. 18: 457–75.

Adam, H. and Moodley. K. (1993) *The Opening of the Apartheid Mind: Options for the New South Africa*. Berkeley: University of California.

Africa, C., Mattes, R., Roefs, M. and Taylor, H. (1998) 'Crime and community action: Pagad and the Cape Flats, 1996–1997', *Public Opinion Service Reports*, No. 4, June.

African National Congress (1994) *The Reconstruction and Development Programme*. Pretoria: ANC.

Alter, P. (1982) 'Traditions of Violence in the Irish National Movement', in J.M. Wolfgang and G. Hirschfield (eds), *Social Protest, Violence and Terror in Nineteenth and Twentieth Century Europe*. London: Macmillan (now Palgrave Macmillan).

Amupadhi, T. (1997) 'Police worried about the rise in mob action', *Weekly Mail and Guardian* (Johannesburg), 14 February.

An Phoblacht (1971) 'Why Tar and Feathers?', N.D. February.

An Phoblacht (1974a) 'Heads Shaved', 26 July.

An Phoblacht (1974b) 'Campaign Against Informers', 2 August.

An Phoblacht/Republican News (1982a) 'Punishment Shootings', 25 March.

An Phoblacht/Republican News (1982b) 'An alternative to punishment shootings?', 26 August.

An Phoblacht (1992) 'Drugs ring smashed by IRA', 5 November.

An Phoblacht/Republican News (1994) 'IRA says woman was informer for nearly two years', 21 July.

An Phoblacht/Republican News (1999) 'IRA investigation locates graves sites', 1 April.

Andersonstown News (1973a) 'Provisionals New "Get Tough" Tactics', 18 July.

Andersonstown News (1973b) 'Community Courts for Social Justice', 9 August.

Andersonstown News (1973c) 'Community Courts', 15 August.

Ashdown v. *Telegraph Group Ltd* (2001) 2 All ER 370.

Auld, J., Gormally, B., McEvoy, K. and Ritchie, M. (1997) *Designing a System of Restorative Community Justice in Northern Ireland: a discussion document*. Belfast: Institute of Criminology and Criminal Justice, Queen's University.

Barclay, G.C. and Tavares, C. (2000) *International Comparisons of Criminal Justice Statistics 1998*. London: Home Office.

Baron, S. and Hartnagel, T.F. (1998) 'Street Youth and Criminal Violence', *Journal of Research in Crime and Delinquency*, Vol. 35(2): 166–92.

Beattie, G. and Doherty, K. (1995) ' "I saw what really happened": The Discursive Construction of Victims and Perpetrators in First Hand Accounts of Paramilitary Violence in Northern Ireland', *Journal of Language and Social Psychology*, Vol. 14(4): 408–33.

Belfast Agreement (1998) *The Agreement Reached in the Multi-Party Negotiations.* Belfast: Northern Ireland Office.

Bell, C. (1996) 'Alternative Justice in Ireland', in N. Dawson, D. Greer and P. Ingram (eds), *One Hundred and Fifty Years of Irish Law.* Belfast: SLS Legal Publications.

Benevides, M.-V. and Fischer Ferreira, R.-M. (1991) 'Popular Responses and Urban Violence: Lynching in Brazil', in M.K. Huggins (ed.), *Vigilantism and the State in Modern Latin America: Essays on Extralegal Violence.* New York: Praeger.

Bernath, B. (1999) *The Prevention of Torture in Europe: The CPT – History, Mandate and Composition.* Geneva: Association for the Prevention of Torture.

Bevir, M. and Rhodes, R.A.W. (2001) 'Decentering tradition: interpreting British Government', *Administration and Society*, Vol. 33(2): 107–32.

Black, D. (1984) 'Crime as Social Control', in D. Black (ed.), *Toward a General Theory of Social Control.* Volume 2. Orlando, FL: Academic Press, Inc.

Blair, T. (1998) *The Third Way: New Politics for the New Century.* London: Fabian Society.

Bloomfield, K. (1998) *We Will Remember Them.* Report of the Northern Ireland Victims Commissioner. Belfast: Stationery Office.

Bond, P. and Khosa, M. (1999) *An RDP Audit.* Pretoria: HSRC Publishers.

Boraine, A. (2000) *A Country Unmasked.* Oxford: Oxford University Press.

Bornmann, E. (1998) 'Group Membership as a Determinant of Violence and Conflict: The Case of South Africa', in E. Bornmann, R. van Eeden and M. Wentzel (eds), *Violence in South Africa.* Pretoria: Human Sciences Research Council.

Bornmann, E., van Eeden, R. and Wentzel, M. (eds) (1998) *Violence in South Africa.* Pretoria: Human Sciences Research Council.

Boulton, D. (1973) *The UVF 1966–1973.* Dublin: Torc Books.

Braithwaite, J. (1989) *Crime, Shame and Reintegration.* Cambridge: Cambridge University Press.

Braithwaite, J. (1993) 'Shame and Modernity', *British Journal of Criminology*, Vol. 33(1): 1–18.

Braithwaite, J. and Mugford, S. (1994) 'Conditions of Successful Reintegration Ceremonies: Dealing with Juvenile Offenders', *British Journal of Criminology*, Vol. 34(2): 139–71.

Brewer, J., Lockhart, B. and Rodgers, P. (1998) 'Informal Social Control and Crime Management in Belfast', *British Journal of Sociology*, Vol. 49(4): 570–85.

Brogden, M. (1998) 'Law, order and the justice question', *Fortnight*, July/August: 14–15.

Brogden, M. and Shearing, C. (1993) *Policing for a New South Africa.* London: Routledge.

Brown, R.M. (1975) *Strain of Violence: Historical Studies of American Violence and Vigilantism.* New York: Oxford University Press.

Bruce, D. (1997) 'Community Safety and Security: Crime prevention and development at the local level', Johannesburg: Centre for the Study of Violence and Reconciliation, www.wits.ac.za/wits/csvr/papafrev.htm.

Bruce, D. (2001) 'Problem of vigilantism raises key questions about community involvement in policing', Johannesburg: Centre for the Study of Violence and Reconciliation, www.wits.ac.za/wits/csvr/articles/.

Bruce, D. and Komane, J. (1999) 'Taxis, Cops and Vigilantes: Police Attitudes towards Street Justice', *Crime and Conflict*, No. 17: 39–44.

Bruce, S. (1992) *The Red Hand*. Oxford: Oxford University Press.

Buckley, P. (1995) 'Thugs who deserve to be beaten', *Newry News*, 10 August, No. 164, requoted from the *News of the World*, 6 August 1995.

Burman, S. (1989) 'The Role of Street Committees: Continuing South Africa's Practice of Alternative Justice', in H. Corder (ed.), *Democracy and the Judiciary*. Cape Town: IDASA.

Burman, S. and Schärf, W. (1990) 'Creating People's Justice: Street Committees and People's Courts in a South African City', *Law and Society Review*, Vol. 24(3): 693–744.

Burton, F. (1978) *The Politics of Legitimacy: Struggles in a Belfast Community*. London: Routledge and Kegan Paul.

Burton, M. (1998) 'The South African Truth and Reconciliation Commission: Looking Back, Moving Forward – Revisting Conflicts, Striving for Peace', in B. Hamber (ed.), *Past Imperfect*. Londonderry: INCORE.

Cabinet Office (1999a) *Modernising Government*. Cm 4310. London: Stationery Office.

Cabinet Office (1999b) *Living without Fear: An Integrated Approach to Tackling Violence against Women*. London: Stationery Office.

Cabinet Office (2000) *Wiring It Up: Whitehall's Management of Cross-cutting Policies and Services*. London: Stationery Office.

Camerer, L. and Kotze, S. (1998) 'The Road to Kimberley', in L. Camerer and S. Kotze (eds), *Special Report on Victim Empowerment in South Africa*. Halfway House: Institute for Security Studies.

Cashman, D.B. (c.1885) *The Life of Michael Davitt and the Secret History of the Land League*. London: Cameron and Ferguson.

Cashmore, E. (1995) *Dictionary of Race and Ethnic Relations*. London: Routledge, 3rd edn.

Cavanaugh, K.A. (1997) 'Interpretations of Political Violence in Ethnically Divided Societies', *Terrorism and Political Violence*, Vol. 9(3): 33–54.

Cawthra, G. (1993) *Policing South Africa*. London: Zed Books.

Cembi, N. (1991) 'Caught reporting – 500 lashes', *The Echo* (Secunda, Mpumalanga), 14 March.

Christie, N. (1986) 'The Ideal Victim', in E. Fattah (ed.), *From Crime Policy to Victim Policy: Reorienting the Justice System*. London: Macmillan (now Palgrave Macmillan).

Citizen Reporter (1992) 'Two men murdered by crowd of 500', *The Citizen* (Johannesburg), 17 July.

Clapham, A. (1993) *Human Rights in the Private Sphere*. Oxford: Clarendon Press.

Collins, E. (1998) *Killing Rage*. London: Granta.

Community Restorative Justice (1999) *Standards and Values of Community Restorative Justice*. Belfast: Community Restorative Justice.

Connolly, J. (1997) *Beyond the Politics of 'Law and Order': Towards Community Policing in Ireland*. Belfast: Centre for Research and Documentation.

Connor, W. (1990) 'Ethno-nationalism and political instability', in H. Giliomee and J. Gagiano (eds), *The Elusive Search for Peace: South Africa, Israel and Northern Ireland*. Cape Town: Oxford University Press.

Consedine, J. (1999) *Restorative Justice: Healing the Effects of Crime*. New Zealand: Ploughshares.

Constitution of the Republic of South Africa, 1996. Act 108 of 1996.

Conway, P. (1994) *Developing a Service Based Response to Those Under Threat from Paramilitaries in Northern Ireland*. Belfast: MSSc (Social Work) Dissertation: Queens University.

Conway, P. (1997) 'Critical Reflections: A Response to Paramilitary Policing in Northern Ireland', *Critical Criminology*, Vol. 8(1): 109–21.

Corrigan, T. (2001) 'Violence gnaws at South Africa's security blanket', *Weekly Mail and Guardian* (Johannesburg), 22 March.

CR v. UK (1996) 21 *European Human Rights Reports*, 363.

Crais, C. (1998) 'Of Men, Magic, and the Law: Popular Justice and the Political Imagination in South Africa', *Journal of Social History*, Vol. 32(1): 49–72.

Crawford, A. and Jones, M. (1995) 'Inter-agency co-operation and community based crime prevention', *British Journal of Criminology*, Vol. 35(1): 17–33.

Criminal Justice Review Group (1998) *Review of the Criminal Justice System in Northern Ireland: a consultation paper*. Belfast: Stationery Office.

Criminal Justice Review Group (2000a) *Review of the Criminal Justice System in Northern Ireland*. Belfast: Stationery Office.

Criminal Justice Review Group (2000b) *Review of the Criminal Justice System in Northern Ireland: A Guide*. Belfast: Stationery Office.

Cusack, J. and McDonald, H. (1997) *UVF*. Dublin: Poolbeg.

De la Roche, R.S. (1996) 'Collective Violence as Social Control', *Sociological Forum*, Vol. 11(1): 97–128.

Department of Finance and Personnel & HM Treasury (1999) *Northern Ireland Expenditure Plans & Priorities: The Government's Expenditure Plans for 1999–2000 to 2001–2002*. Cm 4217. London: Stationery Office.

Department of Justice and Constitutional Development (August 2001) *Victims' Charter Consultative Draft*. Pretoria: www.polity.org.za/govdocs/.

Department of Safety and Security (May 1996) *National Crime Prevention Strategy*. Pretoria: Department of Safety and Security.

Department of Safety and Security (September 1998) *White Paper on Safety and Security 'In Service of Safety' 1999–2004*. Pretoria: www.polity.org.za/govdocs/.

Dickie-Clark, H. (1976) 'The study of conflict in South Africa and Northern Ireland', *Social Dynamics*, Vol. 2: 53–9.

Dickson, B. (1999) 'The Horizontal Application of Human Rights Law', in A. Hegarty and S. Leonard (eds), *Human Rights: An agenda for the 21st Century*. London: Cavendish Publishing Ltd.

Dignan, J. and Lowey, K. (2000) *Restorative Justice Options for Northern Ireland: A Comparative Review*. Belfast: Stationery Office.

Dixon, B. and Johns, L.-M. (2000) *Gangs, PAGAD and the State*. Cape Town: Institute of Criminology, University of Cape Town.

Donnelly, J.D. (1978) 'The Whiteboy Movement, 1761–5', *Irish Historical Studies*, No. 21: 20–54.

Douglas v. Hello Ltd (2001) 2 All ER 289.

Drummond, W. (1998) 'Not trying to undermine police', *Belfast Telegraph*, 3 November.

Duval Smith, A. (1999) 'In a jungle of crime, the leopard changes its spots', *The Sunday Independent* (London), 25 July.

The Economist (1996) 'South Africa Looks for Truth and Hopes for Reconciliation', 20 April: 59–60.

The Economist (1999) 'Mandela's Heir', 29 May: 19–25.

Edgar, K. and O'Donnell, I. (1998) 'Assault in Prison: The "Victim's" Contribution', *British Journal of Criminology*, Vol. 38(4): 635–50.

Eide, A., Meron, T. and Rosas, A. (1995) 'Combating Lawlessness in Gray Zone Conflict through Minimum Humanitarian Standards', *American Journal of International Law*, Vol. 89(1): 215–23.

Ero, C. (2000) 'Vigilantes, civil defence forces and militia groups', *Conflict Trends*, Vol. 1.

Evans, M.D. and Morgan, R. (1998) *Preventing Torture: A Study of the European Convention for the Prevention of Torture and Inhuman or Degrading Treatment or Punishment*. Oxford: Clarendon Press.

Fay, M.T., Morrissey, M. and Smyth, M. (1999) *Northern Ireland's Troubles: The Human Costs*. London: Pluto Press.

Foggo, D. (2000) 'The Young Men who Pay Gunmen to Maim and Kneecap them for £25,000 Compensation', *The Mail on Sunday* (London), 9 January.

Forester, R.F. (1988) *Modern Ireland 1600–1972*. London: Penguin.

Foster, J. (1995) 'Informal Social Control and Community Crime Prevention', *British Journal of Criminology*, Vol. 35(4): 563–83.

Fraser-Moleketi, G. (1998) 'Progress and Prospects', in L. Camerer and S. Kotze (eds), *Special Report on Victim Empowerment in South Africa*. Halfway House: Institute for Security Studies.

Garland, D. (1996) 'The Limits of the Sovereign State – Strategies for Crime Control in Contemporary Society', *British Journal of Criminology*, Vol. 36: 445–71.

Garrett, P.M. (1999) 'The Pretence of Normality: intra-family violence and the response of state agencies in Northern Ireland', *Critical Social Policy*, Vol. 19(1): 31–55.

Giddens, A. (1998) *The Third Way: The Renewal of Social Democracy*. Cambridge: Polity Press.

Gildernew, M. (2001) Northern Ireland Assembly Debate. *Hansard*, 23 January: 356–69.

Giliomee, H. and Gagiano, J. (eds) (1990) *The Elusive Search for Peace: South Africa, Israel and Northern Ireland*. Cape Town: Oxford University Press.

Ginnell, L. (1894) *The Brehon Laws*. London: T. Fisher Unwin.

Gitlitz, J.S. and Rojas T. (1983) 'Peasant Vigilante Committees in Northern Peru', *Journal of Latin American Studies*, Vol. 15(1): 163–97.

Gophe, M. (1999) 'Cops still rounding up vigilante group', *Cape Argus* (Cape Town), 30 July.

Greater Shankill Alternatives (1999) *Principles of Good Practice*. Greater Shankill Alternatives: Belfast.

Greer, D. (1996) (ed.) *Compensating Crime Victims: A European Survey*. Éditions Iuscrim, Freiburg im Breisgau.

Grimond, J. (2001) 'Africa's great black hope', *The Economist Survey*, 24 February.

Guelke, A. (1994) 'The peace process in South Africa, Israel and Northern Ireland: a farewell to arms?', *Irish Studies in International Affairs*, Vol. 5: 93–106.

Guelke, A. (1998) *The Age of Terrorism and the International Political System*. London: I.B. Tauris.

H, Re (2001) *United Kingdom Human Rights Reports,* 717.

Hague, G. (1998) 'Inter-agency work and domestic violence in the United Kingdom', *Women's Studies International Forum,* Vol. 21(4): 441–9.

Hague, G. and Malos, E. (1998) 'Inter-agency approaches to domestic violence and the role of social services', *British Journal of Social Work,* Vol. 28(3): 369–86.

Hall, M. (2000) *Restoring Relationships: a community exploration of anti-social behaviour, punishment beatings and restorative justice.* Newtownabbey: Farset Community Think Tank Project, Island Publications.

Hamber, B. (1998a) 'Dr Jekyll and Mr Hyde: Problems of violence prevention and reconciliation in South Africa's transition to democracy', in E. Bornmann, R. van Eeden and M. Wentzel (eds), *Violence in South Africa.* Pretoria: Human Sciences Research Council.

Hamber, B. (1998b) 'The Past Imperfect: Exploring Northern Ireland, South Africa and Guatemala', in B. Hamber (ed.), *Past Imperfect.* Londonderry: INCORE.

Hamber, B. and Lewis, S. (1997) *An Overview of the Consequences of Violence and Trauma in South Africa.* Johannesburg: Centre for the Study of Violence and Reconciliation.

Hamilton, A. and Moore, L. (1995) 'Policing a Divided Society', in S. Dunn (ed.), *Facets of Conflict in Northern Ireland.* London: Macmillan (now Palgrave Macmillan).

Harris, O. (1996) 'Introduction', in O. Harris (ed.), *Inside and Outside the Law: Anthropological studies of authority and ambiguity.* London: Routledge.

Hartley, R., Jordan, B. and Heard, J. (1999) 'Grim warning after Cape blast', *Sunday Times* (Johannesburg), 3 January.

Hayden, C. and Benington, J. (2000) 'Multi-tier networked governance: reflections from the Better Government for Older People Programme', *Public Money and Management,* Vol. 20(2): 27–34.

Haysom, N. (1986) *Mabangalala: The Rise of Right Wing Vigilantes in South Africa.* Johannesburg: University of Witwatersrand.

Haysom, N. (1989) 'Vigilantes and militarisation of South Africa', in J. Cock and L. Nathan (eds), *War and Society.* Cape Town: David Philip.

Haysom, N. (1990) 'Violence and the policing of African townships: manufacturing violent stability', in D. Hansson and D. Van Zyl Smit (eds), *Towards Justice? Crime and State Control in South Africa.* Oxford: Oxford University Press.

Heywood, A. (1997) *Politics.* London: Macmillan (now Palgrave Macmillan).

Hillyard, P. (1985) 'Popular Justice in Northern Ireland: Continuities and Change', in S. Spitzer and A.T. Scull (eds), *Research in Law Deviance and Social Control,* Volume 7. London: Jai Press.

Hobbes, T. (1651) *Leviathan.* Dent: London, 1973.

Home Office (1990) *Partnership in Crime Prevention.* London: Home Office.

Home Office (1992) *Partnership in Dealing with Offenders in the Community: A Decision Document.* London: Home Office.

Home Office (1995) *Inter-agency Co-ordination to Tackle Domestic Violence.* London: Home Office.

Hough, M. (1986) 'Victims of Violent Crime: Findings from the British Crime Survey', in E. Fattah (ed.), *From Crime Policy to Victim Policy: Reorienting the Justice System.* London: Macmillan (now Palgrave Macmillan).

Human Rights Committee (1999) 'Popular Justice', *Human Rights Review:* 60–87.

Human Rights Watch/Helsinki (1992) *Children in Northern Ireland*. New York: Human Rights Watch.

Human Sciences Research Council (1995) *Omnibus Survey*. Pretoria: Human Sciences Research Council.

Hund, J. (1988) 'Formal Justice and Township Justice', in J. Hund (ed.), *Law and Justice in South Africa*. Johannesburg: Institute for Public Interest Law and Research.

Hund, J. and Kotu-Rammopo, M. (1983) 'Justice in a South African township: the sociology of *Makgotla*', *Comparative and International Law Journal in South Africa*, 16: 179–206.

Hunt, M. (1998) 'The "horizontal" effect of the Human Rights Act', *Public Law*, Autumn: 423–43.

Hunt, M. (2001) 'The "horizontal effect" of the Human Rights Act: moving beyond the public-private distinction', in J. Jowell and J. Cooper (eds), *Understanding Human Rights Principles*. Oxford: Hart Publishing.

Independent Commission on Policing for Northern Ireland (1999) *A New Beginning: Policing in Northern Ireland*. Belfast: HMSO.

Ingram, A. (1998) *Article by Minister for Victims*. Belfast: Northern Ireland Office.

Ingram, A. (2000) 'Restorative Justice', *House of Commons Hansard Debates*, 12 January.

International Council on Human Rights (1999) *Ends and Means: Human Rights Approaches to Armed Groups*. London: ICHRP.

Irish News (Belfast) (1999) '32 years for vigilante', 15 December.

Jennings, C. (1998) 'An Economic Interpretation of the Northern Ireland Conflict', *Scottish Journal of Political Economy*, Vol. 45(3): 294–308.

Jeffrey, A. (1997) *The Natal Story: 16 Years of Conflict*. Johannesburg: South African Institute of Race Relations.

Johnston. L. (1996) 'What is Vigilantism', *British Journal of Criminology*, Vol. 36(2): 220–36.

Joinet, T. (1997) Final Report for the Sub-Commission on Prevention of Discrimination and Protection of Minorities, E/CN.4/Sub.2/1997/20 (26 June 1997).

Kavanagh, D. and Richards, D. (2001) 'Departmentalism and joined-up government: back to the future?', *Parliamentary Affairs*, Vol. 54(1): 1–18.

Keenan v. *UK* (2001) ECHR App. 27229/95. Decision of the European Court of Human Rights, 3 April.

Kelly, G. (2000) 'Coleraine estate in turmoil after girl is shot', *News Letter* (Belfast), 30 August.

Kemp, Y. (2001) 'Vigilante attack gets the thumbs-up', *Cape Argus* (Cape Town), 19 April.

Kennedy, L. (1995) 'Nightmares within Nightmares: Paramilitary Repression within Working-Class Communities', in L. Kennedy (ed.), *Crime and Punishment in West Belfast*. Belfast: The Summer School, West Belfast.

Kennedy, L. (2001) 'An analysis of the age and gender of victims of paramilitary 'punishment' in Northern Ireland', *Northern Ireland Affairs Committee – Relocation Following Paramilitary Intimidation*. Belfast: Stationery Office.

Khupiso, V. and Hennop, J. (1999) 'We paid his bail so we could kill him', *Sunday Times* (Johannesburg), 4 July.

Kiley, S. (1999) 'How Political Violence Can Give Way to Organised Crime', *Sunday Times* (London), 10 September.

Knox, C. (2001) 'The "deserving" victims of political violence: "punishment" attacks in Northern Ireland', *Criminal Justice*, Vol. 1(2): 181–99.

Knox, C. and Monaghan, R. (2000) *Informal Criminal Justice Systems in Northern Ireland*. ESRC Violence Research Report: University of Ulster.

Kotsonouris, M. (1994) 'Revolutionary Justice – the Dàil Éireann Courts', *History Ireland*, Autumn: 32–6.

Koufa, K.K. (1999) First Progress Report on Terrorism and Human Rights, UN Sub-Commission on the Promotion and Protection of Human Rights, E/CN.4/Sub.2/1999/27, para. 44.

Koufa, K.K. (2001) Second Progress Report on Terrorism and Human Rights, UN Sub-Commission on the Promotion and Protection of Human Rights, E/CN.4/Sub.2/2001/31, para. 123.

Le May, J. (2001) 'Mob Justice Claims Two More Victims', *Cape Argus* (Cape Town), 17 November.

Le Roux, C.J.B. (1997) 'People Against Gangsterism and Drugs', *Journal of Contemporary History*, Vol. 22(1): 51–94.

Le Vine, V.T. (1997) 'On the Victims of Terrorism and their Innocence', *Terrorism and Political Violence*, Vol. 9(3): 55–62.

Leggett, T. (1999) 'Mr Fix-it Tackles Crime: An Interview with Steve Tshwete', *Crime and Conflict*, No.17, Spring: 5–8.

Liebenberg, S. and Tilley, A. (1998) *Poverty and Social Security in South Africa*. SANGOCO Occasional Publication Series No. 7. Braamfontein: South African National NGO Coalition.

Louw, A. and Shaw, M. (1997) 'Stolen Opportunities: The Impact of Crime on South Africa's Poor', *Institute of Security Studies Monograph Series*, No. 14.

Lovell, J. (2000) 'Tshwete declares war on Pagad', *Independent Online* (South Africa), 13 September, www.iol.co.za.

Lubisis, D. (1999) 'Vigilantes include white farmers and businessmen', *City Press* (Johannesburg), 2 May.

Macardle, D. (1965) *The Irish Republic*. New York: Farrar, Straus and Giroux.

Macdonald, M. (1986) *Children of Wrath: Political Violence in Northern Ireland*. Cambridge: Polity.

MacGregor, K. (2000) 'FBI joins Cape Town's war on terrorism', *The Independent* (London), 12 September.

MacGregor, K. (2001) 'Guilty and innocent alike fall victim to necklace justice by South Africa mobs', *The Independent* (London) 3 March.

MacKay, A. (1999) 'Terrorist Mutilations (Northern Ireland)', *House of Commons Hansard Debates*, 27 January.

Maluleke, E. (1990) 'Horror assaults at people's courts', *City Press* (Johannesburg), 13 May.

Mama, A. (1989) *The Hidden Struggle: Statutory and Voluntary Responses to Violence against Black Women in the Home*. London: London Race and Housing Research Unit.

Mandela, N. (1996) 'Maskhane – let us build one another together'. Text of Nelson Mandela's address to British Parliament, *New Statesman*, 125, No. 4293: 20–4.

Mandelson, P. (2000a) *Article by the Secretary of State for Northern Ireland for Newsweek*. Northern Ireland Office Information Service, 21 February.

Mandelson, P. (2000b) *Statement by the Secretary of State to the House of Commons*, 19 January. Belfast: Northern Ireland Office.

Marks, M. (2000) 'Transforming police organizations from within: police dissident groupings in South Africa', *British Journal of Criminology*, Vol. 40(1): 557–73.

Martins, J. de Souza. (1991) 'Lynchings – Life by a Thread: Street Justice in Brazil, 1979–1988', in M.K. Huggins (ed.), *Vigilantism and the State in Modern Latin America: Essays on Extralegal Violence*. New York: Praeger.

Matthews, R. (1988) 'Reassessing Informal Justice' in R. Matthews (ed.), *Informal Justice?* London: Sage.

Mbeki, T.M. (1995) *A National Strategic Vision for South Africa*. Address by Deputy President T.M. Mbeki, at the Development Planning Summit, hosted by the Intergovernmental Forum, 27 November, www.anc.org.za/ancdocs/.

Mbeki, T. (2001) 'State of the Nation Address of the President of South Africa at the Opening of Parliament', Cape Town, 9 February.

McCann, E. (1993) *War and an Irish Town*. London: Pluto Press.

McDonnell, J. (2000) MP for Hayes and Harlington. *House of Commons Hansard Debates*, 12 January: 264.

McEvoy, K. (2001) 'Human Rights, Humanitarian Interventions and Paramilitary Activities in Northern Ireland', in C. Harvey (ed.), *Human Rights, Equality and Democratic Renewal in Northern Ireland*. Oxford: Hart Publishing.

McGarry, J. (1998) 'Political Settlements in Northern Ireland and South Africa', *Political Studies*, XLVI: 853–70.

McGarry, J. and O'Leary, B. (1995) *Explaining Northern Ireland: Broken Images*. Oxford: Blackwell.

McGuinness, M. (1999) 'An end to punishment beatings requires measures to tackle anti-social behaviour', *Irish Times* (Dublin), 8 February.

McWilliams, M. (1997) 'Violence against women and political conflict: the Northern Ireland experience', *Critical Criminology*, Vol. 8(1): 78–92.

Mehlwana, A.M. (1996) 'Political violence and family movements: The case of a South African shanty town', in L. Glanz and A. Spiegel (eds), *Violence and Family Life in Contemporary South Africa: Research and Policy Issues*. Pretoria: HSRC Publishers.

Meron, T. (1983) 'On the inadequate reach of humanitarian and human rights law and the need for a new instrument', *American Journal of International Law*, Vol. 77(3): 589–606.

Meron, T. (1990) 'When do acts of terrorism violate human rights?', in the *Israel Yearbook on Human Rights*. Tel Aviv: Faculty of Law, Tel Aviv University.

Merten, M. (2001) 'Apartheid victims' families still wait for reparations', *Weekly Mail and Guardian* (Johannesburg), 26 April.

Migdal, J.S. (1998) *Strong Societies and Weak States: state and society relations and state capabilities in the Third World*. Princeton: Princeton University Press.

Migdal, J.S. (2001) *State in Society: studying how state and societies transform and constitute one another*. Cambridge: Cambridge University Press.

Miers, D. (2000) 'Taking the Law into their own Hands: Victims as Offenders', in A. Crawford and J. Goodey (eds), *Integrating a Victim Perspective within Criminal Justice*. Aldershot: Ashgate.

Minnaar, A. (1995) 'Desperate Justice', *Crime and Conflict*, No. 2: 9–12.

Minnaar, A., Pretorius, S. and Wentzel, M. (1998) 'Political conflict and other manifestations of violence in South Africa', in E. Bornmann, R. van Eeden and M. Wentzel (eds), *Violence in South Africa*. Pretoria: Human Sciences Research Council.

Missionvale Action Committee (1991) Letter addressed to the Regional Secretary of the ANC, 4 May.

Mncadi, M. and Nina, D. (1994) 'A Year After: A Training Programme in Guguletu on Community Policing', *Imbizo*, No. 2, December: 18–24.

Monaghan, R. (2002) 'The Return of "Captain Moonlight": Informal Justice in Northern Ireland', *Studies in Conflict and Terrorism*, Vol. 25(1): 41–56.

Morgan, R. and Evans, M.D. (1999) (eds) *Protecting Prisoners: The Standards of the European Committee for the Prevention of Torture in Context*. Oxford: Oxford University Press.

Morison, J. (2000) 'The government-voluntary sector compacts: governance, governmentality, and civil society', *Journal of Law and Society*, Vol. 27(1): 98–132.

Morrissey, M. and Pease, K. (1982) 'The Black Criminal Justice System in West Belfast', *The Howard Journal*, No. 21: 159–66.

Moses, S. (1990) 'Kangaroo courts take a lashing in Alex', *Sunday Times* (Johannesburg), 27 May.

Motshekga, M. (1998) Premier of the Guateng Province, 'Towards an Integrated Justice System for Social Crime Prevention', Speech at the *International Conference for Crime Prevention Partnerships to Build Community Safety*, October.

Mowlam. M. (1999) *Secretary of State's judgement on alleged breach of the cease-fire*. Northern Ireland Office, 27 August.

Munck, R. (1984) 'Repression, Insurgency, and Popular Justice: The Irish Case', *Crime and Social Justice*, No. 21–22: 81–94.

Munck, R. (1988) 'The Lads and the Hoods: Alternative Justice in an Irish Context', in M. Tomlinson, T. Varley and C. McCullagh (eds), *Whose Law and Order?* Belfast: Sociological Association of Ireland.

Murray, G. (2000) 'No room in the Shankill for refugees of loyalist feud', *News Letter* (Belfast), 7 December.

Murray, M.J. (1994) *The Revolution Deferred: The Painful Birth of Post-Apartheid South Africa*. London: Verso.

Murray, R. (1982) 'Political Violence in Northern Ireland 1969–1977', in F.W. Boal and J.N.H. Douglas (eds), *Integration and Division: Geographical Perspectives on the Northern Ireland Problem*. London: Academic Press.

News Letter (Belfast) (1999) 'Teenager hurt in beating', 24 February.

Ní Aoláin, F. (2000) *The Politics of Force: Conflict Management and State Violence in Northern Ireland*. Belfast: Blackstaff.

Nicholls, T.R. (2000) 'Working to end the back-alley "justice"', *Irish News* (Belfast), 7 October.

Nina, D. (1996) 'Popular Justice or Vigilantism?,' *Crime and Conflict*, No. 7: 1–4.

Nolan, P.C., McPherson, J., McKeown, R., Diaz, H. and Wilson, D. (2000) 'The Price of Peace: the personal and financial cost of paramilitary punishments in Northern Ireland', *Injury*, 31: 41–5.

Nomoyi, N. and Schurink, W. (1998) '*Ukunxityiswa kwempimpi itayari njengotshaba lomzabalazo*: An Exploratory Study of Insider Accounts of Necklacing in Three Port Elizabeth Townships', in E. Bornman, R. van Eeden and M. Wentzel (eds), *Violence in South Africa*. Pretoria: Human Sciences Research Council.

Northern Ireland Affairs Committee (2001) *Relocation Following Paramilitary Intimidation.* Belfast: Stationery Office.

Northern Ireland Annual Abstract of Statistics (2001) Belfast: Stationery Office.

Northern Ireland Executive (2001) *Programme for Government.* Belfast: Office of the First Minister and Deputy First Minister.

Northern Ireland Human Rights Commission (2001a) *Making a Bill of Rights for Northern Ireland.* Belfast: NIHRC.

Northern Ireland Human Rights Commission (2001b) Press Statement, 10 May 2001.

Northern Ireland Office (1998a) *Restorative Justice.* Belfast: Northern Ireland Office, Information Service.

Northern Ireland Office (1998b) *Crime and the Community: A Local Partnership Approach.* Belfast: Northern Ireland Office, Information Service.

Northern Ireland Office (1998c) *Community Responses to Crime: Protocol.* Belfast: Northern Ireland Office, Information Service.

Northern Ireland Office (1999a) *Policing in Northern Ireland.* Belfast: Northern Ireland Office.

Northern Ireland Office (1999b) *Fear of Crime and Victimisation in Northern Ireland.* Belfast: Northern Ireland Office, Statistics and Research Branch.

Northern Ireland Office (2000a) *Fear of Crime and Victimisation in Northern Ireland.* Belfast: Criminal Justice Policy Division – Northern Ireland Office.

Northern Ireland Office (2000b) *Multi Agency Work with Sex offenders in Northern Ireland.* Belfast: Criminal Justice Policy Division – Northern Ireland Office.

Northern Ireland Office (2001) *Criminal Justice Review: Implementation Plan.* Belfast: Stationery Office.

Ntabazalila, E. and Mokwena, M. (1998) 'Crime rate is dropping in Guguletu, say residents', *Cape Times* (Cape Town), N.D. August.

Nxumalo, B. and Valentine, C. (1999) 'Cellphone Snatcher Meets Mob Justice', *Homeless Talk* (Johannesburg), Vol. 6(10): 3.

Ò Broin, L. (1976) *Revolutionary Underground: The Story of the Irish Republican Brotherhood 1858–1924.* Dublin: Gill and Macmillan.

O'Duffy, B. (1995) 'Violence in Northern Ireland 1969–1994: Sectarian or Ethno-National?', *Ethnic and Racial Studies*, Vol. 18(4): 740–72.

Office of the First Minister and Deputy First Minister (2001) *New Targeting Social Need.* Belfast: Corporate Document Services – OFM & DFM.

Omar, A.M. (1996) 'Transformation of the Justice System in South Africa', *Imbizo*, No. 1: 10–15.

Omar, A.M. (1998) Minister of Justice, 'The Role of the Department of Justice in Crime Prevention Partnerships', Speech at the *International Conference for Crime Prevention Partnerships to Build Community Safety*, October.

O'Neill, S. (2000) 'What are the loyalists fighting for?', *Irish News* (Belfast), 11 September.

O'Rawe, M. and Moore, L. (1997) *Human Rights on Duty – Principles for Better Policing: International Lessons for Northern Ireland.* Belfast: Committee on the Administration of Justice.

Osman v. *UK* (2000) 29 *European Human Rights Reports*, 245.

Paine, T. (1790) *Rights of Man.* Harmondsworth: Penguin, 1969.

Painter, C. (1999) 'Public sector reform from Thatcher to Blair: a Third Way', *Parliamentary Affairs*, Vol. 52(1): 94–112.

194   *References*

Paisley, I. (2001) 'Punishment Beatings', *Official Report (Hansard)*, Northern Ireland Assembly, 23 January: 356–70.

Palomino, G.N. (1996) 'The Rise of the *Rondas Campesinas*', *Journal of Legal Pluralism and Unofficial Law*, 36: 111–23.

Parry, R. (2001) 'The role of central units in the Scottish Executive', *Public Money and Management*, Vol. 21(2): 39–44.

Patel, D. (1997) 'Taxi wars in South Africa: Can there be peace?', in A. Minnaar, and M. Hough (eds), *Conflict, violence and conflict resolution: Where is South Africa heading?* Pretoria: Human Sciences Research Council.

Patten Report (1999) *A New Beginning: policing in Northern Ireland*. Report of the Independent Commission on Policing in Northern Ireland. Belfast: Stationery Office.

Pearson, G., Blagg, H., Smith, D., Sampson, A. and Stubbs, P. (1992) 'Crime, community and conflict: the multi-agency approach', in D. Downes (ed.), *Unravelling Criminal Justice*. London: Macmillan (now Palgrave Macmillan).

Pelser, E. (1999) 'The Challenges of Community Policing in South Africa', *Occasional Paper No. 42*. Institute for Security Studies, Pretoria.

Pelser, E. (2001) 'South Africa's criminal culture', *Foreign Policy*, Issue 126: 80–2.

Peninsula Anti-Crime Agency (1998) Leaflet.

Phillips, C. and Sampson, A. (1998) 'Preventing repeated racial victimisation', *British Journal of Criminology*, Vol. 38(1): 124–44.

Police Authority for Northern Ireland (1999) *Listening to the Community: Working with the RUC – a report on police performance in Northern Ireland 1998/99*. Belfast: Police Authority for Northern Ireland.

Police Authority for Northern Ireland (2001) *Listening to the Community: Working with the RUC*. Annual Report 2000/2001. Belfast: Police Authority for Northern Ireland.

Poole, M. (1993) 'The Spatial Distribution of Political Violence in Northern Ireland: An Update to 1993', in A. O'Day (ed.), *Terrorism's Laboratory: The Case of Northern Ireland*. Aldershot: Dartmouth.

Purdy, M. (1998) 'Victims' aid too little, too late', *Belfast Telegraph*, 15 August.

Quinn, G. (2000) 'Restorative justice call to help give Creggan a lift', *Belfast Telegraph*, 25 February.

Randall, E. (2000) 'Lack of schooled cops plagues SAPS', *The Sunday Independent* (Johannesburg), 19 February.

Rauch, J. (2001) 'The 1996 National Crime Prevention Strategy', Johannesburg: Centre for the Study of Violence and Reconciliation, www.wits.ac.za/csvr/papers.

Rawls, J. (1971) *A Theory of Justice*. Cambridge, MA: Belknap Press of Harvard University Press.

Reid, J. (2001) 'Becoming Persuaders – British and Irish Identities in Northern Ireland'. Speech by the Northern Ireland Secretary of State to the Institute of Irish Studies, Liverpool University, 21 November.

Reiner, R. (1992) *The Politics of the Police*. London: Harvester Wheatsheaf.

Reuters (1999) 'Witnesses silent on lynch mob killings', *The Citizen* (Johannesburg), 12 January.

Richardson, D. and May, H. (1999) 'Deserving Victims? Sexual Status and the Social Construction of Violence', *Sociological Review*, Vol. 47(2): 308–31.

Rider, E. (1992) 'Thief flogged to death', *Cape Times* (Cape Town), 30 January.

Rodgers, S. (1999) 'Boy (15) injured in hammer attack', *Belfast Telegraph*, 12 July.

Roefs, M. (1999) 'Anti-virus for the crime plague', *Conflict Trends*, No. 4.

Rolston, B. (2000) *Unfinished Business: State Killings and the Quest for Truth*. Belfast: Beyond the Pale Publications.

Rosenbaum, R.H. and Sederberg, P.C. (eds) (1976) *Vigilante Politics*. Pennsylvania: University of Pennsylvania Press.

Rousseau, J.-J. (1762) *Le Contrat Social*. Paris: S.N.

Salter, M. (1999) 'Terrorist Mutilations, Northern Ireland', *House of Commons Hansard Debates*, 29 January: 383.

Schärf, W. (1990) 'The Resurgence of Urban Street Gangs and Community Responses in Cape Town During the Late Eighties', in D. Hansson and D. Van Zyl Smit (eds), *Towards Justice? Crime and Control in South Africa*. Oxford: Oxford University Press.

Schärf, W. (1997) *Specialist Courts and Community Courts*. Position Paper, Commissioned by the Planning Unit, Ministry of Justice, South Africa, May.

Schärf, W. (2001) 'Community justice and community policing in post-apartheid South Africa', *IDS Bulletin*, Vol. 32(1): 74–82.

Schärf, W. and Ngcokoto, B. (1990) 'Images of Punishment in the People's Courts of Cape Town 1985–7: From Prefigurative Justice to Populist Violence', in N. Chabani Manganyi and A. du Toit (eds), *Political Violence and the Struggle in South Africa*. London: Macmillan (now Palgrave Macmillan).

Schönteich, M. (1999) *Unshackling the Crime Fighters*. Johannesburg: SAIRR.

Schönteich, M. (2000) 'Justice versus Retribution: Attitudes to Punishment in the Eastern Cape', *Institute for Security Studies Monograph Series*, No. 45.

Schönteich, M. and Louw, A. (2001) *Crime in South Africa: A country and cities profile*. Briefing presented at the Institute for Security Studies, 15 March.

Schurink, E. (1998) 'Crimes that Matter the Most? Perceptions on the Seriousness of Crimes', *Nedcor ISS Crime Index*, No. 5: 15–18.

Seekings, J. (1989) 'People's Courts and Popular Politics', *South African Review*, No. 5: 119–35.

Sekhonyane, M. (2000) 'Using Crime to Fight Crime: Tracking Vigilante Activity', *Nedbank ISS Crime Index*, Volume 4, July–August.

Shaw, M. (1996) 'South Africa: Crime in Transition', *Terrorism and Political Violence*, Vol. 8(4): 156–75.

Shaw, M. (1998) 'The Role of Local Government in Crime Prevention in South Africa', Institute for Security Studies, Occasional Paper No. 33, www.iss.co.za/Pubs/Papers/33/Paper33.html.

Silke, A. (1998) 'The Lords of Discipline: The Methods and Motives of Paramilitary Vigilantism in Northern Ireland', *Low Intensity Conflict and Law Enforcement*, Vol. 7(2): 121–56.

Silke, A. (1999a) 'Rebels' Dilemma: The Changing Relationship between the IRA, Sinn Féin and Paramilitary Vigilantism in Northern Ireland', *Terrorism and Political Violence*, Vol. 11(1): 55–93.

Silke, A. (1999b) 'Ragged Justice: Loyalist Vigilantism in Northern Ireland', *Terrorism and Political Violence*, Vol. 11(3): 1–31.

Simpson, G. and Rauch, J. (1999) 'Reflection on the First year of the National Crime Prevention Strategy', in G. Maharaj (ed.), *Between Unity and Diversity: Essays on Nation-Building in Post-Apartheid South Africa*. Pretoria: IDASA.

Singh, A.-M. (1999) 'Changing the Soul of the Nation'? South Africa's National Crime Prevention Strategy', *British Criminology Conferences: Selected Proceedings*,

Volume 2. Papers from the British Criminology Conference, Queen's University, Belfast, 15–19 July 1997: 1–33.

Skosana, W. (1999) 'Thugs assault man who spoils their mission', *City Press* (Johannesburg), 24 October.

Sluka, J. (1989) *Hearts and Minds, Water and Fish: Support for the IRA and INLA in a Northern Irish Ghetto*. London: Jai Press.

Smith, A. (1999a) 'Father gets 7 years for raping daughter', *Cape Argus* (Cape Town), 5 October.

Smith, A. (1999b) 'Death by road in South Africa fuelled by violence', *The Independent on Sunday* (London), 26 December.

Smith, M.L.R. (1997) *Fighting for Ireland*. London: Routledge.

Smyth, M. (1998) 'Remembering in Northern Ireland: Victims, Perpetrators and Hierarchies of Pain and Responsibility', in B. Hamber (ed.), *Past Imperfect: Dealing with the Past in Northern Ireland and Societies in Transition*. Londonderry: INCORE.

Soggot, M. and Ngobeni, E. (1999) 'We must work on their buttocks', *Weekly Mail and Guardian* (Johannesburg), 14 May.

South African Institute of Race Relations (1998) *South African Survey 1997/98*. Johannesburg: South African Institute of Race Relations.

South African Institute of Race Relations (2001) *South African Survey 2000/2001*. Johannesburg: South African Institute of Race Relations.

South African Law Commission (1997) *Alternative Dispute Resolution*. Issue Paper 8, Project 94, July.

South African Law Commission (1999) *Community Dispute Resolution Structures*. Discussion Paper 87, Project 94, October.

South African Police Service (2001) *Crime Statistics*. www.saps.org.za.

South African Police Service (2002) *Organisational Profile*. www.saps.org.za.

South African Press Association (1991) 'Men get 100 lashes for stealing shoes', *The Citizen* (Johannesburg), 18 January.

South African Press Association (1999) 'Man stoned to death', *Sowetan* (Johannesburg), 15 February.

South African Press Association-AFP (1999) 'Intelligence report links 24 killings to Pagad', *Sowetan* (Johannesburg), 25 February.

South African Press Association (2001) 'Court reserves judgment in rapist dad's case', *Independent Online* (South Africa), 5 November, www.iol.co.za.

Sparks, R.F. (1982) 'Research on Victims of Crime: Accomplishments, Issues and New Directions', *Crime and Delinquency Issues*. U.S. Department of Health and Human Services.

Starmer, K. (2001) 'Positive obligations under the Convention', in J. Jowell and J. Cooper (eds), *Understanding Human Rights Principles*. Oxford: Hart Publishing.

Statistics South Africa (1998) *Census '96: National Results*. www.statssa.gov.za.

Steinberg, J. (2001) (eds) *Crime Wave: The South African Underworld and its Foes*. Johannesburg: Witwatersrand University Press.

Sullivan, S. (1998) 'From Theory to Practice: The Patterns of Violence in Northern Ireland 1969–1994', *Irish Political Studies*, Vol. 13: 76–99.

Sutton, M. (1994) *An Index of the Deaths from the Conflict in Ireland 1969–1993*. Belfast: Beyond the Pale.

The Tatler (1972) Ballymurphy, Belfast: An Cumann Liam McParland Sinn Féin.

Taylor, J. (2000) 'Unionist anger as Mandelson rejects RUC link', *The Times* (London), 27 March.

Taylor, R. (1994) 'A Consociational Path to Peace in Northern Ireland and South Africa?', in A. Guelke (ed.), *New Perspectives on the Northern Ireland Conflict*. Aldershot: Avebury.

Thompson, L. (1999) 'Mbeki's uphill struggle', *Foreign Affairs*, Vol. 78(6): 83–94.

Thornton, C. (2000) 'Shankill on edge for march', *Belfast Telegraph*, 2 September.

Tonkiss, F. and Passey, A. (1999) 'Trust, confidence and voluntary organisations: between values and institutions', *Sociology*, Vol. 33(2): 257–74.

Trainor, L. (1999) 'The Alternative to Back-street "Justice" ', *Irish News* (Belfast), 1 March.

The Trauma Centre for Victims of Violence and Torture (1998) *Apartheid's Violent Legacy*. Woodstock: The Trauma Centre for Victims of Violence and Torture.

Trimble, D. (1999) 'Terrorist Mutilations (Northern Ireland)', *House of Commons Hansard Debates*, 27 January: 347–98.

Trimble, D. (2000) 'Restorative Justice', *House of Commons Hansard Debates*, 12 January.

Tromp, B. and Gophe, M. (2001) 'Mapogo Vigilantes to "Clean Up" the Cape', *Cape Argus* (Cape Town), 11 September.

Truth and Reconciliation Commission (1998) *Report of the Truth and Reconciliation Commission*. Volumes 1–5. Cape Town: CTP Book Printers.

Twigg, A. and van der Merwe, H. (1996) 'Proposals from the Coordinating Committee: The State's Initiatives', *Community Mediation Update*, Issue No. 10, April.

Van Zyl Smit (1999) 'Criminological Ideas and the South African Transition', *British Journal of Criminology*, Vol. 39(2): 198–215.

Venables v. *News Group Newspapers Ltd* (2001) 1 All ER 908.

Voluntary Activity Unit (1998) *Building Real Partnership: Compact between Government and the Voluntary and Community Sector in Northern Ireland*. Cm 4167. Belfast: Northern Ireland Office.

Von Hehn, A. (2000) *Engagement with armed groups? General discussion and case study*. Unpublished Masters thesis submitted in the Faculty of Law, Lund University, Sweden.

Wade, W. (1998) 'The United Kingdom's Bill of Rights', in The University of Cambridge Centre for Public Law (ed.), *Constitutional Reform in the United Kingdom: Practice and Principles*. Oxford: Hart Publishing.

Walklate, S. (1989) *Victimology: The Victim and the Criminal Justice Process*. London: Unwin Hyman.

Wall, D. (1999) 'NIACRO's work in the field of community justice', in *Reflections on Restorative Justice in the Community*. Belfast: Northern Ireland Association for the Care and Resettlement of Offenders.

Weber, M. (1958) *Essays in Sociology*. New York: Oxford University Press.

Weissbrodt, D. and Wolfrum, R. (eds) (1997) *The Right to a Fair Trial*. Berlin: Springer.

Weekly Mail and Guardian, (Johannesburg) (2000) 'A Society of Rapists', 7 April.

White, R.W. (1993) 'On Measuring Political Violence: Northern Ireland, 1969 to 1980', *American Sociological Review*, Vol. 58(4): 575–85.

White Haefele, B. (1998) 'Islamic Fundamentalism and Pagad: An Internal Security Issue for South Africa', *Crime and Conflict*, No. 11: 8–12.

Williams, M. (1999) 'Police release kangaroo court victim', *The Mercury* (Durban), 23 February.

Wilson v. First County Trust Ltd (2001) 3 All ER 229.

Wilson, J.P. (1999) *A Place and a Name: Report of the Victims Commission*. Dublin: Stationery Office.

Wilson, R. (2000) *Order on Policing: Resolving the Impasse over the Patten Report*. Belfast: Democratic Dialogue.

Winston, T. (1997) 'Alternatives to Punishment Beatings and Shootings in a Loyalist Community in Belfast', *Critical Criminology*, Vol. 8(1): 122–8.

Winston, T. (1999) 'Shankill Alternatives', *Fortnight*, September: 18–19.

Wittebrood, K. and Nieuwbeerta, P. (1999) 'Wages of Sin? The Link between Offending, Lifestyle and Violent Victimisation', *European Journal of Criminal Policy and Research*, Vol. 7(1): 63–80.

Woods, D. (1995) 'The South African Experience – Lessons for Northern Ireland?' *Ad Hoc Group on South Africa*. Belfast: Irish Network for Nonviolent Action Training and Education.

Zehr, H. (1990) *Changing Lenses: a new focus for crime and justice*. Scottdale PA: Herald Press.

Index

metropolitan councils, 99
Midrand, 65
Miers, D., 52
Migdal, J.S., 169
Minister for Victims (Northern
Ireland), 53, 58
ministries, South African criminal
justice, 99
Missionvale, Port Elizabeth, 31
Missouri Ozarks, 19
mistaken identity, 34, 72, 75–6
Mitchell review on implementation of
Belfast Agreement (1999), 43, 72,
79, 112
mob justice, spontaneous, 49–50, 68,
82, 88, 105, 140, 157
mobile phone theft, 50
Modernising Government (Cabinet
Office), 90
Mogoba, Stanley, 7
Moosa, Dr Ebrahim, 46
Moreland, Caroline, 38
Morrissey, M., 15
Mosikare, Ntombi, 56
Motaung, Johannes, 64
Motshekga, Mathole, 135–6
Motsuenyane Commission,
54
Mowlam, Mo, 9, 37, 52
Mpumalanga, 47
Muendane, Michael, 7
multi-agency approach, 89, 94–5,
98–100
Munck, R., 33
murders, 46, 49, 70–1, 88, 117–18,
122
Murray, R., 15

National Crime Prevention Strategy
(South Africa), 59–60, 93–4,
96–100, 110, 171
aims, 96–7
National Growth and Development
Strategy (GDS), South Africa,
93–4
national law
development of, 158–60
and international law on human
rights, 151–4

National Institute for Crime
Prevention and Reintegration of
Offenders, 108–9, 180n
Community Victim Support Project,
109
National Prosecuting Authority (South
Africa), 167
National Victims of Crime Survey, 65
necklacing, 29, 50, 65, 80, 140, 174
neighbourliness, 17, 126
Nelson, Rosemary, 71, 122
neo-vigilantism, 19
New Labour, 90, 91
Newry, 38
newspapers, human rights standards,
153–4
Ngcokoto, B., 29
Ní Aoláin, F., 57
NIACRO *see* Northern Ireland
Association for the Care and
Resettlement of Offenders
NICRO *see* National Institute for
Crime Prevention and
Reintegration of Offenders
non-governmental organisations
(NGOs)
funding of South African, 109, 110
and PEACA, 49
responses, 100–10
services to victims of crime, 108–9
non-violence, 3, 72, 112
North America, 19–21
Northern Cape, 47
Northern Ireland
community condonation, 85–7
community response to crime, 70–3
compared with South Africa, 3–6
crime statistics, 8–10, 68–70
'deserving' victims, 60–4
and Great Britain *see* British
government
history of informal justice, 23–6,
50
loyalist areas, 38–43
policing reforms, 164–7
political violence and informal
justice, 15–17
population, 4
republican areas, 31–8